1992

CURSING IN AMERICA

CURSING IN AMERICA

A psycholinguistic study of dirty language in the courts,
in the movies, in the schoolyards and on the streets

by

TIMOTHY JAY
North Adams State College

JOHN BENJAMINS PUBLISHING COMPANY
PHILADELPHIA/AMSTERDAM

1992

Library of Congress Cataloging-in-Publication Data

Jay, Timothy.
  Cursing in America : a psycholinguistic study of dirty language in the courts, in the movies, in the schoolyards, and on the streets / by Timothy Jay.
    p.   cm.
  Includes bibliographical references (p.   ) and index.
    1. English language--Obscene words--Psychological aspects--United States. 2. Blessing and cursing--Psychological aspects--United States. 3. Words, Obscene--Psychological aspects--United States. 4. English language--United States--Obscene words. 5. Americanisms. I. Title.
PE3724.O3J38   1992
401'.9'0973--dc20   92-6300
ISBN 90 272 2092 1 (Eur.) / 1-55619-451-X (US) (hb) (alk. paper)   CIP
ISBN 90 272 2093 X (Eur.) / 1-55619-452-8 (US) (pb) (alk. paper)

John Benjamins Publishing Co. · P.O. Box 75577 · 1070 AN Amsterdam · The Netherlands
John Benjamins North America · 821 Bethlehem Pike · Philadelphia, PA 19118 · USA

401.9
J 4 2

Acknowledgments

First, thanks to my teachers: Joseph Danks and James Dooling at Kent State University; Gordon Allen and Arthur Miller at Miami University; and Zoltan Kovecses, who was on a Fulbright at the University of Massachusetts when I met him.

Next, thanks to my colleagues who have supported my work: James May, Harris Elder, Paul Tero, Reinhold Aman, Douglas Herrmann, Robert Treichler, William Brigman, Paul LeSage, and Therese Bruck.

For their interest in exposing my research to the public, many thanks to my friends in various media and entertainment industries: comedian George Carlin, writer Jean Callahan, Nathan Cobb from the *Boston Globe*, Phil Tuckett of NFL Films, Cable Neuhaus formerly with *People Magazine*, Richard Gilbert of NBC Television, Beth Engeler of WAMC Radio, Chip Rowe from *Playboy* magazine, Greg Ptacek, Entertainment Tonight, *Parenting* magazine, *New Woman* magazine, *The Sydney Times*, *TV Guide*, *USA Today*, *Wall Street Journal*, *Cable Choice* magazine, and *American Health* magazine.

Thanks to Robert Broom and Mary Clarkson, attorneys at law.

Thanks to the staff at North Adams State College who have helped in the production of this work: Ray Gaudette, Leon Peters, John Truskowski, Paul Humora and Alan Yagmin. Thanks to the members of the administration who funded my research and travel ventures.

Thanks to my research assistants, who for many years have helped in the collection of the data herein. A special thanks to Alan Claffie who did most of the final word processing chores.

Finally, thanks to the members of my family, especially Jessica, who have been most patient and supportive for many years.

145, 220

Table of Contents

Detailed Table of Contents

Chapter 1

What Are "Dirty" Words?

Parents tell their children not to use dirty words. Adults know that they are not supposed to use dirty words in some situations; but, then again, some other situations seem less intense without them. But what is a dirty word?

"Cursing" as used in the title of this book is meant to cover all sorts of dirty word usage. The term cursing has been chosen over, for example, the term dirty words because cursing is a more widely accepted term for the American public, although language experts might find it somewhat inexact.

In this work, we will consider how cursing is used in particular contexts and identify how the use of certain words affects both the speaker and the listener within the setting of a speech situation. For the study of cursing, the pragmatics of usage, or how the words function in use, is more important than fitting the words into grammatical or etymological categories.

From a pragmatic perspective, we can focus on how people actually curse in real world situations. To start this study we list the categories of usage in which we will place our dirty words, each usage having a different intention or function for the speaker or listener. Immediately it will become obvious that the use of the term dirty words covers a number of different usage intentions. Further, in this work the term dirty words is usually used without specifying a particular semantic or linguistic category, but when a specific type of speech act or intention must be specified, it will be labeled as such. However, the general use of the term dirty words allows the author to refer to many types of acts (insulting, humor, profanity, or ethnic slurs) without needing to refer to a specific act. Thus children's use of dirty words, for example, can be discussed without focusing on a specific type of use.

Following are some terms that "the person on the street" uses to describe dirty words. Provided is a dictionary (*Webster's Seventh New College Dictionary*) definition of the term, followed by a brief psychological and pragmatic interpretation. Finally, a few examples of the particular type of usage are given.

The purpose of the category analysis is to make the reader aware that historically and psychologically the use of offensive language is a coherent event, that such usage fulfills specific types of needs and intentions of the speaker and listener.

Cursing

Curse (vt) : to call upon divine or supernatural power to send injury upon.

Curse (n) : a prayer or invocation for harm or injury to come to one.

The intent of cursing is to invoke harm on another person through the use of certain words or phrases. These words are imbued with power granted to them mainly through religious or social demarcation. In other words, certain institutions like religion, have made a point to note that there exists in language a set of special words. These words are sanctioned by the institution by penalizing or punishing the speaker for such usage. These curse words thus obtain power to cause harm through physical and psychological punishments from the group consensus. Producing a curse is not without danger for a speaker. The curser may be labelled a blasphemer in an attempt to bring harm to the target of the curse, if the words chosen were too sacrilegious. Cursing takes attention from the speaker to the target of the curse and in past times one had to be careful in selecting the target of the curse and of who heard the cursing. Today, what Americans refer to as "cursing" or "cussing" (the person on the street uses "cuss" in non-specific meaning) bears some resemblance to curses and hexes of ancient times. It is doubtful that modern men and women think a curse brings about physical or mental harm, as ancestors of old must have believed.

A religious curse may sound something like:

damn you, goddamn you, damn your hide, to hell with you

Cursing could also be non-religious but still wish harm to the target person, as in:

Eat shit and die.

I hope you break your neck.

You should rot in jail for that crime.

In both types the speaker wants some harm to come to the listener. Some curses are very elaborate and lengthy, as found in the literature (see Montagu, 1967, chapter 3). Most American cursing amounts to fairly short, simple, and direct phrases that are conventionalized expressions of hostility or anger. Both the speaker and the target understand what is going on. The speaker knows that an act of cursing is expressed and the listener knows that he or she is the target or accursed.

Profanity

Profane (vt) : to treat (something sacred) with abuse, irreverence, or contempt.
Profane (adj) : not concerned with religion or religious purposes : *secular* :not holy because unconsecrated, impure, or defiled : *unsanctified*.
Profanity is based on a religious distinction. To be profane means to be secular or behaving outside the customs of religious belief. To be profane means to be ignorant or intolerant of the guidelines of a particular religious order. The profane are outside of the doctrines of the church.

An example of profanity would be a word or phrase which seeks not to denigrate God, religion or holy affairs but would be based more on ignorance of or indifference to these matters.
These might be something like:
> *Jesus H Christ, I'm hungry!*   *For the love of Christ, get off the phone!*
> *Does the Pope shit in the woods?*

These are common expressions employing religious terminology in a profane, secular, or indifferent manner.

Blasphemy

A common confusion in language is to assume that profanity and blasphemy mean the same thing. When one examines the intent of each speech form, one sees that profanity and blasphemy are different.

Blasphemy (n) : the act of insulting or showing contempt or lack of reverence for God : the act of claiming the attributes of deity : irreverence toward something considered sacred or inviolable.

A blasphemy is an attack on religion or religious doctrine. While profanity is related to the secular or indifferent (to religion), blasphemy aims directly at the church. These verbal assaults would take the form of using the Lord's name in vain or cursing the deities. Blasphemy obtains scorn via the power of the church, such that the greater the power of the institution of religion, the more one could be punished for the use of blasphemous language. As the church lost power over its people in this century, so blasphemy has lost its impact as an insult.

Blasphemy would appear as a direct attack on religious figures or religious authority. The blasphemer would be aware of the direct insult to these institutions, whereas the profane might not. These expressions are particularly offensive to the very devout, but may be humorous to the non-believer:

> *Screw the Pope!   Shit on what it says in the Bible!*
> *The church can stick their new fund drive!*

Religious blasphemy was at one point punishable by death or excommunication. Today, this form of word usage has lost its power to offend the average American. However, there are still geographic locations within the United States, the highly devout communities, where blasphemy is not tolerated. Further, church members may be cautioned about certain books or motion pictures and the blasphemous content of such, with the recommendation that members not read the books or attend the films.

Taboo

Taboo or tabu (adj) : set apart as charged with a dangerous supernatural power and
> forbidden to profane use or contact.

Taboo or tabu (n) : a prohibition instituted for the protection of a cultural group
against supernatural reprisal.

Taboo or tabu (vt) : to exclude from profane use or contact as sacrosanct esp. by
> marking with a ritualistic symbol.

A taboo operates to suppress or inhibit certain behavior, thoughts, or in this case, speech. Different cultures, in order to preserve social order, use taboos to control individuals within the group. The power of the taboo or the strength of the taboo is relative to the power of the controlling group to sanction or punish the perpetrator. The larger the threat, the greater the inhibition of the language. The function of the taboo is to prohibit the behavior of a speaker and preserve social cohesion. The focus is on the speaker's behavior.

American taboos may reflect a degree of superstition or fantasy. Hockey players forbid each other from saying "shutout" during a scoreless game. Children tell each other never to say "red or "red hell" to a bull because to do so would cause the bull to charge the speaker, as if the words were the equivalent of the

matador's cape. Parents place restrictions on the vocabulary of their children.
Words for body parts (*dick*), body processes (*piss*), or sex (*screw*) are sanctioned
by washing the speaker's mouth out with soap or sending the offender off to the
bedroom for a bit of isolation therapy. Taboo still surrounds concepts associated
with death and dying. One constantly hears euphemisms at use such as *passed*
away or *met his maker*, while more powerful and direct language, *died*, is avoided.

Obscenity

Obscene (adj) : disgusting to the senses : *repulsive* : abhorrent to morality or virtue
             : designed to incite lust or depravity.
Obscenity as used here is a legal term. The function of obscenity laws is to protect
listeners. In American society there is free speech and only that speech which is
defined or outlined in the law as controlled is subject to restriction. One can speak
as one chooses within reason and within the guidelines of the law. Obscene speech
also means unprotected speech; unprotected speech is not free but subject to the
restrictions of a governing (federal, state, or local) body. To call a word obscene
means that it cannot be used freely; it is subject to restriction; and to use such
speech is to risk sanctioning from the courts. While taboo restricts what speakers
do, obscenity functions to protect listeners from harmful language. Obscenity laws
control the content of books and the content of broadcasts.

In American English obscenities are pointedly sexual in nature. They do not
necessarily have to be so; for example, it could be decided that words that depict
physical violence (*kill* or *murder*) are more dangerous than sexual terms. But,
Americans "chose" sex. It is the sex act and related imagery that have been
deemed by the courts to be so offensive as not to be freely uttered.

Obscene words are considered the most offensive and are rarely, if ever,
used in public media. Words that gain universal restriction would be:
    fuck, motherfucker, cocksucker, cunt, or *tits*
The obscene word "fuck" although restricted in media is one of the most frequently
recorded dirty words in public, especially in the form of an expletive.

The media via the Federal Communication Commission (FCC) also use the
term "indecency" or "indecent language" to restrict or control the content of radio,
television, or cable presentations. This category is more open and would include
milder obscenities and unsavory references through euphemism or circumlocution.

Technically, what is obscene must be determined by the courts and what is indecent may be determined by the discretion of those in control of media content. The fact that speech is banned from the public airwaves, does not mean that it is obscene.

Vulgarity

Vulgar (adj) : generally used, applied, or accepted : having an understanding in the
        ordinary sense : of or relating to common people : lacking in cultivation,
perception, or taste : *coarse* : morally crude, underdeveloped, or
unregenerate : *gross*.
Vulgarity means the language of the common person, "the person in the street", or the unsophisticated, unsocialized, or under-educated. Vulgarity does not serve any particular need or function beyond the normal communication demands of the common human. The distinction serves more as a value judgment placed on the proletariat by the upper classes. After the Normans invaded England in 1066, the French language was identified as the prestige language and to speak in Anglo-Saxonisms was to be vulgar or common. Even as the lower classes gain more standard language terms, the upper classes through social mobility and education continue to control a more prestigious lexicon. To be vulgar is to be common, not necessarily bad or evil.
        Vulgarisms are not necessarily obscene or taboo, they just reflect the crudeness of street language. These words may be considered vulgar:
snot, bloody, up yours, booger, slut, piss, crap, kiss my ass, snatch, on the rag, puke

Slang

Slang (n) : language peculiar to a particular group : an informal nonstandard
vocabulary composed typically of coinages, arbitrary changed words, and
extravagant, forced, or facetious figures of speech.
Slang is a vocabulary that is developed in certain sub-groups (teenagers, musicians, soldiers, drug users, or athletes) for ease of communication. The slang code serves to identify members of the group, while misuse or ignorance of it identifies non-members, which may be especially important in illegal transactions. The words may operate as abbreviations of more wordy or complex notions. The words may

also provide a more specific reference, for example, to specific drug name (*black beauty*), as opposed to general names that non-group members use (*amphetamine*). Sometimes slang terms become popular and are used in standard language, putting pressure on sub-group members to invent a new code. Other terms because of their offensiveness to the general public are never integrated into standard dialects. Slang is easily observed among teenagers, musicians, athletes, soldiers and other sub-groups. Slang terms are:

> *pimp, cherry, dweeb, bennies, mid-term, john, cupcakes, s-o-s, jelly roll, jock*

Slang and jargon will be with us always. The stratification of American culture by profession, income, race and age guarantees that groups will develop special language to be used between in-group members.

Epithets

Epithet (n) : a characterizing word or phrase accompanying or occurring in place of the name of a person or thing : a disparaging or abusive word or phrase. Epithets are brief but forceful bursts of emotional language. They are powerful in presentation (loudness or duration) and in offensiveness than other types of cursing, for example, joking. The epithet is uttered from frustration, as when you hit your hand with a hammer. Epithets may also mark a sense of hostility, as when someone crowds in front of you in a supermarket check-out line. It may be that the epithet is that language which has replaced physical aggression. Epithets may also be habitual in nature, for example always saying the same word or phrase when you hurt yourself.

Epithets are outbursts, "the person on the street" yelling at a selected wrongdoer, or when a person does something stupid or frustrating. These are simple, loud, one- or two-word outbursts:

> *shit, damn, hell, son of a bitch, goddamn it*
> *up yours, fuck you, fuck off, piss off, jesus christ*

Notice that sometimes a target is present even though he or she may be unknown, unidentifiable or anonymous. Other times the epithet is uttered serving no corrective purpose (as with the targeted use) but mainly serving to reduce the anger level of the speaker.

Insults and slurs

Insult (vb) : to treat with insolence, indignity, or contempt : to make little of.
Slur (vt) : to cast aspersions upon : *disparage.*
Insults and slurs are verbal attacks on other people. These words are spoken to harm the other person by the word alone. These insults and slurs do not necessarily gain their powers from religious sanctions or social taboos. They gain their power by denoting real or imagined characteristics of the target. Slurs may be racial, ethnic, or social in nature and may indicate the stereotyping or prejudice of the speaker. Insults may denote the physical, mental, or psychological qualities of the target and are commonly heard on the school playground. They both function to hurt the person directly through the particular word or phrase.

 Some insults use animal imagery:
 pig, dog, bitch, son of a bitch, jackass, sow
 Some are based on social deviations:
 whore, slut, bastard, homo, fag, queer
 Children's insults are commonly based on abnormal physical, psychological, or social characteristics:
 fatty, bubble butt, booger nose, four eyes
 spaz, brain, dumb, weirdo, blabber mouth
 fag, liar, tattle tale, fairy, wimp
 Most readers are familiar with the many ethnic and racial slurs. These are spoken derogatorily to members of those groups:
 honkey, dago, spic, nigger, wop, kike, chink, frog,
 taco, wet back, gook, slope, mick, grease ball, pollack
Each of these insults and slurs is intended to hurt the listener. Members of the ethnic group (e. g., African Americans) on the other hand, may use these terms within their own group as terms of endearment or in joking terms (*nigger*). Members outside the group would be less likely to have the use of such language be interpreted as jokes or terms of endearment.

Scatology

Scatological (adj) : of or relating to excrement or scatology.
Scatology (n) : the study of excrement : interest in or treatment of obscene matters.

Scatological terms refer to human waste products and processes. Such terms are among the early words that children hear and use when they are toilet trained. Americans have a great penchant for coining childish terms rather than using standardized terms or those of scientific origin. Scatological insults are common among children. Different cultures pay attention to different types of taboo. Americans have a penchant for sexual and religious terms; French insults are more sexual than Americans and the Germans appear to be more attentive to scatological references than others.

Since scatological references are about feces and elimination they appear as:

poo poo, ka ka, poop, turd, crap, shit, shit ass

shit for brains, piss, piss pot, piss off, fart

The terms children say are usually different than those that adults would pick for the same referent. Some say only the vulgar would use scatological terms, when a more refined euphemism or technical term could be substituted!

A favorite anecdote about the use of euphemism involves a four-year old girl and her grandmother. The grandmother says, "The kitty went do-do in the litter box." The little girl corrects her saying, "Grandma, that's feces."

What Is the Value of Classification?

Classification of dirty words into categories of usage or semantic taxonomies allows people interested in language to define the different types of reference or meaning that dirty words employ. One can see that what is considered taboo or obscene revolves around a few dimensions of human experience and that there is a logic or purpose behind dirty word usage. They are not simply outbursts of hot air, devoid of meaning or communicative intent.

Notice that some expressions can be cross-categorized, that is, used in more than one way. In fact one has to look at the entire sentence and speech context to see how the word was used. *Son of a bitch* may be an insult or an epithet. *Shit* could be used as scatology, insult, or epithet. *Jesus Christ* could be an epithet or profanity. One does not know for sure by looking at the word alone. One must consider how the speaker used it.

The class of dirty words has some unique qualities about it. All languages are living or growing and changing over time. Some obscene words have been in use for centuries (*fuck*) and others are relatively new entrants (*motherfucker*). To understand the changing nature of words in the dirty word class, one needs to be aware of the forces behind language change.

The remainder of this introduction examines other factors that influence dirty word classification. The factors are connotative and denotative usage, changes in language over time, prosodic or phonological variables and speech context.

Connotative and Denotative Usage

Relative to nontaboo words, taboo words are used for their emotional impact on people rather than for their literal or denotative interpretation. In messages, taboo words are more likely to be interpreted connotatively by listeners, rather than denotatively. For example, *my job is fucked up* is difficult to interpret literally but most listeners would interpret the sentence as indicating that something was wrong or bad at work. Further, *I feel shitty* means that the speaker does not feel well. It does not mean that the speaker is covered with feces. The word *shitty* is more likely to be interpreted with its connotative or emotional overtones dominating the literal or denotative features. A sentence such as *the kid is shitty* is more ambiguous because the word *shitty* could refer to feces or a negative evaluation of the kid. In the majority of the uses of taboo words on the street, the connotative cases outnumber the denotative or literal cases. Needless to say, context and previous conversation play an important role.

Dirty words are used to express connotative meaning, such as the emotional overtones of a word, the feelings, moods, attitudes and power that is comprehended along with the denotative referent. Connotation is not specific or well-defined relative to denotation. While denotation involves truth, analysis, intention, significance or synonymity; connotation is conveyed meaning involved in irony, sarcasm, understatement, overstatement, humor, idiomatic usage and implied requests. Connotative reference can occur with both taboo and nontaboo words, just as both can be used denotatively.

The idea of using dirty words denotatively is not a new one. D. H. Lawrence did so in *Lady Chatterley's Lover*:

"What is cunt?" she said.

"An' doesn't ter know? Cunt! It's thee down theer; an' what I get when I'm i'side the; it's a'as it is, all on't."

"All on't," she teased. "Cunt! It's like fuck then."

"Nay, nay! Fuck's only what you do. Animals fuck. But cunt's more than that..."

(1957, p 234)

Comedian Lenny Bruce was arrested for doing the same, when he used the term *cocksucker* to refer to homosexuals and oral sex acts. Interestingly, the fact that Bruce used *cocksucker* denotatively (or for "semantics", as he pleaded) helped win his acquittal (Bruce, 1963). One need not be a writer or entertainer to put taboo language to such use, however. The author read the following graffiti on a college bathroom wall, "You are all a bunch of fucking nymphomaniacs." Below the encircled adjective *fucking* was added, "There ain't no other kind." Many dirty words are emotion intensifiers, as was the graffiti writer's initial intent.

Within the field of psycholinguistics there is a traditional way to define connotative meaning and measure how it varies from word to word by examining three semantic properties of emotional meaning: 1) is the word good or bad?, 2) is the word active or passive? and 3) is the word weak or strong? Those familiar with semantic research recognize these three scales from the semantic differential scaling technique (Osgood, Suci & Tannenbaum, 1957). Using the semantic differential technique allows researchers to differentiate emotional overtones of power, activity and evaluation across words. Raters are asked to make a 1-to-7 rating scale judgment of the goodness or badness of words such as *money* or *sex* or *penis*. Rather than determining the denotative properties of words, the semantic differential indicates some emotional or connotative properties. Speakers select dirty words for messages because they want to express emotional thoughts or have an emotional impact on listeners. The semantic differential ratings can indicate the emotional content of taboo and nontaboo words. As a class of words, taboo words are clearly rated more bad, for example, than nontaboo words.

Another, but less traditional, manner of looking at meaning is preferred adjective ordering (see Crystal, 1971; or Jay & Danks, 1977 for a discussion). In a string of prenominal adjectives, native speakers prefer the ordering *the large, red swiss clock* relative to other orderings such as *the red, large swiss clock*. While no single theory has been widely accepted to account for prenominal ordering of adjectives, definiteness of denotation, absoluteness or intrinsicalness of the adjectives have been discussed as possible candidates (Jay & Danks, 1977). Taboo adjectives are preferred further away from the nouns they modify relative to nontaboo adjectives in the string. For example, *the shitty, weak person* is preferred to *the weak, shitty person*. The prenominal adjective ordering preferences may support the notion that taboo words are not normally connected with literal or denotative meanings and that connotative meaning predominates. However, Jay and Danks (1977) found that when native English speakers are forced to give literal definitions to taboo adjectives, they prefer them ordered closer to the nouns they modify, than when the same adjectives are interpreted connotatively. Dirty words fluctuate in meaning. Usually they are used connotatively but are also used literally at times, too. The shift in subjects' adjective ordering preferences may be an indication that the semantic features of dirty words can shift from connotative to more denotative reference.

Colorful Metaphors

Dirty word usage also utilizes a great deal of metaphorical imagery, where one idea is understood through reference to another. The insult *shithead* cannot be interpreted literally but it derives its meaning through metaphor. The head is understood as a container for the brains, which represent the seat of thinking or mental ability. If the container was filled with something in place of brains, one would have diminished thinking ability. Thus *shithead* refers to a stupid person, one who committed some thoughtless act, that is with no brains or thought. A speaker could use the term *bonehead* or *knucklehead* or *do-dohead* to express a similar lack of intelligence; however *shithead* or *fuckhead* indicate a greater emotional negativity about the target because they modify the term *head* with more offensive and negative language.

Context is critical

To understand the nature of literal versus emotional reference one has to look at sentences or utterances, not individual words. A pragmatic analysis demands recording *how* words are used in a particular context; one has to record how people swear at other people in the real world.

The context in which a message occurs determines both comprehension and reaction. Physical location, social event, relationship of the speaker to the listener, and intent of the speaker all contribute to the communication context. Dirty words are influenced by context more than any other type of language in modern English. Regardless of how one attempts to define dirty words, the ultimate decision about the offensiveness of words relies on context. Tabooness focuses on the speaker's inhibitions and his or her decision about what can or cannot be said in a given setting. The speaker makes some decision about what is acceptable or unacceptable in a given context after evaluating the listener and the specific social and physical surroundings. Consequently, those expressions that are unacceptable, according to the speaker's rules for editing speech production, are tabooed and inhibited by the speaker. In contrast to tabooness, the notion of obscenity focuses on the listener or recipient of the information. Obscenity laws are intended to protect listeners from offensive speech. To characterize a message as obscene is to say that listeners should be protected from the speech in a particular context.

Words that are inhibited or taboo are not necessarily obscene. On a phonological or speech-sounds level *masticate* may be inhibited because of its approximation in sound to *masturbate*. But *masticate* in any sense would not be considered obscene. Whether a word is taboo or not fluctuates as a function of the speaker-listener relation. The appropriate intonation can make "son of a bitch" a term of endearment. Some words may be very offensive in one context but not offensive at all in another. I may use the word *bitch* with a dog breeder but would inhibit the use of the word around my female colleagues. Similarly, I may use the word *fuck* with most of my friends but would be inhibited from saying *fuck* in the presence of most young children. In some contexts the use of dirty words may be encouraged as terms of endearment (Bloomfield, 1933; Cameron, 1969). Tabooness, then, is not universal for all dirty words, but changes with the speaker-listener relation. Some contexts inhibit dirty words (church, television, stage, dining table); others may encourage their use (bar room, locker room, athletic field, when surrounded by friends).

Physical location and social structure within location also constrain word usage. Some words are inappropriate in some places, for example, saying *motherfucker* at a White House press conference. A word like *motherfucker* is rarely heard in public media and is infrequently used in most public places. Words like *cocksucker*, *motherfucker*, and *fuck* are restricted legally in public media and even mildly offensive words like *damn* or *hell* may be inhibited at highly respected places or in the company of highly respected company such as parents, ministers, or employers. Words such as *screw* and *nuts* are entirely appropriate in a hardware store when referring to hardware, but the homophones may be inhibited in the same time when referring to sexual intercourse or sexual organs. Where we are influences what should be said and what should not be said.

Time perspective

What words are considered dirty also fluctuates as a function of time and usage. Members of the lexicon of dirty words are not static but vary from decade to decade. Many years ago prior to the Norman invasion, Anglo-Saxonisms were used denotatively. *Shit* meant feces, *piss* meant to urinate and *fuck* meant to penetrate. These have now shifted to more connotative use. Other expressions over a period of years undergo a euphemistic-taboo cycle (Pei, 1949, 1973; Sagarin, 1962; Vetter, 1969). The cycle begins when euphemisms are coined to relieve the tension associated with the dirty word. The new euphemism, through its association with the dirty referent becomes contaminated, as well. *Prostitute* may have been the euphemism for the more taboo word *whore*, and when repeatedly associated with *whore*, *prostitute* became taboo, too. A similar process has occurred with anatomical terms; words like *penis* and *vagina* are restricted in usage. Anatomical names are replaced by neologisms, for example, when parents label body parts for their children. With the case of anatomical terms, it is probably the association of the term with the body part (especially sexual organs) that accounts for the tabooness, rather than the association between anatomical names and other words. For example, *wee wee* is taboo because it refers to the sex organ, not because it is a substitute for the word *penis*. One conclusion might be that any word created to denote sexual organs or behavior eventually may become tabooed.

It is interesting to watch the changing attitudes and use of words for birth control prophylactics. A few years ago in New England, one rarely heard the words: *rubber, trojan, condom*, or mild euphemisms used in public. Now that we are forced to deal with the AIDS epidemic and educate children at school and adults through the media, the word *condom* has increased in frequency of usage a thousand fold. The word *condom* has lost its taboo by constant and frequent usage. The repetition of a word thus blunts the original offense caused by inhibition or taboo. This desensitization effect is not particular to dirty words but occurs when any word is used repeatedly. This is the process of semantic satiation and when it occurs with slang terms, the users create new terms to replace some of the exhausted ones.

Summary

The subject of cursing in America covers a variety of different speech acts such as cursing, profanity, blasphemy, slang, obscenity, insults and slurs. The context in which these acts take place also determines how speakers construct messages and how listeners interpret them and react to them. Cursing and dirty word use also change over time and are influenced by social forces such as ethnic group status, subcultures, religion, and the need for professional jargon.

Chapter 2

When Children Use Dirty Words

The purpose of this chapter is to address the issue of how children learn to use dirty words within the normal course of language acquisition. The time frame considered is roughly between the ages of one year to puberty, the time when most of the swearing lexicon has been acquired. The data needed to understand how and why children use dirty words include child interactions with parents initially, then siblings, peers and other adults. Factors that have been found to relate to dirty word usage include emotional expression, anger, sex talk, joking and story telling, and naming objects. From these practices and rituals, dirty words feed into normal language processes.

It should be noted that there are very few long-term studies of language processes, that is, studies which follow a group of children over several years of growth. There are even fewer studies of how children use dirty words. The current puzzle remains: while it is obvious that adults use dirty words at a fairly high rate, we are not sure how they acquired that vocabulary. This chapter will look at both vocabulary growth and the speech acts related to dirty word acquisition. It is divided into three major sections: a lengthy first section on the language of infancy and childhood, a shorter analysis of parental sex talk and the use of dirty language in school settings, and finally two field studies of how children use dirty language in natural settings.

Language Development

Some linguists such as Chomsky (1968) believe that children come into the world pre-wired for many language processes. Others such as Skinner (1957) prefer to believe that most language, if not all, is learned or conditioned by the child's experience. Current views in psycholinguistics indicate that some types of language processes such as phoneme recognition are innate (Condon & Sander, 1974), while others (dialects, diadects) are learned. Much of dirty word usage depends on *learning* the name-calling, insulting, joking, cursing, and emotional expression rituals.

Psychology has a relatively long history of studying children in their natural settings to find out how they speak and think. Certainly the work of Piaget (1955) is a foundation of modern theory and research in this area. Language development, as a topic has more recent roots. Probably the work of Brown (1973) stands as a major starting point. Unfortunately, developmental linguists and developmental psychologists have shed little light on the evolution of cursing. In fact the topic rarely appears in any literature at all. While the research in this chapter is well within the bounds of child language methodology (see Bennett-Kastor, 1988 for a review), the research and theory of children's cursing must draw on several areas outside mainstream psychology and linguistics.

It is important to state that the research in the chapter was derived from natural settings and not in laboratory settings. This language reflects children's speech in day to day living. These data are intended to provide a data base or foundation not only to understand child speech but to understand how these early uses are related to adult personality, emotionality, sexuality and interaction with the world.

Eventually psychologists need to answer these questions: when do the first dirty words emerge? What are the causes of their use? How do those in the context react with punishment or encouragement? How does the child's use compare to adults'? How do vocabulary and language rituals change with time? What is normal and abnormal use of dirty words for children? Because there has been very little research into these questions, the final answer or the truth about the origins of our dirty word usage remains to be discovered.

The literature here is divided into two periods, infancy and childhood. Although childhood is traditionally divided into early and late phases in psychology, there is not sufficient information about dirty word usage in childhood to make clear distinctions.

The Language of Infancy (Birth to Two Years)

Psychologists have always been interested in how children develop certain abilities and behaviors. Language study is a topic which has received its most concentrated scrutiny in the last three decades. One of the landmark efforts to document and describe how children speak is the work of Roger Brown (1973). Based on extensive field data, Brown and his followers began to show how vocabulary, syntax, and semantics unfold during early childhood. The child's language was found to be more limited in power and different from adult speech; however it systematically and predictably evolves into adult-like speech by late childhood. The changes in object naming, syntactic development, question answering, semantic development, and other major linguistic variables have been documented and reported elsewhere (Bennett-Kastor, 1988).

Normal language comprehension and production is systematic and follows syntactic, semantic and phonological rules. Dirty word usage is not unique in syntax or semantics, by and large, and perhaps it is the emotional and social variables that make dirty language different from "normal" language in any systematic way.

The early words of the child are both egocentric and telegraphic. Egocentric means that the speech primarily is from the point of view of the speaker and not the listener or a broader social public. The young child lives in his/her own world, virtually oblivious to the needs of others. Telegraphic characterizes child speech as short and sweet; like a telegram. Speakers omit prepositions, adverbs, and non-essentials. Telegram-like speech occurs because the child has not developed the cognitive abilities, logic, or memory space large enough to construct sentences like those of adults. For example, when the child says, *milk*, it is the parent who must figure out if in the context the word means, "I spilled the milk," "I want more milk," or "Mommy has the milk." This of course assumes the child has used an acceptable, adult word. The word *milk* will be used to represent many meanings until the child develops a more extensive syntax and vocabulary.

The acquisition or early dirty words from parents may take shape similar to the *milk* example. The infant will hear the word *pee pee* used during diaper changes, toilet training and even when parents refer to their own actions. The child hears *pee pee* in a variety of contexts and his use of the single word may mean, "I wet my diaper", "This is my penis", "I have to go to the toilet", or "That is father's penis." At this point the child is using the one word to represent many things, as he did with *milk*. Parents and others around the child may respond to this use in a number of ways. They may tend to the assumed needs of the infant in a nonaggressive manner. They may laugh at the child or smile, rewarding the word, or become angry and physically or verbally punish the child. The reactions provide the emotional background that make some words more powerful and tension-filled than others.

Sometimes dirty word use is not conventional, as the following example illustrates. A neighbor has a two-year-old who uses the term *mutz* for *penis*. Obviously, the child and the parents know what the referent is, but other strangers in the house would be at a loss to interpret his idiosyncratic speech, on first hearing it. The use of *mutz* was functional within the parents' house but once the child went to day care, he began to use *pee pee* at the day care and sometimes at home. Eventually, *mutz* will be dropped from the production vocabulary altogether. Sometimes children will repeat dirty words (and nondirty words) without fully comprehending what the words mean. Once a two-year-old girl dropped a carton of milk, spilling the contents on the kitchen floor in front of her father. The little girl watched for the father's response and said, "Dad are you mad? You didn't *goddamnit* me." The child figured that the word was associated with anger or frustration expression but when later asked what it meant, did not have an answer.

Parents' use of a vocabulary for body parts and products is both conventional (*pee pee*) and idiosyncratic (*mutz*). Outside the home, the conventional will replace the idiosyncratic as the child seeks understanding from a larger audience. Of course the child has to develop a sense that the listener does not understand invented words, a realization that occurs as the child begins to abandon the egocentric form of thought. Attending to others' needs and responses also teaches the infant that some words will make people happy and some will make them angry. The use of dirty words develops, in part, from the reinforcing properties of their use and the ability of the words to achieve certain emotional states, such as expressing anger or insulting listeners (for example, *damn you*).

Anger and Dirty Words in Infancy

In Montagu's book on *The Anatomy of Swearing* (1967), he questions whether there may be some general conditions that give rise to swearing. He develops his answer by tracing the roots of swearing to the child's expression of discomfort and frustration. In this analysis children learn conventionalized ways to express the emotion of anger based on how parents respond both positively and negatively to their needs and words they use, like *damn*. The child has heard *damn* when he or she has done something "bad", when frustration sets in, or when the parents are angry at someone else. *Damn* becomes associated with many negative states, anger being a primary one.

Goodenough (1931) took these speculations one step further by asking parents to monitor and record their children throughout the day. The study indicated that boys express more anger than girls, that verbal expressions of anger replace physical expressions with development, name-calling increases over time, and that anger expression involves predictable sources such as fatigue, illness, hunger, or need for sleep. Another significant variable was the type of parental controls, e. g., punishment, removal of privileges, spanking versus soothing, giving in, and reasoning. Parents are more physical during infancy and compromising or reasoning are rarely used with children under the age of two years. It is during these early episodes of anger and frustration that the child has the opportunity to hear name calling, scatology and any epithets that the parent uses. Anger expression and control may be a significant source of early dirty words for infants, as may more positive emotional states, such as humor.

The Origins of Humor

Humor development, joking, and story telling also undergo age-related changes which are governed in large part by the level of cognitive or intellectual development of the child. As the mind becomes more complex, quick and sure, the nature of humor also evolves. What makes the 2-year-old laugh will not give a smile to the 7-year-old. The important point is that using dirty words in various linguistic routines such as name calling, story telling, or joking takes time and experience. Not only is there variation from child to child, but there is also change over the course of intellectual development (McGhee, 1979). McGhee's account of humor development is closely related to the ideas Piaget expressed about cognitive development.

One can record the child's first words about the time of the child's first steps, around the age of 12 months. At this time the child learns about the names for objects and how they work or function in the physical world. The mind operates on the visual present and language-based memories are very crude, leaving visual thinking at the forefront. Thus the child's sense of humor is also crude; one may see smiling and laughing at routines like peek-a-boo, tickling, and other motor or visually-based actions. After age two, when language is more adult-like and vocabulary is expanding, humor takes a turn away from the physical world and moves to a verbal-abstract base. The child can think about objects that are not present in the visual field and will laugh when a cat is called "dog" or when known words are mispronounced. This humor is not too complicated and relies on changing one or two dimensions of a stimulus, the resulting incongruity causing laughter.

Pre-School Humor. The early form of humor involves a few predictable speech acts: the use of incongruous names, as a cat is called "dog", the use of rhymes and sounds, as when a shoe is called "poo" or "shoe-poo", the construction of ridiculous names, for example, "my name is you-spilled-the-milk." The period is also characterized by the use of much scatology for body parts and products, as in, "ka ka, pee pee, poopie and weiner." These forms will change when the child enters school.

Some Final Thoughts About Infants

Children at two years will use dirty words when they know that the words will make others laugh. They use some words to disparage (*pee pee head*) or insult ("you eat pee pee"). The vocabulary is limited (see Field Study One for data) and contains both conventional and non-conventional dirty words. Some of the words come from emotion, humor, naming and anger speech acts.

The Language of Childhood (Two to Eleven Years)

After the age of two, the child becomes more verbally sophisticated and the use of dirty words reflects changes in memory, comprehension and social awareness. The primitive scatological name calling and the physical humor take on a more verbal nature but not that of the older child or adolescent. The changes in humor, name-calling and object naming have been examined and are discussed next. Unfortunately, there is not enough dirty word research to separate early childhood (two to seven years) from late childhood (seven years to puberty), so both periods appear below. Distinctions between young and old children and the language that they use are made when possible.

Childhood Humor

During the elementary school years, the child will enter the operational stage of thinking. Language based humor becomes dominant and the child can remember if s/he has heard a joke before or not. The older child focuses on social, psychological and physical differences for the source of humor. Jokes include sex and scatology. This mind will begin to tell stories, which are complex and rely on memory, ambiguity and language, as opposed to the younger child's primitive focus on simple, physical humor.

Elementary School Humor. Here we see jokes based on word or grammatical ambiguity. Riddles and cartoons are of interest to the child. The development of the "joke facade" is used to hide sexual and aggressive ideas. They may tell some jokes and stories that they do not entirely understand but laugh at anyway. By the age of five years a child can answer questions such as, "why is a cow called a 'cow'?", with the reply, "because it has horns." For the young child the greater the discrepancy between or incongruity between objects and their labels, the greater is the humor that is experienced (A good general source on object naming is Macnamara, 1982).

During late childhood, about age eight years, the child enters the operational stage that begins the trend into adult thinking. Language based humor becomes dominant and the child can remember if s/he has heard a joke before or not. What sustained laughter in the 2-year-old now seems like baby talk here. The older child focuses on social, psychological, and physical differences for the source of humor. Jokes include sex and scatology. This mind can tell long stories, which are complex and rely on memory, ambiguity, and language as opposed to the younger child's primitive focus on simple, more physical humor.

The specific topics that make one child laugh and not another, of course, vary from child to child. Input from brothers and sisters, friends, and parents make up the universe of humor that will be appreciated as an adult. Joking, story telling, and name calling are all inter-related and their aggressive and sexual content reflect the attitudes and experiences of the speaker. So, by listening to what children say when they are trying to be funny and by watching what makes them laugh as they develop, psychologists are able to determine cognitive, personality, social, and linguistic variables that underlie humor (Analysis of the Field studies will make variables or factors more apparent).

Childhood Name Calling and Insulting

Calling a friend or enemy a hurtful name certainly is related to the expression of anger. On a social level, ethnic-racial slurs, stereotyping, prejudice, tendentious and sexist humor are extensions of calling an object an insulting or denigrating name. In these cases words take on the power of weapons to their users.

In primitive cultures, there are formal and explicit taboos on certain words. A good example would be the name of a dead relative or a deity. At this level the word is power; to use it will bring about sanction from peers and who knows what from the gods. In a similar way, a child finds power in the words he or she uses, as the following anecdote illustrates. Two six-year-olds were discussing what were "bad" things to do and one gave the example of giving "the finger" to older boys. He also added, "never give the finger to a bull or he will charge you." The other added, "And never say *red hell* to a bull or he will charge you, too." For these boys both words and gestures had the power to cause self-destruction if used improperly. Apparently, someone had told them, either in seriousness or jest, something about the taboo nature of giving the finger and saying "hell." Indeed, for these two, such symbols had power, as they did for the boys in the next example.

Two small boys, about age two, were playing on the sidewalk and making a great deal of racket. The author decided to gather some data and inquired if either of them knew any bad language. "I know *goddamn it*" said the noisiest of the pair, "but he knows *son of a bitch!*" Each owned his own word and each word had its own special reference. They knew they were powerful words or they could not have answered the question so directly. The child learns good names and bad names, what their parents say when they are angry and what can be said to hurt their own little friends and enemies.

When the three-year-old heads to school, the name calling from infancy (*pee pee head*) goes too. At this age the source of names is derived from tensions related to toilet training, according to Wolfenstein (1954). Hence, names like *pee pee*, *do do*, and *ka ka*, some from home, are used to amuse and incite teachers and mates. Over the next year or two, the child's own ambiguity about sex roles also leads to the use of girls' names for boys and boys' names for girls. The cross-sex name insulting begins when children recognize the differences between genders but it continues into adulthood, for example when a man wants to taunt another man about sexual preference.

Name calling also operates like primitive cursing. In such a manner the name one curses another with amounts to a type of wish fulfillment. That is, calling someone the name of a dead person among the primitives may be a wish of the speaker that the target of the curse be dead. Calling a classmate a *turd* or *shit* may show that the speaker is attempting to reduce the target to excrement. For young children to use taboo words against other children or adults is not like the "sticks and stones" from the familiar rhyme. The word is intended to harm the other like the curse of old. (see Montagu, 1967, chapter 2 for further discussion of the antiquity of cursing).

The school-aged mind is able to discern physical, psychological, and social characteristics of classmates that deviate from the norm. These apparent differences, noted by friends, become the characteristics that are used for name calling. These would be names such as, *fatty, four eyes, carrot top* (physical), *goofy, weirdo*, or *spaz* (psychological), and *fag, wimp*, or *slut* (social). So, early name calling is based on the recognition of a discrepancy between "normal" kids and deviants in addition to those unresolved tensions about sex and elimination that each brings to school.

All children learn name games and rhyme games by the time they enter school. They also easily acquire games to insult each other and make fun of deviant children. They may change the spelling or pronunciation of a classmate's surname to take on a sexual or scatological nature; Zinkewitz becomes *Stinkyshits*, Potash becomes *Potass*, and Tina Fritz turns into *Freena Tits*. At a later date these routines will no longer be employed. They will not be the source of insult or humor. However, the targets of these insulting name games never forget their nicknames of youthful origin.

American folklorists have recorded our story telling, joking, and naming rituals over the years. David Winslow (1969) studied the derogatory epithets that children use when calling each other names. He divided them into four broad categories. The categories and examples he reported are:

1. Physical peculiarities and Appearance
   Brown Butt, Fatso, Piggy, Flat Face, Mooseface, Bubble Lip
2. Real or Imagined Mental Traits
   Dopey, Dizzy, Dick the Dunce, Jerky, Fudd, Drop Out
3. Social Relationships
   Bully, Chicken Shit, Faggot, Sore Head, Yellow, Blabbermouth

4. A Parody on the Child's Name
    Jerry-Fairy, *Minura-Manure*, *Lester-Fester*, *Bernie-Wormy*,
    Winslow-Winslop
    There are in addition to the four categories above, a few other prominent
dimensions which become sources for names. These dimensions were delineated
from previous collections of name-calling episodes by children and adults (Jay,
1989).

1. Weakness of body or spirit
    Chicken, Wimp, Cry Baby, Sissy, Pussy (for male)
2. Social Deviations
    Whore, Slut, Pimp, Queer, Faggot, Fairy, Homo
3. Animal Names
    Pig, Ass, Cow, Horse, Porky Pig, Dog, Bitch, Chicken
4. Ethnic Slurs
    *Nigger, Kike, Wop, Jew, Slope, Gook, Guinea, Mick, Dago, Frog,
    Taco, Wet Back, Spic*
5. Body Parts
    Tits, Prick, Cunt, Cock, Dink, Dick, Dork, Pussy, Boobs
6. Body Processes and Products
    Fart, Shit, Piss, Poop, Turd, Snot, Booger

These dimensions are included because they are more specific than "social
relationships" from Winslow. Also notice that some names fit in more than one
category: *pussy* is both animal name and social deviation. *Chicken* is also an
animal and used to indicate weakness. It should be noted that these categories are
derogatory terms but children also name people and objects based on positive
features too.

Name calling is not random but tends to focus on a few aspects of children's
lives. It is a means of denoting divergent social, physical, and social features of
their friends, as well as an attempt to assure the speaker that he or she is normal,
relative to the target of abuse. Name calling feeds the need to establish a strong
sense of self in reference to others. Observing the names and targets that children
choose will indicate the nature of the child's friends and enemies and what each
considers normal. These names also extend to the groups that they establish and
to the requirements for inclusion or exclusion. Name calling can also indicate type
and degree of stereotyping on the basis of gender or race. This may stem from
prejudice expressed in the home, among peers, or some combination of the two.

Object Naming

Name calling is not restricted to labels for people. Because children must acquire a working vocabulary for the objects and events in this world they spend much of their early years learning what "it" is and how to describe how it operates. Humorous, scatological, and sexual names are given to many objects. Mechling's (1984) psychoanalytical analysis of the language used at Boy Scout camp will bring back memories of these settings to many readers.

Food is a common category to rename. *Shit on a shingle* is almost a standard at camp. When rice is substituted, *shit on snow* became the new name. *Scours* became the name for banana pudding, a term borrowed from the word for diarrhea in livestock. Instant chocolate pudding was called *scoots* a name also used to describe brown-stained underwear. The word interplay between oatmeal and scrotum provided the name *scroatmeal*. In fact much of the verbal play among these boys combines sex, elimination and food. The soft drink Mountain Dew became the basis for *mountain doo* to describe diarrhea as did the term *hershey squirts* from Hershey Chocolates.

These naming episodes provide developing children with a sense of mastery over the environment when they can name objects and also seemingly manipulate the object or exercise power over it by changing its name. Similarly, calling classmates by different names gives children a sense of superiority, which may be the basis for later racial, ethnic, the sexist forms of humor and insults. Note that when members of an out-group are labelled and targeted, also operating is a sense of in-group solidarity for the non-target group doing the name calling.

Childhood Story Telling

Folklorists and child psychologists have been interested for years in childhood story telling and what it represents. It is almost impossible to study the fascinating joking and story telling episodes that children have in a laboratory. These events commonly occur on the playground, at summer camp, birthday parties, and other interactions, where there is predominantly peer interaction and very little adult monitoring. One wonders whether an adult investigator could ever openly record these exchanges, unless such recording was done surreptitiously; otherwise the openness and spontaneity of the speakers would be somewhat compromised. A more unobtrusive manner of investigation is required, as when a friend threw a birthday party for his 8-year-old daughter and a dozen girlfriends. A mini-tape recorder was placed under a couch and recorded an afternoon of giggles, jokes, and stories. A study of the contents convincingly showed young girls know and say much more than many adults would ever conceive. Many of the stories and jokes contained taboo words. In fact some of the humor relied mainly on the use of a particular word such as *turd* or *fart*, as if, no matter what the storyline was, the word once pronounced was enough to evoke a laugh. Some of the stories contained psychosexual themes such as intercourse or having babies. They were apparently passed down from older schoolmates. It was clear that not all the girls understood these stories but they laughed anyway because the joke frame had been established and laughing at the end of the story was a requisite. Several of the punchlines had to be repeated with the prompt, "get it?" at the end, a clear signal to begin laughing. This anecdotal experience provided a verification of the psychosexual nature of children's humor and story telling to be found in the professional literature.

One informative study of story-telling was done by Sutton-Smith and Abrams (1978). They recorded stories from 150 children ages five to 10 years and found that only a small portion of them, 24 stories, contained psychosexual themes of taboo, sex, or romance. The younger children told stories that focused on dependency, anality, and self exposure. This young humor relied on names for orifices and organs. The older children's tales involved sex acts and aggression. These stories were also more abstract and the humor was indirect. Naturally, the older children told more complicated and involved stories. In difference to a Freudian interpretation that our sexual expression becomes more inhibited as we grow older, these data suggest that there is an increasing violation of taboo with age.

It is interesting to look at some of the particular words used in these stories recorded by Sutton-Smith and Abrams. Here is a brief quote from their report:

> In the present examples 7-year-old-and-under stories seem to be a trifle less extreme, including spitting, shitting, pants down, naked girls, pee fights, biting weeners, sucking buggars, pinching asses, and fucking. From 8 onward there are references to having a boner, farting, tits, being horney, a dickey, animalism, having babies, throwing up, massages, cunts, eating shit, leaping on girls, sexual assaults, being pregnant, whores, vaginas, and incest. (p 524)

The informants' stories combine the use of humor, joking, insulting and sex talk. Listening to them provides an effective method of getting several types of language employing taboo speech. Adults should not be surprised to see the aggressive and sexual nature of children's views of the world. A quick examination of child drawings show similar content. What may surprise adults is that they cannot identify immediately the source of such information. But a sample of children's television and advertising shows a great deal of aggressive and sex-role information to young viewers. Further, because adults do not pay avid attention to the language of children and their peers, they may be missing the actual level of knowledge from these story telling and joking interactions. Researchers interested in obtaining information about taboo language from young informants must take a relaxed and nonpunitive approach for children who have been punished or berated by adults for telling dirty stories or jokes are not willing informants.

From Childhood to Adolescence: Final Thoughts

By the teenage years, we see the mind of the adult beginning to crystallize. The abilities to think hypothetically, inductively and deductively are developing and this more logical and hypothetical thought affects the type of humor that adolescents produce and appreciate. The topic of sex is prominent and the ability to generate sophisticated social and political satire appears. Jokes that seem most funny are not only complex and linguistic in nature but rely on the ability to understand subtle ambiguities in words and their meanings. The young adult now may find some ethnic, sexist and scatological humor somewhat childish, a sign that mature social-psychological and interpersonal attitudes are in place. In short, the adolescent humor appreciation takes advantage of the new, formal reasoning abilities and greater depth of knowledge about the world.

The period of childhood preceding adolescence is marked by the child's appreciation of physical, intellectual, psychological and social differences among people and the things they do. The child takes this awareness and uses it in speech acts involving humor, name calling and insulting, object naming and the expression of anger.

Two General Issues of Sex Talk and Language at School

The "Etiquette" of Dirty Words and Sex Talk

Children learn the linguistic rituals associated with politeness. Parents and siblings go to great lengths to teach young children to say *please*, *thank you*, *may I be excused* or *pardon me*. The child learns what to say, to whom and in what context. Politeness is a linguistic ritual that operates on a number of different social levels from casual to formal. One learns not only when to be polite but what degree of politeness is warranted in a given social setting. Learning to use dirty words should also operate similarly to learning to be polite. The child learns the proper way to curse, the proper place and how to change the style of cursing in context. While the child who forgot to be polite might be prompted with a phrase like, "say the magic word", the child who uses dirty words inappropriately is sanctioned with rituals such as, having the mouth washed out with soap, physical punishment (spanking), or isolation (being sent to one's room). In other words, there is also a dirty word etiquette.

Flexner (1976) has spent a great deal of time and effort to catalog how Americans express themselves with words from English and other languages, showing when and why certain terms have entered our everyday conversation. His observations about children and cursing are pertinent here:

> There is, of course, no logical reason why *fuck, screw, make* (1922), or any other term
> should be "dirty," shocking, or taboo, no logical reason why they should be considered
> any different than such synonyms as *copulate, sexual intercourse*, or *feces*.
> It's a matter of conditioning and etiquette. (p 157)

This etiquette metaphor allows one to describe the way parents talk to their children about the topic of sexual behavior.

One of the more challenging tasks that faces parents is the topic of sex and reproduction. While psychologists have written extensively about this subject, until recently we knew little about what really does happen in the home. One informative book on the matter is *Children & Sex: The Parents Speak* (Berges, et al., 1983), highlighted here due to its frank and unassuming approach and because it is based on parent interviews. The study is based on a sample of 225, primarily middle class, families living throughout the United States. The sample was limited to children ranging in age from three through eleven. Half of the parents interviewed were men and half were women; similarly, half are about girls and half of the interviews are about boys. This work amounts to one of the first extensive set of interviews of parents, regarding their children's sexuality.

The parents' comments are summarized here to relate to the type of language and attitudes about taboo language that children have. Perhaps, the way parents deal with sex talk influences the way children talk and think about sex. Today, according to the text, parents feel that their children are better informed about sex than kids were decades ago. But they admit that the language of sex and reproduction is a common block with their children. For example, parents report that it is easier to call a vagina a *pee pee*. Along with parental concerns, children have their own interests in sex. Parents admit that children want to know: where do babies come from, menstruation, sexual anatomy, erections, wet dreams, orgasms and masturbation. Many parents hope that these matters will be discussed at school rather than in their homes.

Before the age of five, children seek answers to the subjects listed above. Mothers are usually sought for answers and some fathers are excluded entirely. Parents fear that telling too much or too little will cause increased inquisitiveness. Certain topics such as sodomy, oral sex, and orgasms cause parents anxiety and they are reluctant to discuss these matters with children. Children are taught when and where certain topics, for example body odors or flatulence, can be discussed and with whom they may be discussed. The child must derive a sense of context of sex talk and taboo language from the rules of etiquette that parents express in the home.

For the older child, the words and language of sex become a topic of particular focus. Parents generally prefer to talk in euphemisms but some detest them and only use anatomically accurate descriptions. Parents in general do not like children to use slang in the house but even here the kids learn that slang has its place. Parents are more tolerant of slang if their child is overly angry about something or upset. Most realize that they are using it to get their parents' attention. Sanctions on dirty words depend on the word used, the age of the child, and the social and physical setting of the usage. The child learns from all this that the home is merely a microcosm of the outside world and they must learn the "rules" of the name game to avoid getting in trouble.

Some parents treat the "illegal" use of dirty words with penalties. These strategies would appear to be similar to dealing with dirty words used with expressions of anger and aggression. Parents try to tell their children that using dirty words openly is not permissible and rules of etiquette are observed. Breaking the rules can result in physical punishment, such as a slap in the face or having a mouth washed out with soap. Denial of privileges is also used when s/he is sent to the room, denied television privileges, or sent to bed early.

American parents face a contextual problem: a double standard is clearly present in the minds of many fathers. They readily admit to using one language with the guys at work and another at home. Fathers and mothers, too, use one language with their sons and another with daughters. Generally, parents are more lax with boys' swearing outbursts. One has to wonder what might be happening in the single parent home. Is the single parent more or less tolerant of swearing? Does the child learn the rules more quickly or is sex talk delayed?

Conclusions About Sex Talk

As with the behavior associated with the expression of anger, the parents and significant adults in the child's life influence his or her attitude and behavior with regard to sex and language. Simply put, parents and older children in the house tell the younger children about the etiquette of sex talk, behavior, and use of dirty words. This etiquette can occur directly with physical and social rewards and punishments, or indirectly with nonverbal feedback, such as dirty looks or lack of attention. Age differences, sex differences, and place differences are also taught, such as, what little kids can say and what adults can say, that there are multiple standards for home-school-work, double standards for males-females, and that emotions can be expressed in conventional and unconventional forms. To a great degree, sex talk is a form of etiquette taught explicitly and implicitly by parents through their interactions with their children.

The Issue of Dirty Language at School

There is ample evidence that children know and use taboo language in telling stories, name calling and talking about sex. Most of these studies were conducted outside of the school context, a setting where children spend a major part of their lives during the school year. One has to wonder about the nature and extent of the use of taboo language in the school environment. There are plenty of opportunities to interact with peers and, on the other hand, there are strict rules of conduct and behavior administered by the teachers and staff at the school. Certain academic subjects such as sex education, personal health, biology and physical education are likely to employ language for body parts, processes and products but the rules of conduct may sanction the use of slang or taboo language. The school context is also filled with stress from peer pressure, academic performance, athletic competition, intellectual argument and debates and social interactions and disputes amongst all members of the school. The use of taboo language by students and by teachers has been the source of controversy and legal sanctions. This section examines the nature of language at school.

One major problem for the school child is that one's role is very ambiguous. The child should act like a polite adult but is not treated with the same respect or given adult freedoms. The teacher is a law giver but in some schools lacks the respect that parents get. A topic or speech that is freely expressed at home is not permissible at school. Creative and expressive language are stifled in normal classroom conversations and academic performance. Conformity, obedience and passivity are demanded throughout the day.

The teacher role is also constrained and not totally well defined. Teachers have certain liberties and freedoms but they are also bound to teach certain topics in certain ways within the guidelines of their contracts. The use of dirty words or discussion of sex is one area of difficulty for parents, students, teachers and administrators alike. Generally, sex talk from the teacher is absent in the curriculum of most primary school teachers. Yet, we know children are learning about these matters on the street and to a lesser degree at home. The high school setting is where teacher sex talk obtains more scrutiny.

When, or if, an elementary school teacher uses a dirty word in class there is little justification for such use because of the age and course content of the class. At high school the curriculum is attuned to society's needs and the lives of the students after graduation. That is, they must be prepared to become productive members of the community. Teachers who have discussed themes of free speech, protest or obscenity are often subject to personnel action (see Goldstein and Gee, 1980, pp 88-111). In one court case cited (*Keefe v. Geanakos*), an English teacher had his senior class read and discuss an article from the *Atlantic* which contained the word *motherfucker*, when presenting a point of view on protest and dissent in

America in the 1970's. Another case (*Mailloux v. Kelly*) was based on an incident where an English teacher, for his junior class, wrote the word *fuck* on the blackboard and opened a discussion about changes in society and the use of the taboo word and others, in relation to a novel they were reading for class. Such discussions must be justified in terms of their fit to the course or lesson plan, the sophistication of the class (freshmen versus seniors), and the competence and maturity of the teacher.

The teacher who writes *fuck* on the board, or discusses the derivation of the word *motherfucker* is headed for dismissal but will most likely be defended positively by the Federal courts. It is assumed that such use on the part of the instructor was well thought out and contributed to the students' growth and knowledge and fit in society. In other words the use of dirty words at school is mainly a curricular matter, *not* one of academic freedom or freedom of speech. The court or school board will be successful at dismissal when the teacher does something beyond the scope of contractual duties. Adults who hear rumors about teacher language should try to get "the facts" before making judgments. If the teacher was trying to instruct the teenagers about the nature of man in modern times and modern literature by using taboo words, one must consider that the typical teenager has probably heard and maybe said whatever the teacher said in the lecture. If the teacher used a taboo word through some careless act of verbal aggression or slander, that is another matter to be dealt with by the administration. Such lack of control, or demonstration of poor judgment may be evaluated negatively by parents, who think that teachers should always be good role models for the children in public schools.

There is one side issue with respect to language at school and that involves cases of teachers as targets of verbal abuse. Teachers can be abused by other teachers, students and parents; the interference with normal functioning, as a consequence of language, can be great (Greene, 1988). Questions arise as to the location of abuse (school or public places), type of abuse (written or spoken) and the degree to which the speech interferes with normal school activities. While the teacher and his or her speech rights are the focus in these issues, the fact that children may speak or witness these acts causes the topic of teacher abuse to be included in the question of how children learn taboo language. Many of these legal documents include evidence of the use of obscene speech both by students and teachers.

The language at school issue demonstrates the difficulty surrounding children's use of taboo speech in public. They are asked not to use explicit or obscene speech at school. Their teachers are reprimanded when they use taboo speech in front of their students. The school setting provides an additional form of etiquette at odds with the language of the street and social scientists know little about how using taboo speech affects normal or healthy social and psychological development. The last section of this chapter is an attempt to provide a better understanding of how children produce dirty words in natural settings.

The Emergence of an Obscene Lexicon

In these final sections are presented some data that have been collected with respect to the words that children actually use. These words are the mental dictionary or lexicon of dirty words that the child will employ in a variety of speech acts. These were discussed above (name calling, anger, object naming, sexual expressions, etc). In the social sciences researchers must be very careful about the methods they use to obtain data like these. To ensure credibility and reliability the method is usually described in some detail in the research monographs. These reports are more abbreviated than how they appear in technical reports but the important methodological procedures and interesting details remain (see Jay, 1989 for a more technical account). The first field study was an attempt to collect a large sample of taboo language and describe general trends in the data. Its primary function is to plot vocabulary growth, as a function of age and gender of speaker.

The second study was conducted at a summer camp with mainly children from four to 14 years. The focus of the camp study was to identify the causative forces behind male and female swearing episodes, that is, joking, anger, evaluative statements, or other acts. The word frequency data here are much like those obtained and reported from the laboratory on other occasions. Combined with the lexicon study, these two field studies provide a provocative baseline for future field studies involving episodes of children's use of dirty words.

Field Study One

This research is a field study, as opposed to a laboratory based experiment. The control over variables in the laboratory was sacrificed to gain naturalistic observations of what occurs when children use taboo words in everyday settings. Nothing was done to promote or encourage the use of taboo speech, as the research assistants merely recorded what happened spontaneously. These recordings were surreptitious, that is, without the speakers' knowledge. In all cases the speakers remain anonymous and data are never connected with a particular person.

The adults who recorded the data were college students and also research assistants in the psychology research laboratory. There were three females and three males who recorded dirty word use so that the recordings were balanced by the sex of recorder. These students worked in a variety of settings where pre-teenagers gathered (day care, elementary school, recreation centers, Big Sister program, etc).

The Field Card Recording Technique

Previously, language has been recorded with mini-tape recorders (see Jay, 1980a, for example) but these became cumbersome. It took many hours to decode the tape recordings and write words on data sheets. Here the assistants simply used a 3" x 5" file card, which they carried in their pockets to record dirty word episodes when they occur. The pre-printed card had a place for the sentence or expression used, the speaker's age and sex, the target's age and sex, and the ages and sex of any other people in the setting. The card also had room to describe the physical location and the manner in which the word was spoken (joke, anger, loud-soft, etc). Recorders made various comments on a card, such as whether there was parent-child interaction, or what happened after the episode. One card was used per expression.

Recorders carried the cards and noted any expression using insults, expletives, name calling, or regular conversation generated by a pre-teenage child. Also, in many cases the assistants either knew the age of the children who they heard or could estimate age fairly accurately by the child's grade or by the age of their mates. Episodes were recorded when and wherever they occurred: in stores, at ball games, parades, playgrounds, swimming pools, or grade schools.

Below are presented the nearly 700 episodes that were recorded where children uttered an expression with a taboo word or vulgar insult in the expression. The focus of the analysis is on the important contextual variables of the data, such as, sex of speaker, the age of the speaker and the particular word selected. These variables appear in later chapters in the book (Frequency is discussed in chapter 4, Offensiveness in chapter 5) and have been the focus in previous field studies involving adult speakers.

Results: Speaker Age and Sex

Figure 1 shows the size of the taboo lexicon as a function of the sex of the child. It can be seen that the children in and around the community are producing around 30-40 different types of expressions with dirty words by the age of ten years. One can compare the data to adults who were recorded using around 60-70 different expressions in about the same community context. Note that taboo words have been recorded at the age of two, the point where child speech expands beyond the single-word stage a few months earlier. Taboo expressions are simple, one or two word constructions. They, as Wolfenstein would lead us to believe, focus on elimination or aggression and will later be replaced as the child uses more offensive language with sexual themes and learns more adult-like expressions and insults.

In the first two years boys and girls produce about the same small number (4) of dirty words. At three and four years girls are producing more (23 versus 17) words, but after that age, boys begin to clearly outproduce females. This trend of gender differences, where males use more dirty words and use them more frequently will continue through adulthood. The notion that males swear more or females swear less supports gender stereotypes in American culture. It is not clear whether the males are trying to be "macho" by swearing a lot or whether females are trying to be more judicious in their use of swearing. That is, the idea of the female being passive and reserved does not necessarily hold true, if the male is overproducing taboo speech beyond the "norm." The conclusion, whatever the reason for using taboo speech, is that boys produce more dirty words in public than do girls and that this trend may begin as early as the age of 5 years.

Production Lexicon

In Table 1 are listed the words that underlie the graph in Figure 1. Each word is listed and the age and sex of speaker is noted. Table 2 expands the data in Table 1 by showing the sex of the target of the taboo word, as a function of speaker sex. The second table (Table 2) shows that some words are selected by the speaker depending on the gender of the target; what is appropriate to call a male may not hold for a female target. Data are summarized in Table 3.

It can be seen in Table 1 that some of the words cross all age ranges and both sexes (*shit*); others are limited by age (*dink*) or to one sex (*douche bag* for males or the word *vagina* which is produced here only by girls). Some words (*bum bum*) appear but drop out of production later. Other words (*shit*) remain over all age ranges. Obviously, the use of a word like *fuck* by a 3-year-old does not have the same meaning it would have for an adult. These expressions are probably based on what he/she has heard parents or peers say. The speaker probably imitates common insults at this early age. Those interested in how children comprehend sexual terminology would have to test or question young children to find out what these words mean to very young speakers.

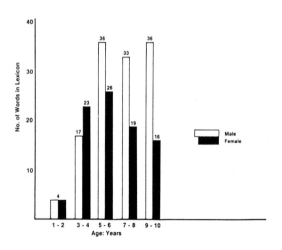

Figure 1. *Lexicon Size as a Function of Gender and Age*

Table 1. *Children's Taboo Lexicon.*

Word	Speaker Gender	(Ages)
Ass	males	1-2,5-6,9-10
	females	3-4,5-6,7-8,9-10
Asshole	males	3-4,5-6,7-8,9-10
	females	1-2,7-8
Asswipe	males	5-6
	females	none
Balls	males	5-6,7-8,9-10
	females	none
Bastard	males	3-4
	females	5-6,7-8
Bingo	males	none
	females	3-4
Bitch	males	3-4,5-6,7-8,9-10
	females	3-4,5-6,7-8,9-10
Brat	males	5-6
	females	5-6
Bum	males	1-2,3-4,5-6,7-8
	females	3-4,9-10
Butt	males	5-6,7-8
	females	none
Bullshit	males	3-4,7-8,9-10
	females	none
Chicken	males	3-4,7-8
	females	none
Christ	males	1-2, 9-10
	females	none
Cock	males	7-8
	females	none

Crap	males	5-6,7-8,9-10
	females	5-6
Creep	males	5-6
	females	5-6,7-8,9-10
Damn	males	5-6,7-8
	females	5-6,9-10
Dick	males	5-6
	females	none
Dink	males	7-8,9-10
	females	7-8
Dipshit	males	none
	females	7-8
Doo-doo	males	none
	females	3-4
Dog	males	3-4
	females	none
Dork	males	7-8
	females	none
Douche bag	males	9-10
	females	none
Dummy	males	5-6
	females	none
Dumb	males	5-6
	females	5-6
Fag	males	5-6,7-8,9-10
	females	3-4,7-8,9-10
Fart	males	5-6,7-8
	females	none
Fat	males	5-6
	females	3-4,5-6
Fool	males	none
	females	9-10
Fraidy cat	males	none
	females	3-4
Friggin	males	7-8,9-10
	females	none

Fuck	males	3-4,5-6,7-8,9-10
	females	3-4,7-8,9-10
Gay	males	none
	females	9-10
Goddamn	males	3-4,5-6,7-8,9-10
	females	3-4,5-6
God	males	9-10
	females	5-6,7-8
Hell	males	7-8,9-10
	females	3-4
Idiot	males	7-8
	females	5-6,7-8
Imbecile	males	5-6
	females	none
Jackass	males	5-6
	females	none
Jerk	males	3-4,5-6,7-8,9-10
	females	3-4,5-6,7-8
Jesus	males	7-8,9-10
	females	1-2,3-4,5-6
Knucklehead	males	none
	females	3-4
Nerd	males	9-10
	females	none
Nigger	males	9-10
	females	none
Nuts	males	none
	females	3-4
Moron	males	9-10
	females	none
Peckerhead	males	9-10
	females	none
Pee	males	9-10
	females	3-4,5-6
Penis	males	9-10
	females	none

Pickle	males	3-4
	females	3-4
Pig	males	5-6,7-8,9-10
	females	5-6,7-8,9-10
Pinhead	males	5-6
	females	none
Piss	males	5-6,7-8,9-10
	females	5-6,7-8
Poo-poo	males	5-6,7-8
	females	3-4
Prick	males	3-4
	females	none
Puke	males	5-6
	females	1-2
Pussy	males	3-4,5-6,9-10
	females	7-8
Queer	males	7-8,9-10
	females	7-8
Retard	males	7-8,9-10
	females	none
Screw	males	5-6,9-10
	females	none
Scum	males	5-6,7-8
	females	5-6,9-10
Shit	males	ALL
	females	ALL
Shithead	males	5-6,9-10
	females	3-4
Silly	males	3-4
	females	3-4,5-6
Sissy	males	5-6,7-8
	females	none
Slob	males	9-10
	females	none
Slum	males	9-10
	females	none

Stupid	males	5-6,7-8
	females	5-6,7-8
Suck	males	3-4,5-6,7-8,9-10
	females	3-4,5-6,9-10
Tit	males	9-10
	females	none
Ugly	males	1-2,3-4
	females	3-4,5-6
Vagina	males	none
	females	5-6
Weenie	males	none
	females	5-6,9-10
Wimp	males	5-6,7-8,9-10
	females	5-6,7-8,9-10
Wuss	males	none
	females	9-10

Table 2a. *Word Frequency by Gender of Speaker and Target.*

WORD	TARGET			
Male Speaker Age	Male	Female	No Target	
Ass				
1-2	1	0	0	
5-6	3	0	0	
7-8	5	0	0	
9-10	3	1	0	=13
Asshole				
3-4	1	0	0	
5-6	4	2	0	
7-8	15	5	0	
9-10	5	0	0	=32
Asswipe				
5-6	1	1	0	=2
Balls				
5-6	1	1	0	
7-8	4	1	0	
9-10	2	0	0	=9
Bastard				
3-4	1	0	0	=1
Bingo	0	0	0	=0

Bitch

3-4	0	0	1	
5-6	0	3	0	
7-8	4	3	0	
9-10	3	1	1	=16

Brat

5-6	1	0	0	=1

Bum

1-2	5	0	0	
3-4	5	1	0	
5-6	2	2	0	
7-8	2	0	0	=17

Butt

5-6	2	0	0	
7-8	1	0	0	
11-12	1	0	0	=4

Bullshit

3-4	1	0	0	
7-8	5	0	0	
9-10	1	0	0	=11

Chicken

3-4	1	0	0	
7-8	1	0	0	=2

Christ

1-2	1	0	0	
9-10	1	1	0	=3

Cock

7-8	2	0	0	=2

Crap
5-6	1	1	0	
7-8	4	2	0	
9-10	1	2	0	=11

Creep
5-6	1	1	0	=2

Damn
5-6	4	0	0	
7-8	2	0	0	=4

Dick
5-6	4	0	0	=4

Dink
7-8	7	5	0	
9-10	3	1	0	=16

Dipshit
	0	0	0	=0

Doo-doo
	0	0	0	=0

Dog
3-4	2	0	0	=2

Dork
7-8	2	2	0	=4

Douchebag
9-10	1	0	0	=1

Dummy
5-6	3	1	0	=4

Dumb
5-6   2   0   0   =2

Fag
5-6   2   0   0
7-8   11   2   0
9-10   4   0   0   =19

Fart
5-6   1   1   0
7-8   1   1   0   =4

Fat
5-6   0   1   0   =1

Fool   0   0   0   =0

Fraidy cat   0   0   0   =0

Friggin
7-8   7   0   0
9-10   1   0   0   =8

Fuck
3-4   1   1   0
5-6   13   4   2
7-8   26   7   0
9-10   16   1   0
11-12   2   0   0   =73

Gay   0   0   0   =0

Goddamn

3-4	0	0	1
5-6	0	2	0
7-8	3	4	0
9-10	2	0	0	=12

God

9-10	0	0	1	=1

Hell

7-8	8	0	0
9-10	5	1	0	=14

Idiot

7-8	2	1	0	=3

Imbecile

5-6	1	0	0	=1

Jackass

5-6	1	0	0	=1

Jerk

3-4	1	2	0
5-6	17	3	0
7-8	13	5	0
9-10	4	1	0
11-12	0	1	0	=47

Jesus

7-8	2	1	2
9-10	1	0	0	=6

Knucklehead

	0	0	0	=0

Moron
9-10   1   0   0   =1

Nerd
9-10   1   0   0   =1

Nigger
9-10   1   0   0   =1

Nuts   0   0   0   =0

Peckerhead
9-10   1   0   0   =1

Pee
9-10   1   0   0   =1

Penis
9-10   0   2   0   =2

Pickle
3-4   4   1   0   =5

Pig
5-6   1   2   0
7-8   1   3   0
9-10   1   0   0   =8

Pinhead
5-6   1   0   0   =1

Piss
5-6   3   0   0
7-8   6   1   0
9-10   1   1   0   =12

Poo-poo
5-6	3	1	0	
7-8	1	0	0	=5

Prick
3-4	1	0	0	=1

Puke
5-6	1	0	0	=1

Pussy
3-4	0	2	0	
5-6	1	0	0	
9-10	3	0	0	=6

Queer
7-8	2	0	0	
9-10	3	0	0	=5

Retard
7-8	2	0	0	
9-10	2	0	0	=4

Screw
5-6	2	0	0	
9-10	1	0	0	=3

Scum
5-6	1	0	0	
7-8	1	0	0	=2

Shit

1-2	2	1	0
3-4	0	0	2
5-6	4	1	1
7-8	11	1	2
9-10	12	1	1	=39

Shithead

5-6	1	0	0
9-10	1	0	0	=2

Silly

3-4	2	0	0	=2

Sissy

5-6	0	1	0
7-8	1	0	0	=2

Slob

9-10	1	0	0	=1

Slum

9-10	1	0	0	=1

Stupid

5-6	5	0	0
7-8	1	0	0	=6

Suck

3-4	2	0	0
5-6	1	0	0
7-8	5	1	0
9-10	2	0	1	=12

Tit

9-10	0	1	0	=1

Ugly				
1-2	4	0	0	
3-4	4	0	0	=8
Vagina	0	0	0	=0
Weenie	0	0	0	=0
Wimp				
5-6	5	0	0	
7-8	2	0	0	
9-10	2	0	0	=9
Wuss	0	0	0	=0
Total	883	98	15	=496

Table 2b. *Word Frequency by Gender of Speaker and Target.*

WORD **Female** Speaker Age	TARGET			
	Male	Female	No Target	
Ass				
3-4	0	2	0	
5-6	1	0	1	
7-8	0	0	1	
9-10	1	0	0	=6
Asshole				
1-2	0	1	0	
7-8	1	1	0	=3
Asswipe	0	0	0	=0
Balls	0	0	0	=0
Bastard				
5-6	2	3	0	
7-8	1	0	0	=6
Bingo				
3-4	6	0	0	=6

Bitch

3-4	0	1	0	
5-6	2	5	0	
7-8	1	1	0	
9-10	1	4	0	=15

Brat

5-6	0	1	0	=1

Bum

3-4	2	1	0	
9-10	1	0	0	=4

Butt	0	0	0	=0

Bullshit	0	0	0	=0

Chicken	0	0	0	=0

Christ	0	0	0	=0

Cock	0	0	0	=0

Crap

5-6	0	1	0	=1

Creep

5-6	4	0	0	
7-8	1	0	0	
9-10	2	0	0	=7

Damn

5-6	0	1	0	
9-10	1	0	0	=2

Dick	0	0	0	=0

Dink				
7-8	1	0	0	=1
Dipshit				
7-8	0	1	0	=1
Doo-doo				
3-4	3	0	0	=3
Dog	0	0	0	=0
Dork	0	0	0	=0
Douchebag	0	0	0	=0
Dummy	0	0	0	=0
Dumb				
5-6	0	1	0	=1
Fag				
3-4	1	0	0	
7-8	4	2	0	
9-10	1	1	0	=9
Fart	0	0	0	=0
Fat				
3-4	0	1	0	
5-6	0	1	0	=2
Fool				
9-10	1	0	0	=1
Fraidy cat				
3-4	3	0	0	=3

Friggin	0	0	0	=0
Fuck				
3-4	1	2	0	
7-8	0	0	1	
9-10	3	1	0	=8
Gay				
9-10	0	1	0	=1
Goddamn				
3-4	0	1	0	
5-6	1	0	0	=2
God				
5-6	1	2	0	
7-8	1	1	0	=5
Hell				
3-4	0	1	0	=1
Idiot				
5-6	1	0	0	
7-8	1	0	0	=2
Imbecile	0	0	0	=0
Jackass	0	0	0	=0
Jerk				
3-4	2	0	0	
5-6	5	6	0	
7-8	2	0	0	=15

Jesus
1-2	0	1	0
3-4	0	1	0
5-6	1	0	0	=3

Knucklehead
3-4	1	0	0	=1

Nerd
0	0	0	=0

Nigger
0	0	0	=0

Nuts
3-4	2	0	0	=2

Moron
0	0	0	=0

Peckerhead
0	0	0	=0

Pee
3-4	3	0	0
5-6	0	1	1	=5

Penis
0	0	0	=0

Pickle
3-4	1	1	0	=2

Pig
5-6	0	2	0
7-8	4	0	0
9-10	1	0	0	=7

Pinhead
0	0	0	=0

Piss
5-6	0	1	0	
7-8	1	0	0	=2

Poo-poo
3-4	1	1	0	=2

Prick
	0	0	0	=0

Puke
1-2	1	0	0	=1

Pussy
7-8	1	0	0	=1

Queer
7-8	1	0	0	=1

Retard
	0	0	0	=0

Screw
	0	0	0	=0

Scum
5-6	1	0	0	
9-10	1	0	0	=2

Shit
1-2	0	0	1	
3-4	0	1	0	
5-6	1	1	0	
7-8	1	2	1	
9-10	2	1	0	=11

Shithead
3-4	1	2	0	=3

Silly
3-4   1   0   0
5-6   1   0   0   =2

Sissy   0   0   0   =0

Slob   0   0   0   =0

Slum   0   0   0   =0

Stupid
5-6   2   0   0
7-8   1   0   0   =3

Suck
3-4   1   0   0
5-6   1   1   0
9-10   1   0   0   =4

Tit   0   0   0   =0

Ugly
3-4   1   0   0
5-6   1   0   0   =2

Vagina
5-6   0   1   0   =1

Weenie
5-6   1   0   0
9-10   1   0   0   =2

Wimp
5-6   1   0   0
7-8   1   0   0
9-10   1   0   0   =3

Wuss
9-10   1   0   0   =1

Totals   100   61   6   =167

Table 3. *Summary of Word Frequency Count.* (Total number of utterances 663)

Male			Female		
496			167		
Target			Target		
Male	Female	No Target	Male	Female	No Target
383	98	15	100	61	6

The "Top Ten"

Male		Female	
fuck	73	bitch	15
jerk	47	jerk	15
shit	39	shit	11
asshole	32	fag	9
bum	17	fuck	8
bitch	16	creep	7
dink	16	pig	7
goddamn	12	ass	6
suck	12	bastard	6
piss	12	bingo	6

An elaborate analysis of the lexicon is not offered in this work, but the reader may find it useful to compare the entries to points made earlier in the chapter with regard to anger, sexuality, joking, name calling and gender differences.

Field Study Two: Summer Camp (Hall & Jay, 1988)

The previous study was designed to collect normative data about speaker age and gender and to determine how the taboo lexicon develops during childhood. Until now the pragmatic function of cursing, using taboo language and the manner in which the speech is produced, have been given less attention. The goal of the second study was to record why children use taboo language: to express anger, tell jokes, express surprise, make insults, or describe connotatively and denotatively their environment. We wanted to look beyond differences in semantics and vocabulary and examine the relative frequencies of pragmatic speech acts discussed in the chapter.

The first author (Peter Hall), while employed as a summer camp counselor, took the opportunity to record children's use of taboo language. The focus was on the speech acts mentioned above and the manner, or speech volume of the utterances. By looking at the speech acts employed, the pragmatic function of taboo speech can be determined. Once the purpose of swearing is known, for example to express anger and frustration, the total variety of speech acts was recorded and relative frequency established. In other words, the most frequent speech act or pragmatic usage is an indication of how important or valuable cursing is to children to achieve the means of the act. If taboo speech is frequently used in expressions of anger relative to expressions of surprise, taboo words may be more valuable to express anger, than non-taboo words. Further, because speech volume has not been analyzed before with regard to taboo word usage, some additional information may be gained to support or challenge previous findings. We suspect that children may try to stifle some uses of taboo language around adults and that females may be more likely to use lower speech levels around males, while males may be less sensitive to listeners' reactions. The point of the study was to determine the value cursing plays in children's language use and to continue to establish a corpus of children's cursing in general.

Method

The study was conducted between June and August of 1987 at a summer camp located in a small community (8,000 population), 35 miles west of Boston, Massachusetts. The camp offered typical activities such as swimming, sailing, baseball, archery, riflery, and horseback riding, which allow campers to express a wide range of skill and emotion. In many of the activities children compete against each other to achieve personal goals. Frustration, surprise and elation along with anger and hostility are commonly expressed emotions.

The camp separates children from parents and other adult authority figures and "home" rules of conduct. Campers use taboo language not only to find out where their new boundaries of conduct lie, but also to challenge the counselors' authority.

The camper population was 350 with an age range from four to 14 years. About 55% were male and 45% were female and the majority of the camp was composed of eight to 12-year olds. The counselors numbered 75 (42 females and 33 males), most of which were college students aged 18 to 25 years. There were also five professional teachers, who carried out the administrative and supervisory duties, without direct contact with the campers. The socioeconomic background of the campers and counselors was similar and most came from within a 15-mile radius of the camp from middle to upper-middle class families.

Procedure

Episodes of taboo or obscene word usage were collected by a male college student counselor, who carried pre-printed 3" x 5" field cards. Speaker age and sex, target age and sex, the utterance including taboo words, the volume (whisper, soft, conversational, loud or yelled) and pragmatic function (joke, anger-frustration, insults, surprise-expletive or description-evaluation) were recorded. The episodes were recorded in a variety of situations around the camp, including, riflery and archery ranges, beach and baseball areas.

The recorder was careful not to disclose the fact that speech was being recorded and tried not to react in an overt fashion when taboo speech was used. In contrast, other counselors reprimanded campers for such usage in many cases.

Classification of Usage

Five functional categories were used and are described here to indicate how episodes were tabulated. Anger and/or frustration were combined due to the difficulty in distinguishing these emotions by language alone. An example of anger-frustration was when a boy who had his basketball field goal attempt blocked responded, "what the fuck." It would be difficult to determine if he was angry at the blocker or himself by that phrase alone.

The Descriptive-Evaluative category was used to indicate how speakers described connotatively or denotatively the objects and events around the camp. "This game sucks" is an evaluation of the baseball game; while "my sneakers are shitty" is a denotative description after stepping in dog feces. Taboo words also intensify descriptions, for example, "he beat the hell out of him" indicates the level of physical energy used in the fight.

The Joking category was used for formal joke frames and humor usage with taboo words. At this camp, non-dirty jokes were often regarded as "corny" and the teller was laughed at rather than his or her joke. At times obscenities were added to jokes and stories to make them appear as funny as possible.

The fourth category was for Surprise reactions to unexpected achievement, loss or other behavior. These usages are typical of expletives and commonly involve religious terms, for example, "jesus" or "oh god."

The last category was for Sarcastic Irony or insults. These episodes involved derogatory words and descriptions, "you fag" or "scum face" are good examples. Here the speaker attempted to mock or criticize the target of abuse in front of peers. Rather than only expressing anger on the part of the speaker, insults served the function of denoting undesirable qualities of the target, whether these were real or imagined by the speaker.

Word Volume

These categories, as listed above, were roughly based on the speech intensity level in decibels of the speaker. A yell was considered to be about 85 decibels, loud was 75, conversational speech was 65, soft was 55, and whispers were 45 decibels or below. The actual speech level in decibels was not recorded but estimated by the recorder.

Results and Discussion

There were a total of 224 episodes recorded. Results are reported by category and frequency of occurrence. An alphabetical listing of word frequencies by sex of speaker appears in Table 4. The most frequent words used overall appear in Table 5, while Table 6 presents the most frequent words as a function of sex of speaker. From these data it can be seen that males were recorded using taboo words at a much higher rate than females (184 versus 40 episodes, respectively) and that males tended to use stronger or more offensive words than did females. Note, for example, that males used the word *fuck* 21 times and females only once. The top ten words in terms of overall frequency (Table 5) account for 118 occurrences or 53% of the total data. A small number of words are used in most of these speech acts. This phenomenon holds true for both males and females. Table 6 indicates that just eight words account for 50% of the males' data. A different set of eight words account for 52% of females' use of taboo words.

Table 4. *Total Word Frequency.*

	Speaker		
Word	Male	Female	Total
Ass	3	0	3
Asshole	2	0	2
Balls	2	0	2
Bastard	1	0	1
Bitch	4	3	7
Bone	1	0	1
Bonehead	2	0	2
Boner	2	0	2
Boobs	1	0	1
Bull	1	0	1
Bullshit	1	0	1
Butt	2	0	2
Christ	0	1	1
Crap	2	0	2
Cunt	1	0	1
Damn	8	2	10
Dang it	2	0	2
Darn it	1	2	3
Dick	4	1	5
Dickhead	0	1	1
Dickless	1	0	1
Dink	2	1	3
Dorks	2	0	2
Dumb	1	0	1
Erection	1	0	1
Fag	2	0	2
Fuck	21	1	22
Gay	5	1	6
Geek	2	1	3
God	6	4	10

Goddamn	2	0	2
Gosh	0	1	1
Heck	3	0	3
Hell	6	1	7
Holyshit	3	0	3
Hump	1	0	1
Idiot	0	1	1
Jesus	9	1	10
Jerk	3	2	5
Knucklehead	1	0	1
Masturbating	0	1	1
Motherfucker	5	0	5
Moron	1	0	1
Motha'	1	0	1
Penis	5	0	5
Pissa'	0	1	1
Pissed off	2	1	3
Pubic hair	1	0	1
Queer	3	0	3
Scum face	1	0	1
Shit	23	3	26
Shithead	2	0	2
Shoot	6	1	7
Shucks	0	2	2
Son-of-a-bitch	2	1	3
Stinks	2	0	2
Stupid	1	1	2
Suck	13	0	13
Sucker	1	0	1
Tick-me-off	0	2	2
Titties	1	0	1
Wacking off	1	0	1
Wench	0	1	1
Whore	0	1	1
Totals	184	40	224

Table 5. *The "Top Ten."*

Word	Frequency
Shit	26
Fuck	22
Suck	13
Damn	10
God	10
Jesus	10
Bitch	7
Hell	7
Shoot	7
Gay	6

Table 6. *Most Frequent: Male & Female.*

Male		Female	
Word	Frequency	Word	Frequency
Shit	23	God	4
Fuck	21	Shit	3
Suck	13	Bitch	3
Jesus	9	Dink	3
Damn	8	Damn	2
God	6	Shucks	2
Hell	6	Tick-me-off	2
Shoot	6	Jerk	2

Table 7. *Pragmatic Word Usage: Most Frequent.*

Pragmatic category	(total frequency)	
Word	Frequency	
Anger/Frustration		(143)
Shit	24	
Fuck	22	
Suck	12	
Damn	9	
Jesus	8	
Description-Evaluation		(31)
Bitch	5	
Hell	4	
Motherfucker	4	
Stinks	2	
Jokes		(27)
Dick	4	
Gay	3	
Penis	3	
Ass	2	
Balls	2	
Boner	2	
Surprise		(12)
Holy shit	3	
God	3	
Jesus	2	
Sarcasm		(11)
Queer	3	
Geek	3	
Fag	2	
Gay	2	

Pragmatic Usage: Speech Acts

The relative frequency of words as a function of pragmatic category appears in Table 7. All of the 224 episodes reported here were categorized or assigned to one of the five types of speech act.

Anger-Frustration. The expression of anger or frustration accounted for the highest number of episodes. A total of 64% of the use of taboo words was for this purpose. At the individual word level, the most frequent was *shit* (24 times), followed by *fuck* (22 times). Interestingly, the word *fuck* was used exclusively to express anger or frustration, as the word was not categorized or recorded as achieving other pragmatic functions.

The strong language conveying anger and frustration was targeted toward others 43% of the time and used as expletives the remainder of its usage. An example of targeted usage was, "what the fuck, Matt?" while expletive usage is exemplified by single word outbursts, such as, "fuck" or "damn."

Description-Evaluation. The use of taboo words to describe or evaluate, although not as frequent as anger-frustration, accounted for the second most popular pragmatic usage. Fourteen percent of the episodes reflected this usage. The words *bitch* and *hell* were the most frequent, occurring five and four times, respectively. These expressions were targeted toward others 77% of the time and the remaining 23% did not target a particular group or individual.

Jokes. Jokes containing taboo and obscene language accounted for 12% of the data. Commonly used words were *dick, gay* and *penis.* The majority of these jokes either referred to body parts or processes related to sexual behavior (*ass, balls, boobs, erection, hump, gay* and *wacking off*).

Surprise. The category of surprise accounted for 5% of the episodes and many of these terms had religious overtones, for example, *holy shit, god* and *jesus.* A larger sample would be needed to determine just how important religious connotations are for the expression of surprise.

Sarcasm. Sarcastic irony was used in only 5% of the total number of episodes. The most popular words were related to suggestions about homosexuality, that is, *queer, fag* and *gay.* Not surprisingly, all of these episodes were targeted at other people.

Did Gender Matter? Yes and No.

The gender of the speaker has often times been found to determine what type of language he or she selects for a given situation (see chapter on Offensiveness). Although sex differences were found in the present study, these data must be interpreted with caution due to the use of only a male recorder and the small size of the sample of words.

Targeted versus Expletive Usage. While males and females used targeted expression at roughly the same frequency, 55%, there appeared to be differences at the type of words each selected for these expressions. For expletive usage, males used words such as *shit*, *fuck* and *damn*, while females used words such as *god* or euphemisms *darn it* and *shucks*. As for targeted expressions, males used *suck*, *fuck* and *hell* and females used *bitch*, *jerk* and *shit* frequently.

Gender and Pragmatics. It seemed clear that the most common function of taboo word usage at the summer camp for both males and females was to express anger or frustration. These episodes accounted for 65% of male usage and 57.5% of females'. These data may reflect the challenging activities within the camp environment and/or the degree of interpersonal conflict for young children and teenagers.

Jokes. Taboo word usage in joke frames accounted for 13.5% of males' data and 5% of females'. The higher frequency of male joking relative to females has been noted before (Coser, 1960) and should be interpreted cautiously, since sex of recorder was not counterbalanced in this study.

Females seemed more likely than males to use taboo speech in an expression of surprise, 15% and 3.5%, respectively. Both sexes used taboo words in descriptions of people and events at about the same frequency with males' descriptive usage at 13.1% and females' at 17.5%. The use of sarcastic irony with taboo words was relatively uncommon with 5% of the overall episodes for both males and females.

Thus there are not dramatic differences in male and female pragmatics. Where there are differences, the data seem to support previous findings with regard to anger expression and for joke telling.

Volume Differences. The speech volume of these episodes showed minor differences as a function of speaker sex. Males were judged to be louder more often than females, 57% versus 45% of the episodes, respectively. Males were estimated to use the conversational level 38.5% of the time and females 50%. The three episodes of the yelling were by males alone and the single recorded incident of whispering was by a female. The "soft" category was used only about 2% of the time by both males and females. It may be that males talk more loudly than females, especially around the male recorder and more data are needed with regard to speech volume at the lower end of the scale to provide a more definitive picture.

Summary of Field Studies

After examining the data from two field studies, it may be observed that children acquire the use of taboo language as early as two years of age, that their vocabulary is small but similar to adults' and that males and females differ in their production of taboo speech at about the age of five or six years in a manner similar to adults. Children use taboo speech primarily in conjunction with frustration or anger provoking events. They also use taboo words frequently to make connotative and denotative statements about their environment and to make jokes. They use them less frequently as expletives to express surprise and in the form of sarcastic remarks. These data are intended to provide a measure of who, what, where and when children use dirty words in public.

Conclusion

Infants enter the world ready to learn language. In the course of language acquisition certain social interactions become associated with the use of taboo and obscene speech. These interactions include anger expression, name calling, object naming, story telling, humor and joking, sex talk and language at school. Dirty words appear as soon as "normal" language does and the lexicon grows and becomes more adult like over time. As the child ages, words are added and some of the childish words are dropped from usage. From the age of five years or so, girls and boys begin to use different words for insults and swearing and they use these words in different manners. For example, boys have a larger and more offensive production vocabulary relative to girls. Boys are also louder and less likely to express surprise when using taboo words. Mainly dirty words are used by children to express anger and frustration and to insult others more than they are used in descriptive statements. Joking, sarcastic irony, along with anger, surprise and descriptive use, account for much of children's use of taboo words in public.

Chapter 3

Anger and Dirty Words

The purpose of this chapter is to examine the relation between the use of dirty words and the expression of anger. The material is divided into three sections. The introductory section covers previous research on anger expression and the figurative language using dirty words to express anger. The next section presents an experiment demonstrating that the "rules" for using dirty words, maybe the "etiquette" of dirty word expressions, have been acquired by native speakers and that these underlying rules are highly contextual in nature. Taking into account the material in the first two discussions, the final section proposes a five-stage model of anger expression with dirty words.

The Emergence and Use of Taboo to Express Anger

In previous writing (Jay, 1985) and others (Goodenough, 1931; Montagu, 1967) it is recognized that infants originally express their anger by howling and crying, which are later replaced by linguistic expressions at or around the first year. These linguistic expressions take the form of swearing or cursing and are clearly part of the child's lexicon by the end of the second year. What specifically the child does say when frustrated or angry depends on the context, that is, what the parents say and what positive and negative reactions they have to these words and episodes of the child's anger.

Much of the content of the child's early humor, story telling, and insulting routines that use taboo words are concerned with the rituals of elimination and those of toilet training. These routines, as Goodenough found, are stressful and frustrating for parents and children alike. Being soiled, wet, messy are experiences that become the semantics of insults and anger. That is, the angry child will use names like *pee pee*, *poop head*, *ka ka*, or the body parts associated with such acts, which result in the names like, *wiener*, *bum bum*, *tinkler*. These are the words that the child hears parents and other children use in association with the toilet rituals.

The speakers who might use the words in anger or periods of stress, signal to the listener, through emphasis on these words, that words are powerful. The child may later repeat these words during a period of stress. Interestingly, these routines are similar to insult rituals used by "primitive" cultures such as the aborigines, according to Montagu. To express anger or incite anger in the enemy one uses words much like the young child would yell at a listener when provoked. Initially, the child is limited to the vocabulary learned in a limited number of contexts. As the child becomes more experienced with the nuances of context and language, a wider variety of words can be selected beyond the early scatological and toilet-training type words.

Montagu thinks that primitive swearing makes references to excrement and filth as if these substances were being thrown at the target of abuse, or used as a means to overpower the enemy. The aborigines may also tell another to "go have sex with your mother" not too far from the American English version, i.e., *motherfucker*. Here, the references to sex organs and sex acts derive their power from the value placed on them by the society in question and the amount of emotion associated with them. In a sense the taboo expression may be a substitute for physical violence in our culture or as Montagu says, "to let off steam" (p 65), and continues:

> "I believe that the evidence so far considered strongly suggests that swearing is a culturally acquired way of expressing anger. Anger is a complex emotion the expression of which may take the form of a hostile response--it may be an oath, it may be a lampoon it may be a laugh or a hundred and one other behaviors. Whatever the truth may be, it is clear that different conditions call forth different forms of anger and that one of these forms of anger the desire to swear, as a learned form of response, occurs in some cultures or segments of a culture but not others." (pp 81-82)

However, Montagu never indicates which cultures do *not* curse! It is probably the case that all cultures have methods of cursing and expressing anger.

Anger Expressed Through Cursing or Blasphemy

Flexner in his book *I Hear America Talking* (1976), notes that "when I hear America talking I hear America cursing" (p 173). He claims that cursing and blasphemy were used to shock or express strong feelings through the Victorian era but started to give way to obscenity and scatology during World War I. By World

War II, blasphemy was replaced almost completely by obscenity. The notion that one form of expression "replaces" another means that the earlier form had lost its power of expression. The milder religious language was replaced by more offensive, more powerful terms that refer to sex. These religious terms are used today to express milder forms of anger relative to that expressed with obscenities. Here are some of the commonly used expressions of anger that are based on religious language:

"goddamn you", and derivatives, "damn you", or
"damn your hide."
"go to hell", "to hell with you", "may you rot
in hell", "I hope you rot in hell", "may you roast in hell."

...these are certainly curses that are intended to do harm to the wrongdoer by the suggestion in the curse. It appears that the speaker wishes for the gods to do these bad things (put you in hell or damn you) to the offender. Exactly what would be experienced in the real, physical world in these modern times is not clear by examining the curse. They seem to operate more as markers of condemnation of unwarranted behavior rather than provoking the religious sanctions used by the church centuries ago. The power of these to do harm to a wrongdoer probably lies in the degree of religious belief of the hearer. Now consider these religious terms that operate on a different level.

jesus, jesus christ, or *christ*
lord, lord in heaven, lord christ

...these are not curses but are a form of blasphemy or perhaps a profane epithet. They may serve the primary function of alleviating the pain of the offended or to signal a wrongdoer, if there is one, that the offended is angry. These expressions do not refer to any particular qualities of the offending event or a wrongdoer. They are used as expletives or as invocations of religious power. The specific harm that is wished to befall the wrongdoer in the expletives is not clear, as in the curses above (*damn you*, etc).

Curses indicate that the speaker wishes to invoke the power of the gods to do harm to the wrongdoer. In this sense a true curse is an act of retaliation in itself. Blasphemy or profanity is not intended to harm the wrongdoer like the curse of old. Blasphemy and profanity reflect a lack of respect for the terms associated with religious figures or religious thought in general.

Anger Expressed Through Reference to Subnormal Thought

Another form of mild anger expression is the use of terms that focus on the thoughtlessness of the offending behavior. These insults express the speaker's anger through the use of a term that indicates that the wrongdoer has subnormal mental functioning. These words usually refer to the wrongdoer's head, brain, or mental abilities.

One of the obvious dimensions of anger expressions is the reference to the thoughtless nature of the provocation. These expressions focus on the head and brains of the wrongdoer. They may be mild in offensiveness or employ obscene qualifiers to make the expression more offensive.

Children may use some of these:

> *dumbhead, do-do head, bum-bum head*
> *numbskull*
> *nuthead, cuckoo head*
> ...these may also use the term *brain* in place of *head*

Other terms that refer to mental subnormality are

> *stupid, dummy, jerk, moron, idiot, retard*

More offensive counterparts of the above examples are:

> *shithead, peckerhead, dickhead, fuckhead*
> *dorkbrain*
> *dumbass, shit for brains, dumb dick, dumb cunt*
> *dumb shit*...in fact using *dumb* to qualify almost
> any other obscenity would do.

These insults tell the wrongdoer that the offending behavior was done without thinking. In other words, they tell the wrongdoer to think before acting the next time. Note that these insults are targeted at human listeners and never at inanimate objects. One would never call the hammer a *moron* after hitting a finger with it.

Anger Expressed Through Obscenity

According to Flexner, the first wide-spread use of *fuck* as an expletive began by the late 1800's. He gives the example of "go fuck yourself" as an indicator of angry rejection. This one example brings under scrutiny the notion that the emotion laden references to sex acts, sex organs, and sexual deviations are widely used to express anger and insult our enemies. In almost all cases these sexually derived terms are more offensive than those based on religious terms or references to mental ability. Following are a few examples of each category of sexual obscenity.

Anger Expressed Through Reference to a Sex Organ

These expressions derive their power of retaliation through association with taboos of sexual body parts. Thus, to call a person a taboo body part is to evoke the understanding that these body parts are powerful or dirty or disgusting and to be called such is to be insulted. If the target is called a body part, then s/he is that body part exclusively; that is, the reference is not intended as a metonymy. It is obvious that these associations are learned and may differ from culture to culture. These references to body parts when used to label a person are in all cases derogatory. Their use differs as a function of the speaker and wrongdoer sex and according to the nature of the offense.

> *prick, cock, dick, wiener, dork, dink*

...these words are targeted at male wrongdoers who have done some unwarranted or undesirable act. The first two words are more offensive than the latter.

> *cunt*

...this word is targeted at a female who is accused of engaging in some sexually promiscuous behavior, or when the offended expected to obtain a sexual favor but was denied it. It is very offensive to women.

Anger Expressed Through Reference to Deviant Sexual Act

This angry insult metaphor means that calling someone a deviant based on taboo sex acts or occupying a sexually deviant social role stands for anger. The examples are:

> *motherfucker (motherhumper, motherjumper, motherraper)*
> *cocksucker*
> *bugger*
> *pigfucker*

To these single word cases are added the following similar expressions.

> *go fuck yourself*

go screw yourself
go bugger yourself
go fuck your fist for five minutes
take a flying fuck

These expressions are not interpreted denotatively (one cannot fuck oneself). They are to be interpreted figuratively or connotatively. In short they express disgust and indicate that the speaker prefers not to be in the company of the accused. In America these are the most offensive forms of swearing and to use these expressions when angered means a high degree of anger is experienced or a high degree of retaliation is intended or both. It is assumed that to speak the most taboo words when angered is to be most angered and that more mild forms of anger would generate milder taboos. The events that trigger strong expressions would be of great offense, high damage or pain, highly unjustified behavior experienced by the offended. They are direct and unambiguous when targeted at the wrongdoer as expressions of anger. With these very offensive expressions, one would expect to note more power in the voice, a red face, strong muscle tension, and other emotional gestures that signal a high degree of anger.

Anger Expressed Through Reference to Being Sexually Violated

These expressions are clearly metaphors for anger. They indicate that the speaker was treated unjustly, *as if* he or she was forced to commit some unwanted or deviant sex act. The unnatural sex act is an indication that the speaker was treated unnaturally, hence is angry. This anger is directed not to the wrongdoer (who is assumed not to be present) but is focused more on the nature of the offending event.

I was fucked over
we got fucked
what a ballbuster(breaker)
we got screwed
he was just jerking us off

...these expressions indicate that the offended has been metaphorically violated like the sexual violation expressed in the words. These focus more on the state of anger in the offended and do not provide a great deal of information about the wrongdoer.

For the speaker the offending event, however, was unwarranted, unjustified, or unexpected.

Underlying the reference to sexual violation is another social model, i.e., the notion that one has been cheated. From the social violation of cheating we use the metaphor of sexual violation, that is, to be cheated is to be sexually violated. Here are some examples

> *The referee called too many penalties on us...*
> *The referee fucked us*

> *The car salesman overcharged me for my new car*
> *The car salesman screwed me*

> *I waited in line for my ticket but there were none for sale*
> *They were just jerking us off*

Thus, the notion of being abused socially is understood and expressed in terms of being violated sexually.

Anger Expressed Through Reference to Social-Sexual Deviation

These expressions are highly dependent on the gender of the offended and the gender of the wrongdoer. Since some of these are labels for deviant sexual behavior, they are used to target behavior that is sexually deviant. *Whore, cunt,* or *slut* would always be targeted at women with the suggestion of questionable moral standards, while *son of a bitch* would more likely be yelled at a male offender for any of a variety of offenses. The woman target actually may have high standards but when her morals are brought into question therein lies the insult. Questioning a man's moral standards is not insulting and the reference to *bitch* in *son of a bitch*, again refers to the woman's morals not the son's.

> *bastard*
> *jerk off*
> *blow job*
> *wanker*
> *pimp*
> *son of a bitch or s o b*

...although these refer to social deviations, they are used to indicate a general disgust with the wrongdoer's behavior. They are less informative as to the nature of the behavior as compared to the expressions that follow.

> *whore*
>
> *slut*
>
> *prickteaser*
>
> *dyke, lesbian, queer, fag, homo, gay, butch*

...these and others specify the nature of the social deviation as rooted in abnormal sexual behavior. The insult serves to label the behavior and the wrongdoer at the same time. They are restricted by the gender of the wrongdoer.

Some insults aimed at women (*dyke, bulldyke, butch, lesbian*) may be based on the notion that women are supposed to be passive and feminine. These terms may be used when the woman in question acted assertively, aggressively or with "masculine behavior."

Anger Expressed Through Racial-Ethnic Reference

In cultures where there are haves and have-nots, in-groups and out-groups, or minorities and majorities there is bound to be social tension and anger that focuses on these group differences. These distinctions may be stereotypes, false attributions, or prejudices unrecognized in the mind of the speaker. They may be taught to children with no sound basis in fact. Ethnic slurs will be used to express hostility and anger among the prejudiced.

Here are but a few examples:

> *spic*
>
> *mick*
>
> *nigger*
>
> *wop*
>
> *dago*
>
> *taco*
>
> *kike*

...actually there are hundreds of these, too numerous to list here. Racial slurs are of course learned and used to derogate a member of an out-group or member of a group of people perceived to be of lower status than the speaker. To express anger they are derogatory in all cases but are at times used as terms of endearment within members of the identified group. The use of these may indicate the speaker's anger with the mere existence of the target without any particular offending behavior in question.

One's social and ethnic class are certainly dimensions that are used to denote inclusion and exclusion. These terms identify outcasts and group members by the use of the term alone.

Anger Expressed Through Scatology

Here the focus is on acts of elimination and the body parts associated with elimination. These insults are common in primitive cultures and they also form the basis for much of children's insults. It is assumed that these words derive their power to offend because they associate the target or wrongdoer with the act of elimination or being soiled by the body product. Many of the expressions are used frequently in our culture to express anger and frustration and these terms are not as offensive as the sexual obscenities.

Anger Expressed Through Reference to Body Product or Process

pissed off, pissed, p o'd, pisser
...these focus on the state of the offended and do not clearly define the nature of the offensive behavior.

> *shit, shithead, shitass, crap, turd*
> *fart, fart smeller, fart face*
> *puke, puke face*
> *ass, asshole, asswipe, asskisser*
> *snot, booger*

...the remainder are targeted at a wrongdoer of either sex and indicate the recognition of some unwanted behavior. The use of the term "head" usually indicates that the behavior was thoughtless or foolish, focusing most directly on the mental (in)abilities of the wrongdoer. "Asskisser" however does indicate some type of overly compliant behavior between a superordinate and subordinate. This category would also include the euphemisms that parents make up to describe these behaviors and would be more idiosyncratic in nature.

Anger Expressed Through Items Associated with Body Products

This category includes objects, tools, or sanitary devices used in conjunction with elimination or sex acts.

> *douche bag, douche*
> *scumbag*
> *shitbag, shit stick*

Anger Expressed Through References to Animals

Referring to someone as an animal can be an expression of anger. One attributes animal qualities to humans (he was a real beast) and human qualities to animals (the dog looks sad). One understands anger in part by relating this emotion to animal properties. The use of animal metaphors and idioms are found in many American expressions of emotion.

Animal names as insults have been used for centuries. The essence of these insults is to reduce a human to an animal form as if the person in question was not a human. The insult may be based on the notion that the person looks like an animal or behaves like the animal.

> *pig, jackass, cock, turkey*
> *pussy* (also *puss, wussy* and *wuss*)
> *cow, bitch, dog, sow, chick*

...the first set of these are targeted at males and the latter more commonly at females. They refer to animal-like behavior, i.e., crude, rude, or socially inept behaviors. They may also refer to physical appearance that the offended chose to focus on with the angry reply. Children commonly use the term *pig* to mean a fat or obese person, or one that is dirty, for example. The term *pussy* generally refers to an effeminate male but is used on occasion to refer to non-assertive females, too. In addition the combination of animal and body products gives us the following expressions of anger.

Anger Expressed Through Reference to Animal Feces

bullshit

horseshit

These two terms are generally used connotatively to indicate that the speaker has uttered some nonsense. Whereas the next reference is to indicate timidity or fear on the part of the offender.

chickenshit

Interestingly, the last example also indicates that besides animal ferocity as an indication of anger, animal referents are used to indicate that passive or feminine behavior in males is interpreted with scorn with animal names and with other taboo referents.

Discussion

Americans express anger with dirty words, using a small number of semantic categories (animals, body products, social deviation). This is not to say that all anger episodes may use dirty words, are limited to verbal expression or are limited to the semantic categories described above. Further, the expression of anger with dirty words may be highly dependent on the context of the episode, the relationship between the speakers, the prosodic features of the speech and other sociolinguistic factors. The next section was designed to elucidate some of the contextual variables and demonstrate how they influence dirty word use.

The Context of Anger Expression

The topic here is a laboratory study to verify that speakers carry around "in their heads" an etiquette for swearing. They know the who, what, when, and where of dirty word usage. This study was conducted with college students by asking them about how likely it would be the case that someone would swear under a set of contextual conditions. Consider the following examples:

the dean said shit in the parking lot
the janitor said shit in the parking lot

the student said hell in his room
the dean said hell in a dorm room

the student said fuck in the dean's office
the dean said fuck in the dean's office

How likely is it that one of the pairs would occur relative to the other? Which of the pairs would be more offensive? If one can make these judgments, and of course he/she can, then the judgments support the contention that speakers have implicitly learned the rules of dirty word use. It would be the high degree of raters' agreements about these language statements that provides credibility to the present claims. The clarity and predictability of these data would provide good evidence that Americans have implicitly learned the rules of dirty word usage.

The following is a look at some influential contextual variables and a test of the notion that Americans understand dirty word etiquette.

Social-Physical Setting

The factors of social and physical settings are difficult to separate for discussion, the reason being that in many cases it is impossible to separate the influence of social climate of a discussion from the physical setting in which it occurs. Take for example the pregame warmup pep talk in a locker room. This point should be kept in mind. Further, some messages have the same interpretation for almost any setting, for example, "your father died of cancer today." Dirty words, however, are very sensitive to setting; *jesus christ* means one thing in a church and quite another when exclaimed in the locker room.

Social climate refers to the dimension of relaxation or formality of the occasion. The climate is determined by the rules of conduct necessary to fit the occasion. Some of the rules may be explicit and shared, such as rules for order for a meeting, or may be inferred by watching how others are acting in the setting. The physical setting refers to the specific location in which the communication is conducted, for example building, rooms, or larger spaces like shopping malls or town commons. Each of these places has rules of conduct specific to the particular location.

Research on dirty word usage as a function of social-physical setting can be found in areas of psychology, sociology, law and mass communication journals. Here is a small sample of that research.

One article of interest is Cameron's (1969) paper, where he sampled speaking in a variety of settings and supported his main hypothesis that traditional word frequency counts like the Thorndike and Lorge (1944) underestimate the frequency of dirty words. He found that dirty words accounted for some 8% of college student conversations at leisure, 3% of adult conversation on the job and 13% of adult leisure conversation. Besides supporting his notions about word frequency, he also demonstrated the influence of setting. The difference between work and leisure in the adult sample is obvious.

Setting also influences the appropriateness of word usage. Some situations demand that dirty words be used, for example, a conversation where the boys on the corner are engaged in a game of the dozens (a game of verbal dueling and insulting between inner-city youth). Other situations may inhibit dirty words. It is hard to imagine swearing at a typical wedding, funeral or White House press conference.

Data have been collected regarding the effect of various physical locations on the likelihood of hearing dirty words. These data are presented in Table 1. In the experiment college students were asked to answer the question, "what is the likelihood of hearing a dirty word in these locations on campus?" They responded with a number from 0 to 100, where 0 means not likely at all and 100 mean most likely possible. These locations were obtained from the campus phone book, which identifies popular campus locations. Mean likelihood values are presented in the table. Locations used frequently or exclusively by students were the most likely to be associated with dirty word usage and those used less frequently are less likely.

Table 1. *Mean Likelihood of Hearing a Dirty Word in Various Campus Locations.*

Location	Value	Location	Value
Taconic Dorm (male)	90.32	Mail Room	35.31
Pub	89.25	Student Senate Office	35.31
Berkshire Dorm (coed)	88.75	Radio Station	34.69
Athletic Field	88.37	Student Affairs Office	34.38
Townhouse Apartments	86.25	Bookstore	33.44
Hoosac Dorm (female)	83.32	Veteran's Affairs Office	32.50
Greylock dorm (female)	82.19	Swimming Pool	31.56
Game Room	79.63	Media Center	29.69
Gymnasium	78.94	Supply Room	28.75
Training Room	63.25	Piano Lab	23.44
Athletic Office	62.12	Copy Center	20.94
Maintenance Room	57.13	Payroll Office	19.38
Newspaper Office	55.31	Campus School	18.75
Parking Lot	54.06	Registrar's Office	16.62
Sidewalk	53.13	Health Center	15.31
Security Office	44.37	President's Office	14.50
Library	43.44	Financial Aid Office	12.06
Biology Lab	40.94	Career Planning Office	11.69
Theater	40.94	Placement Office	10.63
Resourceful Living Center	39.69	Admissions Office	7.25
Computer Center	37.81	Dean's Office	7.25
Chemistry Lab	37.81	Day Care Center	1.44
Faculty Lounge	35.88		

Scale values are: 0=not likely at all, 100=most likely possible

Speaker-Listener Variable

Another force in the communication context is the relation between the speaker and the listener. Previous research has focused on the comprehension aspect of this factor, while less attention has been paid to production aspects. Some of the dimensions that have received attention include: gender, intimacy, age and status.

Most information about production and comprehension with regard to the speaker-listener variable deal with the dimension of sex role. Sex differences have been demonstrated in both production and reaction to dirty words. Lakoff (1973) reported that women use expletives that are different than men: women were more likely to use non-referent particles like, *oh, dear, goodness* or *fudge*, while men use stronger expletives like *shit* or *damn*. Other production differences as a function of gender have been demonstrated for degree of restraint in usage. This has been a reliable finding over the last 40 to 50 years, where females are more restrained in usage than males (see Hunter & Gains, 1938), the use of sex related slang (Kutner & Brogan, 1974), the use of terms for menstruation (Ernster, 1975), the use of terms for sexual intercourse (Walsh & Leonard 1974) and recall memory for dirty words (Grosser & Walsh, 1966).

As for sex differences in reaction to dirty words, the finding that females react with more inhibition to, or are more offended by the perception of dirty words, as compared to males, has been repeatedly demonstrated since the beginning of research in the area known as perceptual defense in the late 1940's (Erdelyi, 1974; or McGinnies, 1949).

When age becomes a factor in the speaker-listener relation, the attention switches to the use of dirty words by children. Here the concern is about children's use of dirty words and the possible relationship to normal growth and development. The reports typically focus on the relationship between the child and parents or peers (Hartmann, 1973; 1975). It is interesting to note that psychiatrists treat this phenomenon as a contextual problem, although they never make that explicit in their reports. They discuss setting, the listeners present, and so on, but then return to psychodynamics for answers. It would seem that age is not important unless the speaker is a child. Once identified, the "problem" is not only the child's, but belongs to the parents and siblings, as well.

Sociolinguistics has clearly shown that children's or adults' use of language can characterize certain qualities about the user, for example, profession, intelligence, education, status, or abstractness of thought. The speaker's use of dirty words provides information about speaker-listener dimensions such as sex, values, attitudes and social group. Sociologists use the production of dirty words to indicate the degree of socialization, or degree of in-group behavior for youth subculture (Gibson, 1963; Kulik, Sarbin & Stein, 1971; and Lerman, 1967). The speaker has at his/her disposal the ability to disclose as much of this information as necessary by the words chosen for the listener present.

If speaker and listener characteristics, such as occupation or status influence dirty word use, then varying characteristics in scenarios of dirty word episodes should affect subjects' likelihood estimates of dirty word use. Judgment data are presented in Table 2 with respect to speakers' occupations. Here subjects were asked to make likelihood judgments about dirty word usage as a function of campus occupation. These occupations were derived from rankings of occupational prestige in previous sociological research. The occupations which were represented on the author's campus were selected for examination. Again, the differences in perceived likelihood of using dirty words as a function of occupation is obvious from the mean ratings in Table 2.

Table 2. *Mean Likelihood of Using Dirty Words for Various Campus Occupations.*

Male Occupation	Rating	Female Occupation	Rating
Athletic Coach	82.50	Athletic Coach	49.37
Janitor	62.81	Cook	36.88
Policeman	62.50	Maid	33.44
Groundkeeper	58.13	Secretary	31.87
Building Superintendent	57.50	Bookstore Employee	28.44
Cook	51.88	Business Office Clerk	27.56
Teacher	44.50	Cashier	26.25
Mail Carrier	37.50	Teacher	24.69
Bookstore Employee	36.87	Admissions Officer	20.62
Business Office Clerk	32.81	Receptionist	20.06
Dean	28.75	Guidance Counselor	20.00
President	26.56	Nurse	19.37
Admissions Officer	25.00	Dean	14.38
Registrar	23.44	Librarian	7.87

Scale values are: 0= not likely at all, 100= most likely possible

Other likelihood ratings point out gender differences in dirty word usage. The general effect, cited above, is for females to show more restraint than males, or that males show less restraint in reaction to dirty words. Looking at Table 1 shows that gender is an important moderator in the likelihood ratings, especially in the dorm room locations. The most likely place to hear a dirty word is in a male's room, followed by a coed dorm room, and finally the least likely place to hear dirty words is the female's room (interestingly the upperclass dorm for females is a more likely place than the freshmen women's dorm). Looking at the ratings as a function of occupation in Table 2, it can be seen that a significant difference in likelihood exists as a function of gender for those occupations using both males and females, for example, athletic coach, cook, teacher, dean, admissions officer, bookstore employee or business office clerk, all have higher ratings for males.

Here is one final test of the model of production and comprehension as a decision making process based on the elements of the communication context. These final experiments construct combinations of various speakers, various locations and various words. College students were asked to rate: (a) the likelihood of occurrence and (b) the degree of offensiveness of a particular combination of people, places and words. For example, a possible item would be, "the janitor says hell in the library." The student subject rated the likelihood and later the offensiveness of this particular combination. The subjects received all combinations of three people, three places and three words. It was assumed that the combination of the pieces of information would be similar to what actually happens in communication contexts in the real world; i.e., people pay attention to factors like these when producing, interpreting or reacting to any type of language.

The results are plotted in the next four figures. Figure 1 represents the mean likelihood responses, ranging from 0 to 100, for the various combinations. The top of the figure represents the same data as the bottom, the difference is that likelihood ratings are plotted as a function of location at the top and as a function of speaker at the bottom. These data indicate significant differences in: (a) type of speaker, (b) type of location and (c) type of word used. There is no statistical interaction of speaker, location and word used. Figure 2 represents the offensiveness ratings for the same set of speakers, locations and words. These ratings are the opposite of those for likelihood judgments in the sense that high offensiveness indicates low likelihood of occurrence of dirty words and low offensiveness indicates high likelihood, when the reader compares Figure 1 data with those in Figure 2. In other words, a highly likely word like *hell* is very low in offensiveness; a highly likely person is low in offensiveness and a highly likely location is low in offensiveness. The correlation between likelihood and offensiveness is r= -.97, supporting the previous interpretation.

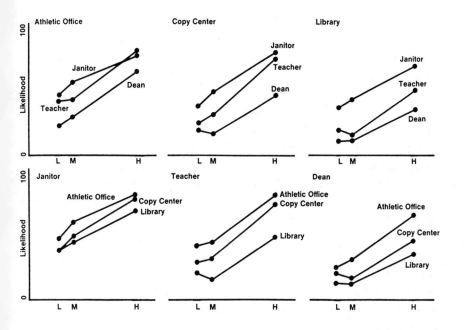

Figure 1. *Mean Likelihood Ratings as a Function of Speaker, Location, and Word.*

Note   Scale values are: 0= not likely at all, 100= most likely possible. Likelihood ratings are plotted vertically. The horizontal plot is obtained word likelihood: L=low, M=medium, H=high.

The bottom of the figure represents the same data as the top. However, data at the bottom are plotted as a function of location at the top of the figure.

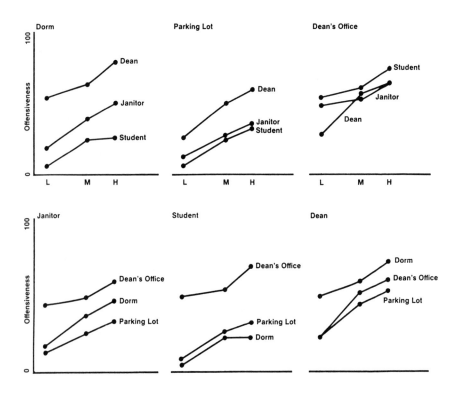

Figure 2. *Mean Offensiveness Ratings as a Function of Speaker, Location, and Word.*

Note   Scale values are: 0= not offensive at all, 100= most offensive possible. Offensiveness ratings are plotted vertically. The horizontal plot is obtained word offensiveness: L=low, M=medium, H=high.

The bottom of the figure represents the same data as the top. However, data at the bottom are plotted as a function of location at the top of the figure.

Although the results of the first experiment here were quite clear, there are some puzzling findings. Originally, the library was rated as a moderately likely place to hear dirty words. These data were from students (see Table 1) but the people in the library in the combinations in the present experiment, include the teacher and the dean. The students in the present experiment were probably indicating that it was all right for students to use dirty words in the library but not for the higher status teacher and dean. The teacher and dean were out of place, so to speak. In other words, some places are all right to use dirty words. These may be places like one's home office, dorm room, or in other words, one's own "turf." However, when one is out of place or "on another's turf", it is not all right to use dirty words uncritically. Here lies the rationale for the last experiment.

In the final experiment speakers are described in their own environment versus others' environments. To be more specific, it would be predicted that there will be a statistical interaction between speakers, locations and words in the final experiment.

The results from the last experiment are presented in Figures 3 and 4. The interaction was obtained indicating that it is all right, for example, for the student to say a dirty word in his or her dorm room but not in the dean's office. Similarly, it is more likely that the dean will use a dirty word in the office (and less offensive) than when the dean uses a dirty word in the student's dorm room. Again, there was a high correlation, r= -.96, between likelihood and offensiveness, as in the previous experiment.

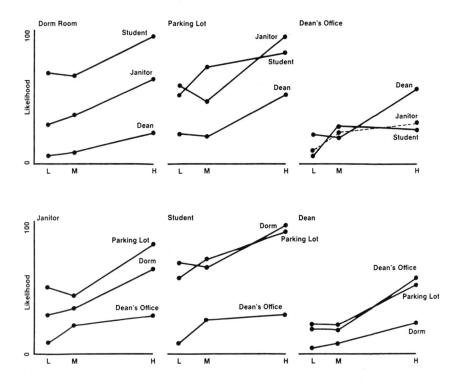

Figure 3. *Mean Likelihood Ratings as a Function of Speaker, Location, and Word.*

Note   Scale values are: 0= not likely at all, 100= most likely possible.
        Likelihood ratings are plotted vertically. The horizontal plot is obtained
        word likelihood: L=low, M=medium, H=high.

        The bottom of the figure represents the same data as the top. However, data
        at the bottom are plotted as a function of location at the top of the figure.

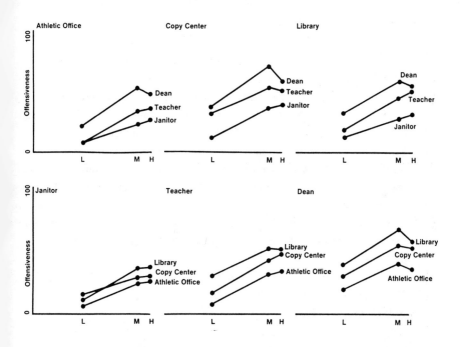

Figure 4. *Mean Offensiveness Ratings as a Function of Speaker, Location, and Word.*

Note   Scale values are: 0= not offensive at all, 100= most offensive possible.
        Offensiveness ratings are plotted vertically. The horizontal plot is obtained
        word offensiveness: L=low, M=medium, H=high.

        The bottom of the figure represents the same data as the top. However, data
        at the bottom are plotted as a function of location at the top of the figure.

Discussion

Although the results in these experiments may appear trivial to some readers, they indicate quantitatively, that Americans carry around information integration devices that make decisions about when, where, and how to produce or comprehend dirty words. In these final studies the decisions were limited to likelihood and offensiveness but in any event are much similar to other production and comprehension decisions used in the real world. Americans learn an etiquette for dirty word usage, as has been claimed with regard to children's acquisition in the previous chapter and the issue returns when the topic of gender-related insults is addressed in chapter 5.

The concluding section is the formulation of a model of anger expression based on the discussion of the semantic and contextual variables in the preceding sections.

The Etiquette of Anger Expression with Taboo Words

One analysis of expressing anger with taboo words is through the notion of a speech act. A speech act indicates that there is a hearer and a speaker with a message to be transferred or communicated between the two. There must be some set of conditions or events that caused the speaker to choose the particular expression used. There is an intention or final effect that the expression is to fulfill. Speech acts involved with anger are based on rules of communicating that emotion. These amount to the etiquette of anger expression. Something causes, incites, provokes, or evokes the anger. The causal event is interpreted in terms of its nature, justification, cost, and qualities of the wrongdoer in question. The expression of anger, as spoken, is coded to the nature of the provocation. The retaliation, embodied in the taboo expression, is intended to notify the wrongdoer of the misdeed and change the behavior in question.

A Five-Stage Model of Anger

Here is a five-stage model of how Americans express anger with language. In particular it specifies how one expresses anger with taboo words. The point of the model is to show that taboo or obscene speech when used to express anger is coded speech. The taboo word selected to express anger is related to the events that caused the person to experience anger. Furthermore, the model of anger is meant to represent a culturally shared notion of anger and how to express it. The fact that Americans have a ritual or shared model of anger means that they know when another person is angry, how angry the person is, and what is the nature of the cause or source of the anger.

The pragmatic value of the underlying model of anger is that knowing when someone is angry provides important information. Bystanders know that a wrongdoer has offended a speaker and that this wrongful behavior should be weakened to prevent further aggression on the part of the speaker. The function of expressing anger with words and not physical acts of violence is to perform a corrective operation. The wrongdoer has been identified and the nature of the offense has too. The verbal anger may be intended to cause the wrongdoer to change and restore a sense of calm or balance that was disturbed without resorting to violence. Sometimes the anger may be intended to provoke anger in the wrongdoer or it may be intended to influence or benefit a third party. The wrongdoer or offending event does not have to include another person. Anger is provoked by animals, objects or the weather. In these cases the language used is coded to nonhuman conditions.

The model is temporal in nature so that the five stages unfold in order in real time. The stages are not entirely independent of each other but what happens early in the emotional experience may influence what happens in the later stages. It is also important to note that not all anger episodes include the use of taboo words and that not every use of taboo words means that the speaker is angry.

A great deal of the language of emotions has to do with prosodic features of speech. The way a particular set of words or even a single word is pronounced may evoke entirely different emotions. "You old son of a bitch" may be an angry retort to an old man who cheated you out of some money. The same expression may be a term of endearment for an old college roommate, when pronounced with a grin. Anger is also tied to physiological agitation and gesturing. Many studies have indicated that by facial expression or gesture alone, one can tell what basic emotion is being expressed. Voice quality and nonverbal cues are part of the stream of information available to provide emotion cues. What is presented here concentrates on the language of anger, taking into account that language is only part of the picture of any emotion.

Stage 1: The Offending Event

The major elements of the offending event involve the person or event that evokes the anger and the social-physical location of the event. These factors amount to the who, what, where, and when of anger. What provokes anger can vary from person to person and from time to time. What is sought are the correlative features of the event and offender which provoke anger in general in our culture. When the features of the offending event change, for example the offender's age, the words selected to express anger change too. When a man crowds in front of someone in a long ticket line, he may be called an "asshole". If a young boy does the same he may be called something like "you little shit" or maybe one would not be angered and hence say nothing at all because of the offender's youth. The elements of the offending event are the *most* important in determining how anger is expressed verbally. Exactly which elements are weighted most heavily is not totally known and such weights may be different for different speakers. Here are what seem to be the most salient features, in line with current psychological and sociological studies of language.

The Offender. The offender or wrongdoer has certain qualities, real and imagined, accurate and inaccurate. The important point is that these offender factors will be used to select the appropriate semantic dimensions when retaliating with a taboo word.

Age- child, teenager, adult, elder are the most salient features. Very young and the very old offenders evoke less anger than teenagers and adults, the typical targets of anger. The young and the old may lead the speaker to inhibit his anger by using mild taboo words or to suppress the expression of anger completely. As in the example of crowding in line above, a young offender may be called "you little..." in the same respect and older offender may be labelled, "you old..."

Sex- one of the more powerful dimensions of human communication is the gender of the speaker or listener, especially with respect to swearing and insulting behaviors. The word *bitch* is targeted at females and the term *son of a bitch* is targeted at males, for example. Gender differences are addressed in chapter 5.

Status - perceived social or economic status such as rich/poor, amount of education, employer/employee, occupation, or religious authority affect the way one uses anger. High status, rich, employers, or religious figures are less likely to be the targets of spoken anger or direct anger speech acts relative to others. The presence of a police uniform, military uniform, or other types of dress may signal the inhibition of direct expression.

Ethnic Group - racial/minority or assumed ethnic origin is a feature that is used to select an expression when the speaker is angered by the (ethnic) offender. Americans use a large number of words to denote race and ethnic origin in a derogatory manner. It may be the presence of an ethnic minority member that provokes anger or racial hatred. As one would expect, the use of racial slurs would depend on the social context, too. A speaker might be less likely to use a slur if there were a large number of the minority in the setting.

Physical Appearance - any noticeable deviation from "normal". This dimension seems particularly salient in the names that children select to insult each other. Body size, abnormal facial features, weight, deformities, and body movement or locomotion cover the majority of these angry insults noting physical differences. In this case, the offended would use the abnormality as a subject of the insult, such as calling an obese person a "pig" or "slow poke". Physical appearance may be assessed in another fashion that affects the expression of anger. Here, if the offender is much larger or stronger than the offended, the latter may think twice before aggressing someone who could retaliate physically.

Social-Physical Setting - relaxed/business, private/public, homogenous/mixed grouping, relatives/strangers. In each of the first of these pairings there are less constraints on communication. One is more likely to hear anger expressed under these conditions where its expression is not highly sanctioned. Strangers, new acquaintances, or those who the speaker cannot change through anger will be less likely to be the targets of it relative to those offenders with a close relationship with the offended.

Non-human Wrongdoer - chased by dog, hit with bird droppings, seeing poor weather conditions. These events occur where a person did not cause the anger; instead the anger came from some event or action that was more accidental or non-intentional in nature. This dimension is included in the event scenario because many of the anger expressions that use taboo words are of this non-human category. In these instances the person is angry and emits an expletive, the force and offensiveness of which are related to the degree of insult or injury experienced. The intent is not to communicate anger to another but to express frustration.

Self as Wrongdoer - in this case the offending person or behavior is one's self. The purpose of self-directed anger is to perform a self-corrective procedure. For example, you shut the car door on your new raincoat and say to yourself, "Next time pull the jacket in before you shut the door, dumb ass!" The expression performs a teaching function and at the same time allows you to let off a little steam.

The use of a full sentence is probably less likely than the use of one word expletives, such as, *dammit, shit* or *you dumb ass* in a case of self-frustration.

The Event. Here the focus is on the nature of the action or lack of action on the part of the wrongdoer that offended the person. The event could be some type of behavior that was expected but not provided, some type of language or communication, or the manner in which the event occurred. The temporal and physical qualities of the event are weighed, in conjunction with the spontaneity or intentionality of the cause of the event. The major dimensions are listed here.

Behavior - unexpected, deviant, ill-mannered, aggressive, crude or vulgar. Examples of these would be crowding in a line, cheating in a game, or sneezing on someone. The behavior may be evaluated by its morality or its legality, which are used especially in the cases of undesirable sexual or social behavior.

Language - speech or comment that incites the source. Besides physical action, what another person says or the manner in which the language is spoken may provoke another. These linguistic or verbal behaviors are the basis of slander, libel, verbal abuse, and "fighting words" laws in the culture. The verbal behavior may provoke immediate anger or delayed retribution through legal or officially sanctioned channels.

Intentionality - whether the event was caused, or occurred by accident. That is, intentionality influences the perception of a wrongful act. The more intentional the act appears to the speaker, the greater the justification for an angry response. If the event was purely accidental, less anger is expressed. There is a custom of labeling accidents by saying out loud to those around us, especially children, that a certain event was an accident. One probably learns in these situations not to get angry if the behavior was unintentional. For the young child who gets upset over the amount of damage done, s/he is taught that intentionality is more important than the degree of damage. For adults, the label of "accident" also means, "don't yell at me." Children learn this very early; "I didn't do it on purpose. It's not my fault.

Damage - The event can be measured in terms of its duration, degree of physical pain, cost in dollars, waste of time or energy. The more damage done by the event and the more likely that the damage cannot be repaired, the more anger is associated with the event. In other words big damage means big anger. As noted above the child must learn to separate damage from intent when determining if anger is justified.

Stage 2: The Degree of Anger

The experience of anger and the expression of anger as an emotional state is a combination of three types of information. First is a set of autonomic nervous system reactions to the eliciting event. These nervous system events may include changes in blood pressure and heart rate, respiration, pupil dilation, blood sugar level, gastrointestinal tract movements and perspiration. A second set of information comes from the person's cognitive appraisal of the situation, such as the social and physical setting, the nature of the eliciting event, perceived control over the situation, level of unpleasantness and the effort one anticipates expending on the situation. The third piece of information is the nature of the emotional expression, such as facial feedback, muscles used, cultural expectations or learned responses to the eliciting situation and attention to cues in the surrounding setting including others' reactions.

Anger is basically a response to an obstacle in the setting. The degree of emotion expressed is a function of the three pieces of information to which the person may or may not be aware. The amount and degree of cursing in anger should be related to the amount of emotion experienced, such that increasing the emotional experience increases severity, duration and strength of cursing.

This second stage remains to be tested but suffice it to say that language must be correlated with emotional intensity and arousal (blood pressure, muscle tension or negative appraisal).

Stage 3: Attempts to Control Anger

In American culture the normal or prototypical response to the feeling of anger would be to control or contain anger. The notion of civilization, etiquette, and social interaction views the unchecked expression of anger as primitive, uncultured, and ill-mannered. Members of the upper classes are schooled in etiquette and how to inhibit anger. Children are taught to show respect (not anger) to others such as elders, parents, religious figures, authority figures, and people with high status positions. One is taught manners and how to be good little boys and girls, which means not attacking others either physically or verbally.

The ability to control anger at others has social consequences that are realized by speakers. One conforms to social rules in order to maintain status in social groups or to advance to more prestigious groups. Learning social rules and behaving by them is motivating to those who do not want to be labelled outcasts or socially inept. The value of rule learning or conformity is related to the attractiveness of group membership. Maintaining control over anger is then a function of individual motivation and the group's ability to sanction one's progress in life.

Individuals vary in their ability to control anger as a function of age and experience. Some may be taught that to suffer an insult without retribution is a weakness or that anger has its place in a given group setting. People use a concept of self-image or self-esteem when they operate socially. One tries to maintain an image of control when interacting with others. Verbal aggression should be controlled but for some it cannot be stopped.

Cursing in anger may be in response to accidental or unforseen events. Hitting oneself with a hammer instead of hitting the nail may cause the utterance of a strong oath or epithet. The reaction may be so automatic or well-learned that inhibiting or controlling the curse is next to impossible. Losing control under such circumstances would not be evaluated as negatively as less painful but more controllable events by those innocent bystanders overhearing the oath.

Getting angry is also a function of the intentionality of the offending event. The more accidental the event, the less likely one should get angry about it. Anger may be controlled in the presence of certain types of offenders, intentional or otherwise.

Anger is controlled when the wrongdoer is very young or very old. Offenders of high status (minister) or certain social roles (mother) may trigger control. The loss of control over one's anger with high status or special role offenders results in a lowering of one's esteem. Special mental or physical features of the offender such as mentally incompetent, physically superior, or non-human (dog) may cause the offended to suppress anger. In these cases anger would have no effect on the offender. The assumed reaction of the offender, when physically superior, may be more damaging than the first offending event. Anger is also voluntarily suppressed when there are legal implications of expressing it, such as with obscenity, slander, libel, or verbal abuse charges as possible reactions to anger.

Some believe that verbal aggression is the civilized form of earlier, more primitively evolved, physical aggression. Which is to say I'll beat you with words, not hands or clubs. It would seem that every society has sanctions against aggression and physical violence, as well as verbal attacks. Those who live in controlled societies must learn the rules controlling the expression of anger by violence or verbal attack.

Controlling anger may take more than one form. Control may result in the suppression of anger in order to stop feeling angry or to protect the wrongdoer. Control may mean giving the wrongdoer a less offensive level of abuse than the event merits. Nontaboo replies, joking, or sarcasm may function as less aggressive forms in response to larger offenses.

The major dimensions of a speech context that cause speakers to control anger even though they have experienced the physiological effects of it, are the following:

Age - anger is inhibited toward very young and very old wrongdoers by healthy adult speakers. In fact laws in many states define extensive cursing and insulting of children as a form of child abuse.

Status - anger is suppressed for an employer or superior. This may be clearly labeled by rank or title. Anger is also controlled as a function of the perceived high status positions, such as religious figures, police or celebrities.

Relation- grandchildren, grandparents, others related by blood may cause the speaker to inhibit aggression especially in public. Telling jokes, making sexual remarks or suggestions about sexual behavior may be a form of sexual harassment on the job.

Physical size - anger is inhibited around a wrongdoer who may look like "the type of person" who would return your anger with physical punishment.

Reasoning ability - anger is suppressed around retarded people or the mentally deficient because they are not not able to interpret the speaker's anger and adjust their behavior accordingly.

Overreacting

Consider the case when a speaker produces what he/she considers to be an appropriate expression of anger but the hearer overreacts by feeling unjustly attacked or overly insulted. This may occur with a child as the wrongdoer, or with someone who is not familiar with insulting rituals. In this case the wrongdoer takes offense even though s/he did something wrong in the first place but does not necessarily perceive or believe that s/he did.

In an attempt to control these overreactions to anger expressions, the angered has to provide more information or cues to the wrongdoer that s/he *was* provoked but that the offender should "not get so upset about it." Other expressions to control wrongdoer (hearer) overreacting include:

> *Can't you see what you have done?*
> *I was only trying to point out that you made me angry in the first place*
> *Well, it was your fault, wasn't it?*

These post-anger comments are to let the wrongdoer know that s/he originally did something wrong but that the wrongdoer is overreacting to the appropriate nature of the speaker's retaliation.

Stage 4: Loss of Control

As just explained, a common reaction to provocation is to suppress anger. However, when anger is not suppressed, a person will then lose control and swear at or verbally abuse an offender. This loss of control is not generally immediate, except with the use of expletives, i.e., producing a short burst of taboo words in a conditioned manner. For example, some have learned to say *shit* to the accidentally inflicted pain, like hitting oneself with a hammer.

Expletives and Exclamations. The first stage of loss of control with taboo words is the short one or two word exclamation or expletive. Words like: *damn*, *goddamn (it)*, *shit*, *fuck*, or *christ* serve as good examples. Even with expletives there is a range of anger from mild religious taboos (*damn*) to obscenities (*fuck*). The degree of anger may also be dampened by the use of euphemisms, such as *darn*, *goshdarn (it)*, *shoot*, *fudge*, or *cripes*, which parallel those given in the previous sentence. Expletives are not semantically tied to the wrongdoer or the event in a direct way; and in that respect they serve the speaker's need to let off some steam. Since these words are conditioned in nature they may be idiosyncratic to the particular speaker. Some speakers when they become angry habitually use the same word or phrase as exclamations of anger; these cases support the notion that expletive primarily serve the speaker.

Expletives are uttered without thinking or time to control. This would be the case where the offender is not a person, or the self is the wrongdoer, or there is a lack of social or physical constraint on the speaker, such as when the speaker is alone, or is anonymous in a crowd, or will never again see the people with whom s/he is assembled. Expletive choice and degree of offensiveness is related to the amount of damage experienced. The greater the damage the more immediate and stronger the response to it. The function of the expletive may be to perform a self-corrective action, a signal of pain, or a signal for help. The particular word chosen is a matter of learning, since the particular word has little communicative or semantic value.

Loss of control over anger or the perception that control over anger was not necessary would seem to be maximized by the following dimensions of the offending event:

Offender -is an adult male, not young or old

Status - the offender is of equal or lower in status

Ethnic- out-group offenders would prompt ethnic slurs

Physical Appearance- a body type that is not physically imposing

Social/Physical Setting- corrective swearing would be among friends, in a close physical and social setting. Expletives are used in isolation, or in public when the speaker is not identified. Expletives are commonly yelled from passing cars, at sporting events, on a darkened street, or in large gang settings (where the speaker cannot be attacked for doing so).

The event- is intentional, a repeat of a previous offense, and causes a large amount of physical, economic, or social stress (i.e., *damage*). There may also be some social situations that by their very nature call for the loss of control over anger and the use of expletives. Getting "psyched" for a sporting event (football or boxing), attempting to intimidate an opponent, using anger to control a crowd, using anger to cause fear in a group to establish dominance status, or using anger to make others keep their social-physical distance . Here is where loss of control of anger is rewarded by obtaining a state of affairs that the speaker wants to obtain.

The level of retaliation is not open-ended. There are limits to what can be said to another which take the form of legal sanctions and punishments for illegal retaliations. The concept of sexual harassment, obscenity, spouse abuse, child abuse, libel, slander, verbal abuse, and fighting words set restrictions on ability to verbally retaliate against a wrongdoer. It would seem reasonable to believe that people vary in their sensitivity to these legal doctrines, so that, law and order suppresses some speakers but not others.

Beyond the stage of loss of control over anger comes the act of retaliation or retribution.   Mere loss of control, as in the use of the expletives, may not perform this function but mainly serves the speaker's needs. Some loss of control, to intimidate others, may not be directed to the goal of retaliation for a misdeed. In this non-retaliation loss of control, the anger expression itself serves the speaker through control or intimidation of others, even though they did nothing to provoke the anger in the first place.

Underreaction. The author was walking into a toy store. A mother told her son that if he whined or got upset she would spank him right in the store. The little boy giggled and ran into the store ahead of his mother.

> *"You think I'm kidding.   Well, I'm not.   I'm serious.   You'll see..."*

Here is a case where the child did not understand the nature of the mother's anger (at a prediction of the child's negative behavior). The point is that sometimes one gets angry and the wrongdoer *fails* to see (we are angry).   As in the case of "overreacting" the speaker has to provide extra information about the severity of the offense.   Other expressions might include:

> *You don't think I'm serious.*
> *I am serious!*
> *Did you hear what I said?*
> *I mean it...I am angry.*

The final example occurs with other types of emotional situations where the speaker presents one type of emotion and the hearer fails to comprehend or pick up on it. In this case the speaker just interprets the emotion for the hearer in explicit terms.

Stage 5: Retribution

The act of retribution is what swearing, cursing, and insulting is all about. One does not select words to express anger lightly. The expression selected at this stage is a function of the offending event, how much anger is expressed, and the need to control our anger. It is probably the nature of the offending event that imposes the most control over the expression of anger. Assuming that the offended one is seeking a verbal act of retribution, that act may be less than, equivalent to, or greater than the amount of anger called for by the event.

Retribution may be minimized when certain features of the offending event are salient to the offended: when the wrongdoer is young or very old, has high status, is a new acquaintance or stranger, or if the offended assumes that s/he cannot influence the wrongdoer with an expression of anger. Need to retaliate is also minimized when the event is accidental or of very low damage. These conditions call for a suppression of anger or the use of a very mild expression.

Retribution beyond what is called for is another special case of expressing more anger than is required by the nature of the event. The speaker may wish to stop any future language or behavior on the part of the wrongdoer. The speaker may want to bully the offender or may get rewarded for overreacting, as in the case of teenage gang members, verbal dueling games, or attempts to achieve status through swearing ability. It is in these cases of overreacting where legal and moral sanctions are applied. The control of anger expressions through legal, religious, or social standards serves to protect the wrongdoer from unjustified aggression. These sanctions are also part of the etiquette that all speakers must learn, or face the penalties.

"Getting even" is the concept in which the offended swears on a level equivalent to the offense. The typical or common notion of verbal retaliation is to match the level of offense with the type and level of word(s) chosen to retaliate. Experience says that the reason for retaliation through the expression of anger with taboo words is to identify the wrongdoer, the nature of the offense, and ultimately seek correction of the offending event (apology, penalty, or stop the undesirable behavior). Thus, retribution or retaliation is a *necessary* functional component of human communication because it tells wrongdoers the who, what, where, and when of their offensive acts.

The Value of Expressing Anger

One of the authors who has influenced this writing about the the nature of anger and aggression is Averill (see 1983), who focuses on anger to examine a number of issues in the study of emotion. Because Averill's work is so relevant to the discussion of the act of swearing and verbal aggression, the general findings are summarized here. In Averill's study subjects were asked a number of questions about their experiences with anger and what function anger performed. First, when people get angry they do not immediately become aggressive. Averill's subjects tried to engage in some non-aggressive or calming activity. When they did become aggressive, most of these episodes resulted in verbal or symbolic aggression *not* physical aggression. So, when people become angry they do not immediately fly off the handle but they try to control the anger. If they do express the anger it is in verbal terms. These data mean that using language to express anger is a highly probable act that Americans carry out, but what is the function of these verbal attacks?

Part of the answer is the nature of the target of the anger. In most cases the target is a close friend or loved one and both males and females are equally likely to be targets of anger. The lack of sex differences in targets stands counter to common sense experience with public episodes of anger. In public where the target is highly likely to be a stranger (who angers another) these episodes are more likely to involve male targets. Averill concludes that most anger expressions are interpersonal events and are not those found in public among strangers. The next question would be to consider what caused this angry expression between friends in the first place?

As indicated by the model there are many potential sources of behavior, language, and conduct that cause us to experience anger. The important point is that what specifically causes the anger is secondary to a) the justification of the behavior on the part of the wrongdoer and b) the later consequences and changes of the behavior if justified. The behavior, if justified, serves the purpose of blaming or passing a value judgement on the actions of the wrongdoer. The attribution of blame leads to the final consequences of the anger episode, the beneficial correction of wrongful behavior. The point of expressing justified anger among friends is to correct their behavior.

In sum, Averill's outline has shown that anger functions in American society by correcting misdeeds among friends. One can now understand why one sees frequent expression of the emotion, i.e., because in the end anger expression performs a positive function of stopping the repetition of unwanted behavior.

Summary

Americans express anger toward other people with a limited number of categories of dirty words. The rules for cursing in anger are learned early in life and form a type of "etiquette" or rule-based method of dirty word use. The hypothesis that anger expression is context bound was demonstrated by the experiment in which subjects were asked to make offensiveness and likelihood judgements of language samples where only the contextual factors varied. The five-stage model of anger should be used to test the nature and purpose of cursing.

Note - The data from the contextual analysis of anger expression were originally presented at the Interdisciplinary Conference on Linguistics in Louisville, Kentucky in 1978 by the author.

Chapter 4

The Frequency of Dirty Word Usage

How frequently are dirty words used in American culture? How often does one person use them throughout the day? Although many people in broadcasting, education, law, and social science make judgments about the frequency of dirty word usage, there are no sound data on which to make those decisions. If one examines the literature on general word frequency, one finds little information on dirty word usage. Entries in standard dictionaries are standard speech. Studies of word frequency tend to be studies of standard word frequency. One can examine colloquial dictionaries or those dedicated to argot, slang, or jargon. These provide no indication of how frequently such terms are used. A few minutes on a busy street corner convinces the listener that Americans use dirty words frequently in public but how frequently? This chapter is about determining the relative frequencies of dirty words in American English using standard empirical techniques. We will look at traditional means of establishing word frequency and some of the problems with establishing how often people swear. The conclusion from the available data is that these words are used relatively frequently.

Why Word Frequency?

For many years those interested in human communication and verbal behavior have known that words are used with different frequencies in communication. The notion of variable frequency has led investigators to study how frequency differences affect a wide variety of language-related activities (reading, creativity, language learning, problem solving, or comprehension). Given that dirty word usage is a behavior that most social scientists have constantly ignored, how can we tell how often dirty words are used? What impact does differential usage have?

One of the early concerns was the role of word frequency in both face-to-face communication and through electronic media like radio, short wave, or encoded channels. It was pointed out by Zipf (1949), for example, that relatively few words were used extremely often in communication and that the higher the frequency of occurrence a word had, the more likely it was to be used in general. Shannon and Weaver (1949) incorporated "Zipf's Law" into their grand theory of communication, using word frequency to make predictions about the probability of various sayings or messages during communication. These predictions were important to produce efficient and quick communication and to eliminate errors by using predictable words. These findings were applied in military and government communication systems following World War II. However, the grand theory building that dominated psychology in the 1950's has died out and contemporary psychologists now focus on specific issues and problems involving human communication. Interest has shifted to how word frequency influences a specific type of language processing. The frequency question remains present in almost every aspect involving information processing abilities, such as attention, problem solving, pattern recognition, learning, rehabilitation, and memorization. Below are some of the recent applications of word frequency in contemporary investigations to show why the dirty word frequency question has remained unanswered.

Word frequency has been a fairly consistent predictor of response time differences in language processing tasks. High frequency words are processed faster and more easily than words at low frequencies. The result has been called "the word frequency effect" in whatever process is under investigation. In a lexical decision task, for example, subjects are shown a string of letters and asked to tell whether the string forms a word. One of the best predictors of response time is how frequently the word is used; the higher the frequency, the lower the reaction time.

Word frequency effects have been reported in other language and memory tasks. In an object-naming task, where subjects are asked to name objects as fast as possible, results indicate that word frequency is related to the ease of naming the object. In word legibility tasks, frequent words were found to be as legible as single letters, although infrequent words are less legible than either. In lexical access tasks, word frequency effects the time it takes to decide if a target word has occurred in a sentence. Word frequency effects have been found in many memory tests of recall, recognition, and others (see Jay, 1980a). People who study reading and learning to read know that frequent or familiar words make information processing tasks easier and faster than obscure or low frequency words.

It should be clear that in each of these studies dirty words are *never* used. What is known about linguistic processes has had little or nothing to do with dirty words. If all science on language stopped now, we would know little about dirty word usage or how dirty word usage relates to more normal language use.

A recent question has been whether word frequency is related to the age of acquisition of a language by children. Carroll and White (1973 a,b) found that frequent words tend to be those that are acquired early in life. Another variable related to acquisition is the number of different meanings that a word has. One point here is that frequent words have more interpretations than low frequency words. So, age of acquisition depends both on meaning and frequency aspects of word usage. It is important to know what children learn early in life when examining patients with brain damage. Lesser (1978, pp 110-112), for example, shows that word frequency is needed to study aphasic (language loss) patients. Patients may use childish or highly frequent language when recovering from brain damage. Some of these aphasics may use only dirty words when recovering because the words were learned early and well, and may be stored in parts of the brain untouched by the trauma.

There should be no doubt that word frequency has an important influence on communication and communication problems. But, have we stopped to ask the question, where did all these frequency data come from in the first place?

The Frequency Estimation Problem: Why There Are No Dirty Words

There are hundreds of millions of speakers of English using tens of thousands of words on thousands of different occasions. To accurately count actual word usage is impossible. Therefore, *estimates* must be used. Throughout the history of frequency research, the question of proper frequency estimation has received minimal attention, and one wonders whether any of these previous estimates were accurate. While the tasks mentioned above have been conducted with appropriate methods, those interested in taboo language estimation would find them inadequate and inaccurate to estimate taboo language frequency. Future interest in controlling taboo language frequency or offensiveness requires an alternative to traditional methods and reports.

One major problem is the use of inappropriate normative samples of word frequency. Since its publication, psychologists and others interested in language frequency have been using the Thorndike and Lorge (1944) norms to estimate word frequency. However, the count (or others like it) are inadequate for three reasons:

(a) the sample is restricted only to *written*, not oral usage, (b) the written sample is restricted to a limited domain of reading materials (mostly children's and popular adult literature), and (c) it is outdated (language changes with time). Eriksen (1963) has demonstrated quite clearly that the Thorndike-Lorge count is inadequate to estimate *oral* usage and that it in fact underestimates the frequency of many colloquially used words. Two collections of written word frequency norms were published by Kucera and Francis (1967) and more recently by Carroll, Davies, and Richman (1971). These are updated and less restricted than Thorndike-Lorge, but they are still limited to written samples.

The problem with written norms is not that they are inaccurate, but that they are used incorrectly by researchers. The written norms generally are appropriate when applied to tasks involving textual material; that is, reading processes. The written norms are *not* appropriate for research concerning oral usage, however. Written norms do not apply directly to colloquial, conversational situations such as parent-child interaction, discourse processes, or language influenced by sociolinguistic variables (social or physical setting). The point is that sociolinguistic variables are crucial to understanding dirty word usage. It is context that controls dirty word usage and these factors must be accounted for.

The bottom line on studies of written samples is that one is rarely going to find dirty words used in the sample because they are collected from biased material, even though that material may be appropriate to design children's reading texts, for example.

Counting Oral Frequency: Almost Good Enough

Written and oral speech are two different forms of language. In addition to different rules (e.g., the future perfect does not seem to exist in oral speech) and different distributions of rules they have in common (e.g., the perfect form of the verb appears much more in written speech), written language has the benefit of more polish. Oral speech is marked by hesitations, interruptions, incomplete expressions, is more prone to imprecise or incorrect definitions -- all of which can be corrected with a little proofreading in the written form.

Oral speech is also at the mercy of a number of sociolinguistic influences. Spoken language, particularly in its more colloquial form, is more sensitive to the relation between speaker and listener, the degree of social relaxation, and the topic of discussion (see Jay, 1978c). When these variables flucuate, so does the kind of language selected and used in conversation. In light of these contextual constraints, then, the estimation of oral frequency requires looking at oral -- not written -- samples of language for taboo speech.

Several attempts have been made to examine the frequency of word usage in conversational English (Jay, 1980a). One widely mentioned study is French, Carter, and Koenig's (1930) collection of words and sounds from telephone conversations. This study is cited because it provides information about vowel, consonant, and word frequency data. The study has one major flaw. They omitted some 25% of the data representing utterances such as exclamations, interjections, proper names, titles, letters, numbers, and *profanity*. In fact profanity was 40% of the material omitted! While the study could give a relatively accurate picture of conversations, it compromised a true picture of dirty word usage. Fairbanks (1944) updated the French et al. study and compared the spoken language samples of college students with diagnosed schizophrenics. More recently, Black, Stratton, Nichols, and Chavez (1985) published a word count based on college student classroom language, as did Berger in 1968.

Several studies concentrate on children's oral language. The need for these data in reading, learning, and comprehension applications should be clear. These data serve the purpose of designing age-appropriate textbooks but do not indicate anything about how children use dirty words or how often. One of the best collections and most current counts is *Spoken Words* (1984) by Hall, Nagy, and Linn. These investigators report the data as a function of situation and social status of the children's family. However, when speech was recorded in classes or at the dinner table, very few dirty words were spoken. Dirty words are highly context dependent and even young children have learned not to use them most of the time at school or at the dinner table. Thus few of them appear in the corpus. While these norms provide a useful foundation for writing or evaluating children's reading texts, as intended, they give the impression that children do not produce dirty words. Consequently, there is a risk of thinking children are much more naive about matters involving sex and aggression than they are, if the conclusion is based on biased word counts. Cameron (1969) made one of the more natural attempts to collect adult language data as a function of social setting. His sample, though restricted to a few college settings, is useful to indicate how speech changes from relaxed to formal social environments. The major problem with the Cameron norms stems from an inadequate sampling procedure. He asked his "overhearer" to record by hand "the first three words they heard during the conversation at 15 second intervals" (p 102).   Such recording is subject to constraints from attention, perception, or recording bias, especially when overhearers knew he was interested in certain types of words. Howes (1966) collected oral word samples from both a hospital and university interview sessions.

Howes' sample is restricted to a formal interview setting in which language is constrained by the content of the interview and the impression that the interviewee tries to convey in the formal communication context.

In some cases, experimenters have used subjective frequency estimation as an alternative to field recording techniques (Shapiro, 1969). In these studies, the subject is considered as an informant capable of estimating relative word frequency using (e.g., 1-to-9 rating scales). Shapiro has indicated that these ratings fit traditional scaling abilities and are reasonable alternatives to counting techniques. However, these studies do not include colloquialisms or dirty words, nor are they concerned with how language processing changes with context.

The investigator interested in word frequency of colloquial English is left in the dark. Restricted sampling procedures, restricted sampling domain, restricted setting and methodology make the previous findings suspect to answer the question of how frequently Americans use dirty words.

The remainder of this chapter is a report on a series of four experiments designed to converge on the question of how frequently dirty words appear in usage. Two laboratory studies use the item rating technique to estimate usage; the other two provide data from observations and recordings of how Americans use dirty words "on the street."

A Frequency Count of Students' Colloquial English (Jay, 1980a)

In order to obtain comparative data for laboratory research and to establish a set of colloquially derived word norms, we recorded elementary school student and college student conversations. With mini-tape recorders hidden from view, 15 minute segments of student conversations were recorded on a college campus and the campus elementary school, both set in western Massachusetts. After cassettes were filled with data, research assistants, who also collected the conversations, transcribed and then entered these data for computer sorting and counting.

The data set is not described in fine detail, as it exists elsewhere in more convenient format (Jay, 1980a). The results are explained here as they apply to estimating dirty word frequency. Every utterance that was interpretable as a word was transcribed and counted for both an elementary school sample and a college campus sample. The result was 11,609 word tokens of 1171 unique word types for the college student sample, which is discussed next.

College Sample of Dirty Words

As in previous frequency counts, much of the conversations are accounted for by the use of a few words. The rank ordering of the top 60 words (of the 1711) accounts for 50% of the data. The top 15 words account for 25% of the data.

Amongst the words recorded were many dirty words. They included (frequency in parentheses): *bastard* (3), *bozo* (1), *christ* (2), *damn* (1), *fatso* (1), *friggin* (1), *fuck* (8), *fuckin* (2), *god* (11), *goddamn* (1), *hell* (5), *humpin* (1), *jerk* (1), *jesus* (1), *nerds* (5), *nuts* (2), *penis* (1), *pissed* (2), *screw* (1), *screwed* (3), *shit* (10), *shitfaced* (1), *stupid* (2), *suck* (1), *tits* (1), and *weirdos* (2). Notice here that a few words (*fuck(in)*, *god(damn)*, *hell*, and *shit*) account for most of the dirty words recorded in spontaneous, public conversations.

For comparison purposes, the top 60 words were correlated with some of the other frequency counts of college student and adult conversational English. The highest correlation was with Berger's (1968) data, r= .94 (n= 42), followed by the French et al. study (1930), r= .86 (n=50), Fairbanks (1944), r= .86 (n= 47), and finally Cameron's (1969) sample, r= .68 (n= 23). These correlations are high and positive, indicating a very reasonable amount of agreement across researchers, methods and settings. The agreement between studies is important to establish validity and consistency checks. More important is the recording of the use of dirty words in public settings, a phenomenon that previous researchers have either not heard, ignored or expurgated.

The field study was not designed to capture dirty words. It was designed to capture how students speak at school. It just so happened that students used dirty words in those settings. Of course there are better places to find incidences of swearing, as the recording uses locations off campus or in restricted (non-public) areas such as locker rooms or dorm rooms. However, to make the setting comparable in scope to the elementary school sample, only public school buildings (campus center and classrooms) were used. Following are the data from the elementary school.

Elementary School Dirty Words

The elementary school sample included 5858 tokens of 1130 different words. Among these words were the following dirty words (with frequencies in parentheses): *bum* (1), *farted* (1), *fink* (1), *hog* (1), *jerk* (1), *motha'* (2), *pig* (1), *slob* (1), *stupid* (4) and *weenie* (3).

Most of these school-setting recordings were taken from formal lunchroom settings, rather than on playgrounds or in classrooms. The presence of adult teachers and teacher aides certainly constrained these children more than on the school bus or on the playground, where it was reported that more dirty language occurred but was not sampled by the technique chosen for this study. Nonetheless, dirty words were among the very sample of words from a very selective (and constrained) setting.

Discussion

The point of the study was to demonstrate that when a large word count was obtained in public, it would contain dirty words, and that the method would be fairly free of contamination or bias from the assistants' ears.

The rate of dirty word usage, less than 1% of both samples, was low but not surprising. Dirty word usage is highly influenced by contextual variables. One would not expect children to curse around adults, who might punish them for such dirty word use. It would be more likely that children would use these words while playing or arguing with each other on the playground away from adult supervision. Similarly, the public locations of recordings of college students are not those associated with dirty word use. Spontaneous use of dirty words would be more likely at parties, in barrooms, at sporting events and private residences. Studies which capitalized on the effects of freedom from sanctions and likelihood of aggression predictably would capture a higher percentage of dirty word use. The picture of even the low percentage of dirty words in the sample is informative, relative to previous studies where none were found.

Field Studies Versus Laboratory Studies

From the period of 1970 to 1980 most word research was conducted in a college psychology laboratory using college students in a variety of paper and pencil tasks involving dirty words. They rated words on 1-9 scales, made judgments about how much they would like a person who was described with dirty words, wrote lists of dirty words, and used them in sentences. These tasks began to seem artificial and lacked ecological validity. The truth of dirty word usage was to be found in the streets. Recently the field of psycholinguistics has begun to look at more natural or real-world communication processes. Dirty words just could not be understood fully without a new emphasis on analysis of speech in social-physical context.

Both laboratory and field studies have a place in answering psychological questions. Both are important and necessary to understand how people use words or think about language. In the laboratory people can behave or think in terms that are not observable in the real world. Many times in the real world they will do and say things they would never consider appropriate in the laboratory setting.

There are three remaining studies to provide convincing evidence of the frequent use of taboo language. After the taping method, comparative data were needed from less constrained settings. These data and methodology are reported next. Even though field recordings provide a picture of language usage, there are additional questions that are more properly answered by laboratory methods. The final two studies use native English speakers' judgments about frequency. In the end these tables of words and numbers may appear to be just that, words and numbers. Other frequency counts are just words and numbers, too. But the interesting questions only begin to emerge when we look at these data. Why do men swear more than women? Why do people use dirty words more than nontaboo counterparts? Why are some words used by women and not by men? Why are some words more frequently used than others?

All of the answers to those questions have not been found but those interested in communication now have some foundations on which to base an answer.

A Field Study of Offensive Speech

The understanding of dirty words and the data base is limited at present. A stage of observational research is proposed, especially in natural, real-life situations to establish a body of normative data. Then one can account for past and present laboratory data with this comprehensive model. The phenomenon of offensive speech, like other sexually explicit expressions, is highly subject to ecological or contextual influence; so, a contextual or sociolinguistic model is suggested to account for the inherently social nature of these episodes. The basis of a contextual account of dirty words (Jay, 1978c) focuses on speaker-listener relation, social-physical setting, intent of the message and other more or less obtrusive factors. The model is briefly outlined below.

The goal here is to widen the understanding of offensive word usage. First, if the phenomenon is to be appreciated from the contextual point of view, the critical dimensions, such as speakers, listeners, and situational characteristics influencing usage need to be studied. Next, field data can be collected via observation in a variety of different settings. Thirdly, lab and field data can be contrasted. Finally, different disciplines with different research priorities can incorporate and integrate these contextual data where necessary in their research.

The Contextual Approach

The model for understanding how people use dirty words is based on the assumption that people communicate to others as a function of the major sociolinguistic factors in the environment. These factors include the speaker, listener, topic, intent, physical surrounding, each of which can be further examined in terms of a number of variables (for example, speaker age, status, education, occupation, and so on). The advantage of the contextual approach is that it allows one to make comparisons both within and across these major factors. The factors are limited both physically and socially in a laboratory setting.

Method

Data Collection. Dirty word utterances were recorded by 6 male and 6 female college students, as these utterances occurred spontaneously in a variety of settings on and off campus.

   Field Cards. Each recorder carried a number of 3" x 5" field cards on which they wrote the utterance and recorded the characteristics of the setting. Figure 1 is a representation of these cards. Each card contained categories for speakers, listeners, and others in context (those who were assumed to be able to hear the utterance. Speaker, listener, and others' age categories were estimated. These age categories conform roughly to pre-school, elementary school, teenage, college age, graduate student-teacher, middle aged, and old age stereotypes.

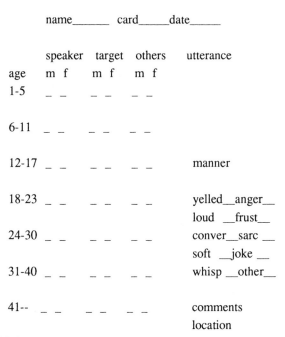

Figure 1. *Fieldcard Information*

Procedure. The recorder's task was to first record the utterance, then note the number, age, and sex of others present. They further noted the physical location and the manner in which the utterance was produced (e.g., anger or joking).

Although previous studies from the laboratory were based on unobtrusive tape recordings (Jay, 1980a), the field card method was easier, simpler, cheaper, and provided a fast and direct analysis. Recorders in general were satisfied that the card technique was efficient and as accurate as mechanical recordings used before. They were instructed to record any and all words and utterances that were offensive and stemmed from profanity, taboo, obscenity and other insults. The author made the final decision about whether an episode would be included in the final analysis, based on words which appeared in previous dirty word research in the author's laboratory and in other research in the literature on dirty word use.

Results

Here, 2171 dirty word episodes were recorded. A rank ordering of the 10 most frequently used words, as a function of speaker sex and sex of company or listener is reported in Table 1. Table 2 contains a relatively complete report of all words, including semantic usage, and distribution of age of speakers involved. Most of the data were obtained from teenagers, college students, and those in the 20-30 year age category. Recognizing apparent limitation, age, as a contextual variable was not examined further.

Sex of Speaker. Males were recorded making far more dirty word utterances than females with overall episodes of 1482 and 689, respectively. It is not surprising that males use dirty words more often than females, a finding in line with much previous research (Jay, 1980b).

In all of these episodes, some 60 root words account for all the data. Further, the top ten in terms of frequency of occurrence account for half of the data. Males produced a range of 58 different root words, while females were recorded using only 29 different words, many of which had extremely low frequencies. Only the words *dike* and *moron* occurred in the female corpus but not the males'. These two words only occurred once. On the other hand many of the words that the males used were never recorded from female speakers. Basically, in public males produce more dirty words than do females. Males also produce a larger vocabulary of them, relative to females.

Sex of Company. The sex of those listening to or in hearing range of the speaker had a noted effect on the emergence of dirty word usage. Both male and female speakers are more likely to swear in the company of same sex companions. The ratio here is two to one for both speakers. Speakers are less restricted by a group of listeners who are similar in background or are friends of the speaker. When speakers are in a context with minimal social constraints, they are more likely to use explicit or dirty language. Studies on the topic of the use of terms for sexual behavior have demonstrated that more explicit language use depends on the relationship between the speaker and listener and the listener's gender.

Table 1. *Summary of Field Data.* (Total Number of Utterances 2171)

Sex of
Speaker

MALE   FEMALE
1482   689

Sex of
Company

SAME   MIXED   SAME   MIXED
1095   387   485   204

Ten Most
Frequent Words

fuck	287	fuck	92	fuck	112	shit	48
shit	166	shit	58	shit	111	fuck	24
asshole	75	hell	39	asshole	38	ass	18
jesus	68	bitch	31	hell	36	hell	17
goddamn	56	ass	29	goddamn	35	bitch	16
hell	48	goddamn	19	ass	32	asshole	14
ass	49	damn	18	bitch	27	jesus	11
bitch	40	bastards	16	jesus	25	goddamn	10
suck	34	jesus	16	damn	16	damn	10
piss	26	suck	15	suck	13	piss	6

Table 2a. *Dirty Word Production Lexicon.*

Male Speaker

	Male Listener								Female Listener							
Age*	1	2	3	4	5	6	7	Tot	1	2	3	4	5	6	7	Tot
Word Usage																
Ass																
Body Part	0	2	3	17	0	5	6	33	0	0	1	10	3	2	7	33
Soc Dev	0	2	2	5	2	0	0	11	0	0	0	2	0	0	0	2
Pain in	0	0	0	3	0	1	1	5	0	0	0	2	0	0	2	4
								(49)								(29)=78
Asshole																
Body Part	0	0	0	3	1	1	0	5	0	0	0	0	0	0	0	0
Soc Dev	0	4	1	47	8	6	2	68	0	3	1	5	1	0	0	10
Expletive	0	1	0	0	1	0	0	2	0	0	0	0	0	0	0	0
								(75)								(10)=85
Balls																
Eval	0	2	0	2	0	0	0	4	0	0	0	0	1	0	0	1
Expletive	0	0	0	0	0	0	0	0	0	0	0	0	0	0	0	0
Body Part	0	2	0	2	0	0	1	5	0	0	0	3	0	0	1	4
Strength	0	0	0	9	0	0	0	9	0	0	0	3	0	1	0	4
								(18)								(9)=27
Bastard																
Eval	0	0	0	2	0	0	0	2	0	0	0	0	0	0	0	0
Soc Dev	0	0	2	4	2	4	2	14	0	0	0	5	1	2	8	16
								(16)								(16)=32

Bitch

Soc Dev	0	0	2	5	2	1	1	11	0	1	0	10	0	0	0	11
S O B	0	0	0	5	4	8	8	25	0	1	0	3	0	0	3	7
Complain	0	0	0	0	0	0	0	0	1	0	0	5	1	2	1	10
Difficult	0	0	0	3	0	1	0	4	0	0	0	3	0	0	0	3
								(40)								(31)=71

Blows

Sex Act	0	0	0	1	0	0	1	2	0	0	0	0	0	0	0	0
Der	0	0	0	5	0	0	0	5	0	0	0	0	0	0	0	0
								(7)								(0)=7

Blow Job

Sex Act	0	0	0	1	0	0	1	2	0	0	0	0	0	0	0	0
								(2)								(0)=2

Bull Shit

Expletive	0	1	0	5	0	1	0	7	0	0	0	3	0	0	0	3
Nonsense	0	0	0	1	0	2	2	5	0	0	0	0	0	0	1	1
Anger	0	0	0	0	1	0	1	2	0	0	0	1	0	0	0	1
								(14)								(5)=19

Cock

Genitalia	0	0	0	1	0	0	0	1	0	0	0	0	0	0	0	0
-teaser	0	0	0	2	0	0	0	2	0	0	0	0	0	0	0	0
								(3)								(0)=3

Cocksucker

Soc Dev	0	0	0	1	0	2	0	3	0	0	0	0	0	0	0	0
								(3)								(0)=3

Crap

Function	0	0	0	0	0	0	0	0	0	2	0	0	0	0	0	2
Nonsense	0	0	2	0	0	0	0	2	0	0	0	0	0	0	0	0
Product	0	0	0	0	0	0	0	0	0	1	0	0	0	0	0	1
Soc Dev	0	0	0	0	0	0	0	0	0	1	0	0	0	0	0	1
								(2)								(4)=6

Crotch

Body Part	0	0	0	0	1	0	0	1	0	0	0	0	0	0	0	0
								(1)								(0)=1

Cunt
 Soc Dev   0 0 0 0 2 3 0 5   0 0 0 0 0 0 0 0
 Genitalia   0 0 0 0 0 2 0 2   0 0 0 0 0 0 0 0
                              (7)   (0)=7
Damn
 Expletive   0 0 0 2 0 0 1 3   0 0 0 1 0 0 5 6
 Verb   0 0 0 1 0 0 0 1   0 0 0 0 0 0 0 0
 Adv-Adj   0 0 2 4 1 6 3 16   0 0 2 2 0 2 7 13
                              (20)   (18)=38
Dick
 Genitalia   1 0 0 0 0 0 0 1   0 0 0 0 0 0 0 0
 Soc Dev   0 0 2 3 0 0 0 5   0 0 0 0 0 0 0 0
 -teaser   0 0 0 2 0 0 0 2   0 0 0 0 0 0 0 0
                              (8)   (0)=8
Dike
 Soc Dev   0 0 0 0 0 0 0 0   0 0 0 0 0 0 0 0
                              (0)   (0)=0
Dildo
 Soc Dev   0 0 0 0 0 0 1 0   0 0 0 0 0 0 0 0
                              (1)   (0)=1
Dink
 Soc Dev   0 5 7 3 0 0 0 15   0 2 0 0 0 0 0 2
                              (15)   (2)=17
Dog
 Soc Dev   0 0 0 0 0 1 0 1   0 0 0 0 0 0 0 0
                              (1)   (0)=1
Dork
 Soc Dev   0 1 2 0 0 0 0 3   0 1 0 0 0 0 0 1
                              (3)   (1)=4
Douche
 Soc Dev   0 0 0 2 0 1 0 3   0 0 0 0 0 0 0 0
                              (3)   (0)=3
Douche-bag
 Soc Dev   0 0 1 5 0 0 0 6   0 0 0 0 0 0 0 0
                              (6)   (0)=6

Fag
Soc Dev 0 5 4 1 0 0 0 10   0 1 0 0 0 0 0 1
         (10)   (1)=11

Fart
Process 0 0 1 1 0 0 0 2   0 0 0 0 0 0 0 0
Soc Dev 0 1 0 0 0 0 0 1   0 0 0 0 0 0 0 0
-around 0 1 0 0 0 0 0 1   0 0 0 0 0 0 0 0
         (4)   (0)=4

Fuck
Expletive 0 0 2 35 0 0 0 37   0 0 2 0 0 0 0 2
-you 0 2 0 26 4 1 0 33   0 1 0 12 2 0 0 15
Sex Act 0 0 1 4 0 5 0 10   0 0 0 2 0 0 0 2
Soc Dev 0 1 3 7 2 0 0 15   0 0 0 2 0 0 0 2
Fucked up 0 0 0 10 1 1 0 12   0 0 0 4 0 3 2 9
Adjective 0 9 9 116 17 22 7 180   0 2 3 32 6 7 12 62
         (287)   (92)=329

God
Expletive 0 0 0 3 1 0 1 5   0 0 0 0 0 0 2 2
         (5)   (2)=7

God Damn
Expletive 0 1 1 2 0 1 3 8   0 0 0 0 1 0 1 2
-you 0 0 0 0 0 0 0 0   0 0 0 0 0 0 0 0
Adjective 0 0 2 20 2 7 17 48   0 2 0 0 3 6 6 17
         (56)   (19)=75

Head
Soc Dev 0 0 1 0 1 0 0 2   0 0 0 0 0 0 0 0
Sex Act 0 0 0 1 1 0 0 2   0 0 0 0 0 0 0 0
         (4)   (0)=4

Hell
Expletive 0 4 1 11 6 11 11 44   0 0 0 8 6 3 17 34
Go To 0 0 1 0 0 1 0 2   0 0 1 1 0 0 0 2
Adjective 0 0 0 1 0 1 0 2   0 0 0 1 0 0 2 3
         (48)   (39)=87

Hole
Der	0	2	1	0	5	0	0	8		0	1	0	0	0	0	0	1
Soc Dev	0	0	0	0	0	1	0	1		0	0	0	0	0	0	0	0

(9)   (1)=10

Homo
Soc Dev	0	0	0	3	0	0	0	3		0	0	0	0	0	0	0	0

(3)   (0)=3

Honkey
Soc Dev	0	0	0	0	0	1	0	1		0	0	0	0	0	0	0	0

(1)   (0)=1

Jesus/Christ
Expletive	0	3	3	22	17	8	15	68		0	1	3	1	1	2	8	16

(68)   (16)=84

Jew
Soc Dev	0	0	0	0	0	0	0	0		0	0	0	0	0	0	1	1

(0)   (1)=1

Laid
Sex Act	0	0	0	6	0	0	0	6		0	0	0	0	0	1	0	1

(6)   (1)=7

Masturbate
Sex Act	0	0	1	0	0	0	0	1		0	0	0	0	0	0	0	0

(1)   (0)=1

Moron
Soc Dev	0	0	0	0	0	0	0	0		0	0	0	0	0	0	0	0

(0)   (0)=0

Mother of Christ
Expletive	0	0	0	1	1	0	0	2		0	0	0	0	0	0	0	0

(2)   (0)=2

Mother Fucker
Soc Dev	0	0	1	6	1	3	1	12		0	0	0	2	0	2	0	4

(12)   (4)=16

Nigger
Racial Slur	0	0	0	2	1	0	0	3		0	0	0	0	0	0	0	0

(3)   (0)=3

Nuts
  Body Part   0 1 0 1 0 0 0 2   0 0 0 0 0 0 0 0
                              (2)   (0)=2
Pig
  Soc Dev   0 1 1 3 0 0 0 5   0 0 0 0 0 0 0 0
                              (5)   (0)=5
Piss
  Process   1 3 0 11 0 0 0 15   0 0 0 1 0 0 0 1
  Soc Dev   0 1 0 0 0 0 0 1   0 0 0 0 0 0 0 0
  Angry   0 2 0 7 1 0 0 10   0 2 0 2 0 0 0 4
                              (26)   (5)=31
Prick
  Genitalia   0 0 0 4 2 1 1 8   0 0 0 0 0 0 0 0
  Soc Dev   0 1 0 4 1 2 2 10   0 0 0 0 0 0 0 0
                              (18)   (0)=18
Puke
  Soc Dev   0 0 1 0 0 0 0 1   0 0 0 0 0 0 0 0
                              (1)   (0)=1
Pussy
  Soc Dev   0 3 1 3 0 0 0 7   0 0 2 1 0 0 0 3
  Body Part   0 0 0 1 0 0 0 1   0 0 0 0 0 0 0 0
                              (8)   (3)=11
Queer
  Soc Dev   0 1 0 1 0 0 0 2   0 0 0 0 0 0 0 0
                              (2)   (0)=2
Screw
  -you   0 0 1 0 0 0 0 1   0 0 0 0 0 0 0 0
                              (1)   (0)=1
Shit
  Expletive   0 4 4 46 9 6 8 77   0 1 1 16 2 6 0 26
  Soc Dev   0 1 0 7 0 0 2 10   0 0 0 2 0 1 1 4
  Process   0 2 2 4 0 1 1 10   0 0 1 1 0 0 0 2
  Adjective or Noun 0 6 4 38 10 7 4 69   0 0 0 4 5 8 9 26
                              (166)   (58)=244

Slut
 Soc Dev 0 0 0 0 0 0 0 0 (0) | 0 0 0 2 0 0 0 2 (2)=2

Spic
 Racial Slur 0 0 0 1 0 0 0 1 (1) | 0 0 0 0 0 0 0 0 (0)=1

Suck
 Sex Act 0 0 0 1 0 0 0 1 | 0 0 0 0 0 0 0 0
 Soc Dev 0 1 0 3 0 1 0 5 | 0 0 0 0 0 0 0 0
 Der 0 3 3 17 2 2 0 27 (34) | 0 0 1 13 0 1 0 15 (15)=49

Tits
 Body Part 0 0 0 9 0 0 0 9 (9) | 0 0 0 0 1 0 0 1 (1)=10

Twat
 Body Part 0 0 0 1 0 0 0 0 (1) | 0 0 0 0 0 0 0 0 (0)=1

Wackin-off
 Sex Act 0 0 1 0 0 0 0 1 (1) | 0 0 0 0 0 0 0 0 (0)=1

Whimp
 Soc Dev 1 1 0 0 0 0 0 2 (2) | 0 1 0 0 0 0 0 1 (1)=3

Whore
 Soc Dev 0 0 1 2 0 1 0 4 (4) | 0 0 0 0 0 0 0 0 (0)=4

Wond
 Body Part 0 0 0 1 0 0 0 1 (1) | 0 0 0 0 0 0 0 0 (0)=1

Table 2b. *Dirty Word Production Lexicon.*

Female Speaker

Word Usage	Female Listener								Male Listener							
Age*	1	2	3	4	5	6	7	Tot	1	2	3	4	5	6	7	Tot
Ass																
Body Part	0	0	1	13	1	0	0	15	0	0	0	2	2	2	0	6
Soc Dev	0	0	2	12	0	1	0	15	0	0	0	4	0	1	3	7
Pain in	0	0	1	0	1	0	0	2	0	0	1	3	0	1	0	5
								(32)								(18)=50
Asshole																
Body Part	0	0	0	0	0	0	0	0	0	0	0	0	0	0	0	0
Expletive	1	0	0	1	0	0	0	2	0	0	0	1	0	0	0	1
Soc Dev	0	0	2	33	0	0	1	36	0	0	3	6	1	0	3	13
								(38)								(14)=52
Balls																
Eval	0	0	1	6	0	0	0	7	0	0	0	0	0	0	0	0
Expletive	1	0	0	1	0	0	0	2	0	0	0	1	0	0	0	1
Body Part	0	0	1	1	0	0	0	2	0	0	0	1	0	0	0	1
Strength	0	0	0	0	0	0	0	0	0	0	0	0	0	0	0	0
								(9)								(2)=11
Bastard																
Eval	0	0	0	0	0	0	0	0	0	0	0	0	0	0	0	0
Soc Dev	0	0	0	2	0	0	0	2	0	0	0	2	0	1	2	5
								(2)								(5)=7

Bitch

Soc Dev	0	1	2	10	0	0	0	13		0	0	2	5	0	1	0	8
S O B	0	0	0	4	0	0	0	4		0	0	0	1	1	2	0	4
Complain	0	0	1	3	0	0	1	5		0	0	0	2	1	0	0	3
Difficult	0	0	1	4	0	0	0	5		0	0	0	1	0	0	0	1

(27)   (16)=43

Blows

Sex Act	0	0	0	0	0	0	0	0		0	0	0	0	0	0	0	0
Der	0	0	0	0	0	0	0	0		0	0	0	0	0	0	0	0

(0)   (0)=0

Blow Job

Sex Act	0	0	0	0	0	0	0	0		0	0	0	0	0	0	0	0

(0)   (0)=0

Bull Shit

Expletive	0	0	0	2	1	0	0	3		0	0	0	1	0	0	0	1
Nonsense	0	0	0	0	1	0	0	1		0	0	0	0	0	0	0	0
Anger	0	0	0	0	0	0	0	0		0	0	0	0	0	0	0	0

(4)   (1)=5

Cock

Soc Dev	0	0	0	0	0	0	0	0		0	0	0	0	0	0	0	0
Genitalia	0	0	0	0	0	0	0	0		0	0	0	0	0	0	0	0

(0)   (0)=0

Cock Sucker

Soc Dev	0	0	0	0	1	0	0	1		0	0	0	0	0	0	0	0

(1)   (0)=1

Crap

Function	1	0	0	0	0	0	0	1		0	0	0	0	0	0	0	0
Product	0	0	0	0	0	0	0	0		0	0	0	0	0	0	0	0
Nonsense	0	0	0	0	0	0	0	0		0	0	0	0	0	0	0	0
Soc Dev	0	0	0	0	0	0	0	0		0	0	0	0	0	0	0	0

(1)   (0)=1

Crotch

Body Part	0	0	0	0	0	0	0	0		0	0	0	0	0	0	0	0

(0)   (0)=0

Cunt
  Soc Dev   0 0 0 0 0 0 0 0   0 0 0 0 0 0 0 0
  Genitalia   0 0 0 0 0 0 0 0   0 0 0 0 0 0 0 0
                                (0)   (0)=0

Damn
  Expletive   0 0 0 5 0 0 1 6   0 0 1 0 0 1 1 3
  Verb   0 0 0 1 0 0 0 1   0 0 0 0 0 0 1 1
  Adv-Adj   0 0 0 5 1 0 3 9   0 0 0 5 0 1 0 6
                             (16)   (10)=26

Dick
  Soc Dev   0 0 0 0 0 0 0 0   0 0 0 0 0 0 0 0
  Genitalia   0 0 0 0 0 0 0 0   0 0 0 0 0 0 0 0
  -teaser   0 0 0 0 0 0 0 0   0 0 0 0 0 0 0 0
                                (0)   (0)=0

Dike
  Soc Dev   0 0 0 1 0 0 0 1   0 0 0 0 0 0 0 0
                                (1)   (0)=1

Dildo
  Soc Dev   0 0 0 0 0 0 0 0   0 0 0 0 0 0 0 0
                                (0)   (0)=0

Dink
  Soc Dev   0 0 1 4 0 0 0 5   0 0 0 0 0 1 0 1
                                (5)   (1)=6

Dog
  Soc Dev   0 0 0 0 0 0 0 0   0 0 0 0 0 0 0 0
                                (0)   (0)=0

Dork
  Soc Dev   0 0 0 0 0 0 0 0   0 0 0 0 0 0 0 0
                                (0)   (0)=0

Douche
  Soc Dev   0 0 0 2 0 0 0 2   0 0 0 0 0 0 0 0
                                (2)   (0)=2

Douche-bag
  Soc Dev   0 0 0 0 0 0 0 0   0 0 0 0 0 0 0 0
                                (0)   (0)=0

Fag
  Soc Dev   0 0 0 0 0 0 0 0   0 0 0 4 0 0 0 4
                        (0)   (4)=4
Fart
  Soc Dev   0 0 0 0 0 0 0 0   0 0 0 0 0 0 0 0
  Process   0 0 0 0 0 0 0 0   0 0 0 0 0 0 0 0
  -around   0 0 0 0 0 0 0 0   0 0 0 0 0 0 0 0
                        (0)   (0)=0
Fuck
  Expletive 0 0 1 19 0 0 0 20   0 0 0 2 2 0 0 4
  -you   0 0 9 20 0 0 0 29   0 0 0 4 1 1 0 6
  Sex Act   0 0 0 0 0 0 0 0   0 0 0 0 0 0 0 0
  Soc Dev   0 0 0 1 0 0 0 1   0 0 1 0 0 0 0 1
  Fucked Up 0 0 0 2 0 0 0 2   0 0 0 2 0 0 0 2
  Adjective 0 0 1 15 1 5 1 23   0 0 0 3 0 0 2 6
                        (112)   (24)=136
God
  Expletive 0 0 0 0 0 1 0 1   0 1 1 0 0 1 0 3
                        (1)   (3)=4
God Damn
  Expletive 0 0 0 10 0 0 0 10   0 1 1 0 1 1 0 4
  -you   0 0 0 2 0 0 0 2   0 0 0 0 0 0 0 0
  Adjective 0 0 1 15 1 5 1 23   1 0 0 3 0 0 2 6
                        (35)   (10)=45
Head
  Soc Dev   0 0 0 0 0 0 0 0   0 0 0 0 0 0 0 0
  Sex Act   0 0 0 0 0 0 0 0   0 0 0 0 0 0 0 0
                        (0)   (0)=0
Hell
  Adjective 0 0 0 0 0 0 0 0   0 0 0 1 0 0 0 1
  Go To   0 0 0 24 0 1 11 36   0 0 0 12 0 0 4 16
  Expletive 0 0 0 0 0 0 0 0   0 0 0 0 0 0 0 0
                        (36)   (17)=53

Hole
 Der   0 0 0 0 0 0 0 0   0 0 0 0 0 0 0 0
 Soc Dev   0 0 0 0 0 0 0 0   0 0 0 0 0 0 0 0
                                (0)   (0)=0
Homo
 Soc Dev   0 0 0 0 0 0 0 0   0 0 0 0 0 0 0 0
                                (0)   (0)=0
Honkey
 Soc Dev   0 0 0 0 0 0 0 0   0 0 0 0 0 0 0 0
                                (0)   (0)=0
Jesus/Christ
 Expletive 3 0 1 16 2 0 3 25   0 0 0 6 1 2 2 11
                               (25)   (11)=36
Jew
 Soc Dev   0 0 0 0 0 0 0 0   0 0 0 0 0 0 0 0
                                (0)   (0)-0
Laid
 Sex Act   0 0 0 0 0 0 0 0   0 0 0 0 0 0 0 0
                                (0)   (0)=0
Masturbate
 Sex Act   0 0 0 0 0 0 0 0   0 0 0 0 0 0 0 0
                                (0)   (0)=0
Moron
 Soc Dev   0 0 0 1 0 0 0 1   0 0 0 0 0 0 0 0
                                (1)   (0)=1
Mother of Christ
 Expletive 0 0 0 0 0 0 0 0   0 0 0 2 0 0 0 2
                                (0)   (2)=2
Nigger
 Racial slur 0 0 0 1 0 0 0 1   0 0 0 0 0 0 0 0
                                (1)   (0)=1
Nuts
 Body Part 0 0 0 0 0 0 0 0   0 0 0 0 0 0 0 0
                                (0)   (0)=0

Pig
 Soc Dev   0 0 0 0 0 0 0 0   0 1 0 0 0 0 0 1
                                        (0)   (1)=1
Piss
 Process   0 0 0 0 0 0 0 0   0 0 0 0 0 0 0 0
 Soc Dev   0 0 0 0 0 0 0 0   0 0 0 0 0 0 0 0
 Anger   0 0 1 6 0 0 0 7   0 0 2 4 0 0 0 6
                                        (7)   (6)=13
Prick
 Genitalia   0 0 0 0 0 0 0 0   0 0 0 0 0 0 0 0
 Soc Dev   0 0 0 0 0 0 0 0   0 2 0 0 0 0 0 2
                                        (0)   (2)=2
Puke
 Soc Dev   0 0 0 0 0 0 0 0   0 0 0 0 0 0 0 0
                                        (0)   (0)=0
Pussy
 Soc Dev   0 0 0 0 0 0 0 0   0 1 1 0 0 0 0 2
 Body Part   0 0 0 0 0 0 0 0   0 0 0 0 0 0 0 0
                                        (0)   (2)=2
Queer
 Soc Dev   0 0 0 0 0 0 0 0   0 0 0 0 0 0 0 0
                                        (0)   (0)=0
Screw
 -you   0 0 0 2 0 0 0 2   0 0 0 0 0 0 0 0
                                        (2)   (0)=2
Shit
 Expletive   0 0 3 63 4 2 1 73   0 0 2 14 1 1 2 20
 Soc Dev   0 0 0 5 0 0 0 5   0 0 0 2 0 2 2 6
 Process   0 0 0 0 0 0 0 0   0 0 0 0 0 0 1 1
 Adjective or Noun 0 1 0 25 0 6 0 33   0 0 3 10 5 1 2 21
                                        (111)   (48)=159
Slut
 Soc Dev   0 0 0 3 0 0 0 3   0 0 0 0 0 0 0 0
                                        (3)   (0)=3

Spic
Racial Slur   0 0 0 0 0 0 0 0   0 0 0 0 0 0 0 0
                              (0)   (0)=0
Suck
Sex Act   0 0 0 1 0 0 0 1   0 0 0 0 0 0 0 0
Adjective   0 0 0 1 0 0 0 1   0 0 0 0 0 0 0 0
Der   0 0 3 8 0 0 0 11   0 0 1 2 1 0 0 4
                              (13)   (4)=17
Tits
Body Part   0 0 0 0 0 0 0 0   0 0 0 1 0 0 0 1
                              (0)   (1)=1
Twat
Body Part   0 0 0 0 0 0 0 0   0 0 0 0 0 0 0 0
                              (0)   (0)=0
Wacking-off
Sex Act   0 0 0 0 0 0 0 0   0 0 0 0 0 0 0 0
                              (0)   (0)=0
Whimp
Soc Dev   0 0 0 0 0 0 0 0   0 1 0 1 0 0 0 2
                              (0)   (2)=2
Whore
Soc Dev   0 0 0 0 0 0 0 0   0 0 0 0 0 0 0 0
                              (0)   (0)=0
Wond
Body Part   0 0 0 0 0 0 0 0   0 0 0 0 0 0 0 0
                              (0)   (0)=0

---

*Note - 1 to 7 refer to seven age ranges on Field Card. For example, 1 represents ages one to five years.

Semantics. Note that only two words, *fuck* and *shit*, account for a large part of the data. This could be so because when speakers use them, especially as expletives, they stand out more to our recorders, and are highly probable in the lexicon of speakers.

Although males and females were recorded using the same words, they use many of these words (e.g., *ass*) to denote different properties of the referent in question. For example, the word *ass* was used by females to denote either a social deviation or a body part; it was used mainly as a body part by males. *Cock, cunt,* and *dick* appeared as body parts in males' data but were not recorded for females. Similarly, neither *tits* or *pussy* were used by females. For males, *tits* was a body part and *pussy* referred to a social deviation. *Piss* referred to anger for females but was more likely to mean a process for males. *Balls, fuck, shit,* and *suck* were used more or less the same by both males and females.

Company Dependent Words. Several words were recorded predominantly (twice as often) in the same sex company, an indication that sex of company may influence word selection. Males were more likely to use the following words with other males: *asshole, balls, blows, bullshit, dick, dink, fag, fuck, goddamn, jesus, laid, motherfucker, piss, shit,* and *suck.* Similarly, female speakers were more likely to use *asshole, fuck, goddamn, hell, jesus, shit,* and *suck* in the context of other female company. The remainder of the corpus was more flexibly used in both same and mixed company contexts.

Discussion

Until the presentation of these data, there had been no extensive field study of the use of taboo or offensive language. The data in Table 2 are intended to provide frequency data and information about the semantic use of these words as a function of speaker and listener gender.

There is support for the stereotype that swearing is dominated by male speakers but that each gender uses dirty words more frequently around same sex crowds than in mixed company. Observe that swearing occurs across a wide age range, although mainly concentrated in the adolescent and young adult years. When people swear in public they use only a few words of the hundreds possible. The words used are not unidimensional in semantic meaning. Dirty words have several possible interpretations and one has to look at the utterance in which they occur and the context of use to determine meaning. Males and females may use one type of meaning for a particular word and not others. Perhaps a complete understanding must await the examination of these data by sociologists, linguists, anthropologists, and other psychologists.

There are some limitations here due to the method of field data collection and by the nature of swearing alone. To gain more insight about taboo language usage and comprehension, one must look at some additional data obtained in the laboratory. Field studies alone may not capture words that people use in private or off the street. Any field study is limited by its location, method of collection, and extent of its data. This field study provides a fairly accurate glimpse of how the average American swears in public. There are few claims about minority or ethnic group use of taboo words or language restricted to a single setting.

Laboratory Studies of Offensive Speech

There have been several studies using dirty words as items to be rated by college students in a laboratory setting (see literature reviews on the topic for example, Jay, 1980b; 1985). The main reason for conducting lab experiments is to control the phenomenon under investigation, as to nature, number, and presentation of materials. One can imagine that there are many words that subjects know, that were not recorded in the field study. There are words that subjects would never say in the laboratory in front of other people. By using pre-printed word lists one can ask subjects to make a number of decisions (frequency, offensiveness, etc) about the words on the list. Otherwise, by waiting for the words to occur in public, one would waste a great deal of time and effort. The laboratory setting sacrifices naturalness for control and efficiency.

Here are the results of two laboratory studies where subjects were asked to make linguistic decisions about taboo and nontaboo words on a list of words. The first study was conducted in Ohio in the early 1970's. The second was done six years later in western Massachusetts.

The purpose of presenting these tables of dirty word ratings is: a) to compare ratings with frequency counts in natural settings, b) to compare these ratings with previous methods and ratings, c) to examine the nature of word differences and sex of subject differences, and d) to estimate the stability of these ratings over time and geographic location. Until those interested in swearing establish the existence and nature of the phenomenon under investigation, we can only guess at what Americans are saying or not saying and how they feel about what they say, when they talk.

Jay 1977 Ratings

These data were originally obtained for a Master's Thesis at Kent State University in 1972-4. The results were published later in *Maledicta* in 1977 as part of an article on "How To Do Research With Dirty Words." The experiments were designed to find tabooness and frequency ratings for purposes of control.

Method

A list of 60 words was selected to be rated. 28 taboo and 28 nontaboo words were taken from Foote and Woodward (1972). The taboo words were those most frequently reported by university students. Four additional words from Kucera and Francis (1967) were added as low and high frequency "anchors." The list was randomized and given to a group of 29 female and 23 male students in introductory psychology courses. The subjects were asked to provide estimates of frequency of usage and tabooness on one-to-nine scales.

First, subjects were asked to rate how frequently each word was used in "everyday communication by college students" in typical interaction. The scale values ranged from 1 (never heard at all) to 9 (heard very frequently).

Next, they were asked to judge how obscene they thought the same list of words were to "a significant part of the population." They were asked to rate the words in relation to the general public because some students may think that they are not offended by anything. The results were intended to reflect general standards not college students' values. The rating scale was from 1 (not obscene at all) to 9 (the most obscene word imaginable).

Results

The frequency ratings indicate that taboo words were heard more frequently, 5.87, than the nontaboo words selected for the the list, 4.50 (see Tables 3 and 4 for word ratings). These data suggest that college students use taboo words very frequently in a setting that is socially relaxed. The range of ratings was from a high of 8.52 for *shit* to a low of 2.63 for *spic* (see Table 3). It is important to remember that these ratings are of relative, not absolute, frequency. The finding that these taboo words are rated as occurring more frequently than nontaboo words is important. That native speakers can estimate word frequency was known from previous research but if one believes that these previous reports using nontaboo words were accurate, then one must accept that these ratings of taboo words are also accurate and that *taboo words are used very frequently.*

A validity check on the ratings proved encouraging. Frequency ratings for *nontaboo* words correlated positively (r= .67) with the Kucera and Francis norms. Similarly, *taboo* words were correlated positively with Cameron's (1969) data (r= .56). Both taboo and nontaboo correlations were acceptable relationships in light of the fact that each measure is based on a different procedure of estimating word frequency, as well as using different subjects in different contexts.

One unexpected result was the *lack* of a sex of subject effect. Overall, males and females rated these words about the same, although differences do occur at the level of individual words. This lack of a finding tells us that what is observed in the real world and the laboratory are different. Perhaps males and females do indeed use these words at the same frequency *but* in different non-laboratory settings.

Table 3. *Frequency and Tabooness Ratings for Taboo Words.*

Word	Frequency			Tabooness			Cameron*
	Mean	Male	Female	Mean	Male	Female	
Motherfucker	5.52	6.13	5.03	8.56	8.43	8.65	---
Cocksucker	3.38	4.52	2.48	8.04	8.17	7.93	
Fuck	7.13	7.78	6.62	7.98	8.26	7.76	311
Pussy	4.48	6.13	3.17	7.06	6.70	7.34	10
Cunt	4.37	5.09	3.79	7.04	6.65	7.34	---
Prick	5.15	5.26	5.07	6.96	6.82	7.07	136
Cock	3.52	5.09	2.27	6.90	7.35	6.55	52
Bastard	5.83	5.30	6.24	6.19	5.65	6.62	234
Son of a bitch	6.94	6.78	7.07	6.13	6.00	6.24	13
Asshole	6.83	6.13	7.38	5.88	5.48	6.21	16
Suck	5.44	5.26	5.59	5.77	5.61	5.90	9
Nigger	4.33	4.39	4.28	5.73	5.65	5.79	---
Tits	5.08	6.39	4.03	5.65	5.39	5.86	3
Whore	4.94	5.22	4.72	5.51	5.35	5.66	---
Goddamn	7.87	7.39	8.24	5.44	5.22	5.62	218
Shit	8.52	8.30	8.69	5.38	5.57	5.24	266
Bitch	7.21	6.57	7.72	5.31	5.39	5.24	189
Piss	5.98	6.00	5.97	5.23	4.61	5.72	115
Slut	4.87	4.74	4.97	5.19	4.65	5.62	---
Queer	6.09	5.70	6.41	4.96	5.00	4.93	57
Bullshit	7.63	7.00	8.14	4.94	5.09	4.83	119
Ass	7.46	6.65	8.10	4.77	4.52	4.97	89
Spic	2.63	2.17	3.00	4.21	4.91	3.66	---
Blow	4.88	5.00	4.79	4.13	4.91	3.52	22
Jesus Christ	6.94	6.35	7.41	3.92	3.39	4.34	208
Damn	8.38	7.78	8.79	3.73	3.61	3.83	404
Hell	7.48	7.17	7.72	3.40	3.43	3.38	378
Pig	5.40	4.91	5.79	3.10	2.96	3.21	---

* Occurrences per 48,918 words sampled from college student conversations. Blanks indicate that no data were available.

Table 4. *Frequency and Tabooness Ratings for Nontaboo Words.*

Word	Frequency			Tabooness			Kucera Francis+
	Mean	Male	Female	Mean	Male	Female	
Dirty	6.11	5.04	6.97	1.63	1.26	1.93	36
High	7.06	6.87	7.21	1.40	1.69	1.17	497
Danger	4.42	4.04	4.72	1.33	1.17	1.45	70
Glow	2.30	2.09	2.48	1.31	1.35	1.28	16
Command	2.98	2.96	3.00	1.29	1.39	1.21	73
Wagon	2.67	2.78	2.59	1.23	1.09	1.34	55
Bitter	3.56	3.43	3.66	1.21	1.13	1.28	53
Run	5.75	5.00	6.34	1.17	1.13	1.21	212
Nurse	4.40	3.74	4.93	1.17	1.09	1.24	17
Plain	4.50	4.00	4.90	1.15	1.09	1.21	48
Yellow	3.90	2.83	4.76	1.15	1.09	1.21	55
Moth	2.75	2.52	2.93	1.15	1.00	1.28	1
Sword	2.44	2.65	2.28	1.13	1.22	1.07	7
Truth	5.38	4.65	5.97	1.13	1.30	1.00	126
Art	5.42	4.87	5.86	1.12	1.26	1.00	208
Money	7.61	7.87	7.41	1.10	1.13	1.07	265
Music	7.00	6.57	7.34	1.10	1.13	1.07	216
Boat	3.65	3.52	3.76	1.08	1.00	1.14	72
Faith	5.04	4.83	5.21	1.08	1.17	1.00	111
Joy	4.11	4.00	4.21	1.06	1.13	1.00	40
Silk	2.58	2.22	2.86	1.04	1.00	1.07	12
Dawn	3.06	2.83	3.24	1.04	1.09	1.00	28
Stars	3.98	3.52	4.34	1.03	1.08	1.00	25
Slow	5.09	4.70	5.41	1.02	1.00	1.03	60
City	5.88	5.83	5.93	1.02	1.00	1.03	393
Wise	4.04	3.78	4.24	1.00	1.00	1.00	36
Flower	4.96	4.17	5.59	1.00	1.00	1.00	23
Table	5.23	4.47	5.62	1.00	1.00	1.00	198
Resign*	3.48	3.13	3.71	1.24	1.44	1.10	2
Acrobats*	1.93	1.92	1.96	1.07	1.00	1.14	1

| Life* | 5.96 5.46 6.36 | 1.00 1.00 1.00 | 715 |
| My* | 7.87 7.63 8.04 | 1.00 1.00 1.00 | 1319 |

+ Occurrences per 1,014,000 words.

* Word was not included in analysis of variance

The Massachusetts Study (1978)

These norms were obtained using roughly the same methodology as the Kent study. However, the setting shifted 6 years later from the Midwest to New England.

To date these are the most extensive set of ratings obtained in the laboratory. There were several points that needed clarification from previous rating studies. First, most word rating studies were limited to a small number of taboo or offensive words. Even though ratings were obtained, they were informative of only a small set of the thousands of offensive words available. Taboo word lists usually include only one version of a concept, for example, *tits* but not *bosom*, *boobs*, *breast* and *knockers*. These probably differ in both offensiveness and frequency. Thirdly, word lists did not contain both vulgar terms (*fuck*) and clinical terms (*intercourse*). They should differ greatly in offensiveness but not necessarily in frequency. Finally, no one has compared the verbal form of the insult "*fuck*" to a behavioral form of the same, that is, a rating of actually "witnessing intercourse." The current list was constructed to overcome all four limitations.

Word List

The word list was constructed with three sets of items. One set of words were obscene, taboo, or vulgar words for body parts, processes, products, religious terms, racial-ethnic slurs, social deviations, animal insults, and euphemisms. These were taken from *The Dictionary of Contemporary and Colloquial Usage* (1972). A second set were items that were acceptable, nontaboo, or clinical references to many of the vulgar terms. Finally, a set of items that were *not* words but were prompted by "witnessing" certain acts, behaviors, and mannerisms. This last set was behavior to be evaluated not oral usage alone.

The final list included 117 unique words and 32 separate behaviors to be rated. Seven of the words were repeated on the word list for control purposes. The final list had 155 items.

Method

Subjects. The subjects were college students enrolled in an introductory psychology class, who received course credit for participation. There were 49 subjects, 25 females and 24 males. Most were white, middle-class natives of Massachusetts. All subjects were native English speakers.

Procedure. The experiment was run in group fashion. Subjects were given booklets containing the randomized list of 123 words, followed by another randomized listing of the acts and deeds to be evaluated. Before beginning the experiments subjects were told the nature of the stimuli and were given the opportunity to leave the experiment. No subjects left, however. Subjects first judged the list on frequency of occurrence. When all were finished with the first judgments, they then rated the same list on the basis of offensiveness.

Both judgments employed a one-to-nine rating scale on computerized answer sheets. For frequency estimation, subjects were asked to rate how frequently they heard the words or witnessed the actions or behaviors. The scale values ranged from 1 (never hear or witness the word or deed) to 9 (most frequently hear or witness). For offensiveness subjects were asked to determine how offensive the words and deeds were to a significant part of the population using a 1 (not offensive at all) to 9 (most offensive imaginable) scale.

For the word section of the list, instructions indicated that each item was to be considered as a word used in language. They were to consider them as part of any general conversation when making judgments and not think of specific speakers or listeners. They were asked to work quickly and indicate their first impressions of the words.

Following the word list, a written set of instructions for the acts and deeds appeared before the next set of items. Subjects were instructed to consider the items as acts or deeds (*not words*). They were to make judgments of them as if the given behavior was occurring and they were witnessing that act or deed.

Results

Mean ratings of frequency and of offensiveness were calculated for each term, as a function of sex of subject. Overall means for both judgments for each term were also calculated. Terms that were repeated for control purposes were averaged together. Averaged scale values appear in an alphabetized list for words, then acts in Table 5.

The goal of the frequency estimation study here is to obtain a more accurate picture of how often people use dirty words. One way to judge how these data approach that goal is to compare them with previous studies. For that reason, mean frequency ratings from the (a) Jay (1977) word ratings, (b) the Field Study norms, and (c) the present data from Table 4 were intercorrelated. The same 28 words (see Table 3) were compared to see how consistent these different methods of frequency estimation were. These correlations proved most satisfying.

The correlation with the two rating studies (Jay, 1977 and Massachusetts) were very high, r= .92, despite the fact that they were obtained several years apart and in different parts of the country. The correlations between the laboratory ratings and the field study were also strong. The 1977 ratings and the Field data correlation was r= .58 and the Massachusetts ratings and Field data was also r= .58. The same magnitude of correlation was obtained in the Jay (1977) study with Cameron's (1969) field study. Since laboratory and field data are obtained under such vastly different methods, correlations in this range are quite acceptable.

Table 5. *Tabooness and Frequency Ratings (1978).*

	Word	Tabooness				Frequency			
		Male	Female	Mean	R-O	Male	Female	Mean	R-O
1.	Anus	4.33	2.76	3.53	120	4.13	3.72	3.92	100
2.	Ass	3.17	3.04	3.10	134	7.83	8.16	8.00	4
3.	Asshole	4.79	3.60	4.18	86	7.83	8.16	8.00	5
4.	Ball	4.00	4.68	4.35	72	6.79	5.72	6.25	31
5.	Bastard	3.92	3.60	3.76	110	7.38	7.40	7.39	14
6.	Beat-off	6.83	4.40	5.59	26	5.46	3.00	4.20	90
7.	Beaver	4.00	4.48	4.25	77	5.75	3.44	4.57	78
8.	Bitch	4.42	3.72	4.06	91	7.58	7.68	7.63	12
9.	Blow-job	5.50	6.68	6.10	15	6.33	3.76	5.02	63
10.	Bone	3.75	2.84	3.29	130	5.00	3.72	4.35	83
11.	Boobs	3.84	3.56	3.69	115	5.42	6.64	6.04	34
12.	Brown-hole	4.79	4.96	4.88	48	2.92	1.48	2.18	139
13.	Breast	2.58	1.72	2.14	147	5.42	5.68	5.55	45
14.	Bull-dyke	3.96	4.44	4.20	82	2.17	1.36	1.76	147
15.	Bullshit	3.38	2.84	3.10	135	7.33	8.40	7.88	6
16.	Buns	3.29	2.96	3.12	133	4.92	4.76	4.84	69
17.	Butch	3.62	4.72	4.18	85	3.67	2.04	2.84	123
18.	Buttocks	3.13	1.92	2.51	144	4.21	4.00	4.10	97
19.	Castration	5.25	3.84	4.53	61	3.58	3.20	3.39	113
20.	Cherry	4.62	4.32	4.47	65	5.50	3.12	4.29	87
21.	Chicken-shit	3.92	2.80	3.35	126	4.58	3.96	4.27	88
22.	Chink	5.04	4.12	4.57	57	4.13	4.80	4.47	79
23.	Climax	4.04	3.40	3.71	113	4.79	3.80	4.29	86
24.	Clitoris	5.13	3.68	4.39	70	4.79	3.60	4.18	93
25.	Cock	5.83	5.80	5.82	18	6.29	4.16	5.20	61
26.	Cocksucker	6.13	6.92	6.53	9	6.17	4.32	5.22	60
27.	Cockteaser	6.38	6.68	6.53	10	6.37	3.36	4.84	70
28.	Coitus	3.54	3.48	3.51	122	3.17	1.80	2.47	132
29.	Come	5.17	4.92	5.04	39	5.63	4.68	5.14	62

0.	Coon	4.71	4.64	4.67	55	4.88	3.32	4.08	98
1.	Copulation	4.21	3.32	3.76	109	2.79	2.56	2.67	126
2.	Corn-hole	4.79	5.08	4.94	46	3.13	1.20	2.14	141
3.	Crabs	5.79	4.84	5.31	32	4.96	3.36	4.14	94
34.	Crap	3.92	2.84	3.37	125	6.13	6.56	6.35	28
35.	Cunnilingus	4.38	4.20	4.29	73	3.54	1.16	2.32	135
36.	Cunt	6.37	7.20	6.80	8	6.88	3.00	4.90	68
37.	Damn	2.38	1.76	2.06	149	7.46	8.04	7.76	8
38.	Dang	3.71	3.92	3.82	103	3.17	1.60	2.37	133
39.	Defecation	4.21	3.60	3.90	99	2.87	2.44	2.65	127
40.	Dick	5.00	5.56	5.29	33	5.79	4.16	4.96	66
41.	Dildo	5.67	4.52	5.08	37	5.67	3.20	4.41	81
42.	Dink	4.46	3.88	4.16	87	5.13	5.40	5.27	55
43.	Dipshit	4.38	3.84	4.10	89	5.29	5.28	5.29	53
44.	Dog	2.92	1.96	2.43	145	5.75	7.44	6.61	21
45.	Dong	4.29	4.20	4.25	78	4.29	1.72	2.98	120
46.	Dork	3.96	3.64	3.80	105	3.00	1.76	2.37	134
47.	Douche-bag	6.33	5.40	5.86	17	6.50	4.32	5.39	49
48.	Ejaculation	4.92	3.52	4.20	81	4.75	3.16	3.94	99
49.	Erection	4.90	3.64	4.25	75	4.73	3.92	4.32	84
50.	Fag	5.25	2.44	3.82	102	6.58	7.40	7.00	15
51.	Fart	4.17	3.00	3.57	118	6.00	7.24	6.63	20
52.	Fornication	3.71	3.80	3.76	108	2.87	2.60	2.74	125
53.	Fox	2.25	3.12	2.69	141	5.25	3.04	4.12	95
54.	Frig	3.87	3.72	3.79	104	3.33	4.41	3.75	106
55.	Fuck	6.04	6.72	6.39	12	7.79	7.48	7.63	13
56.	Fur-burger	5.38	5.88	5.63	25	3.63	1.48	2.53	129
57.	Goddamn	3.37	3.32	3.35	127	7.67	7.80	7.74	9
58.	Hairpie	4.25	4.48	4.37	71	2.58	1.56	2.06	143
59.	Hand-job	5.17	5.64	5.41	29	5.00	2.72	3.84	105
60.	Hard-on	4.88	4.96	4.92	47	6.00	4.64	5.31	52
61.	Hebe	5.21	4.32	4.76	52	2.42	2.04	2.22	137
62.	Hell	2.63	1.64	2.12	148	7.54	8.56	8.06	2
63.	Homo	5.00	3.44	4.21	84	5.92	6.52	6.22	32
64.	Homosexuality	5.16	3.42	4.27	74	5.16	6.28	5.73	41
65.	Honky	4.83	4.08	4.45	66	4.21	5.52	4.37	82

66.	Horny	3.21	3.44	3.33	128	6.63	7.00	6.82	16
67.	Horseshit	4.38	3.16	3.76	111	4.79	5.68	5.24	59
68.	Hump	4.67	5.24	4.96	44	5.58	3.72	4.63	75
69.	Intercourse	3.33	2.76	3.04	137	5.54	5.56	5.55	46
70.	Jerk-off	3.08	5.24	5.65	24	5.83	3.72	4.76	72
71.	Jesus Christ	4.88	3.36	4.10	90	7.25	8.08	7.67	11
72.	Jism	5.17	4.32	4.74	54	2.79	1.16	1.96	145
73.	Kike	4.74	4.74	4.74	53	3.31	2.82	3.07	121
74.	Knockers	3.46	4.56	4.02	96	5.21	3.32	4.25	89
75.	Knock-up	4.88	5.92	5.41	30	4.96	3.68	4.31	85
76.	Lay	4.54	5.04	4.80	50	7.12	5.76	6.43	25
77.	Lesbian	6.13	3.92	5.00	42	5.17	5.48	5.33	50
78.	Masturbation	5.54	4.60	5.06	38	4.46	3.80	4.12	96
79.	Menstruation	4.33	2.36	3.33	129	4.00	5.92	4.98	65
80.	Motherfucker	6.42	7.44	6.94	5	6.46	5.20	5.82	40
81.	Nigger	5.21	5.84	5.53	27	6.50	4.92	5.69	42
82.	Nipples	4.08	3.84	3.96	97	6.08	4.48	5.27	54
83.	Nymphomaniac	4.08	3.72	3.90	100	4.00	2.92	3.45	110
84.	Orgasm	4.04	4.04	4.04	92	6.04	5.16	5.59	44
85.	Pecker	5.00	5.20	5.10	36	6.58	3.96	5.25	56
86.	Penis	4.50	3.56	4.02	95	5.33	5.16	5.24	57
87.	Peter	3.92	3.56	3.74	112	4.58	2.48	3.51	109
88.	Pig	3.35	3.08	3.21	132	5.33	6.58	5.97	36
89.	Piss	4.50	3.40	3.94	98	6.33	6.48	6.41	26
90.	Polock	4.54	3.88	4.20	83	4.92	5.72	5.33	51
91.	Poontang	3.83	4.20	4.02	93	3.17	1.24	2.18	138
92.	Prick	5.08	6.36	5.74	21	6.38	4.92	5.63	43
93.	Pubic	3.96	3.12	3.53	119	4.75	4.08	4.41	82
94.	Pud	4.25	4.76	4.51	63	4.63	2.04	3.31	116
95.	Pussy	5.38	6.16	5.78	19	7.21	5.24	6.20	33
96.	Queer	5.08	3.40	4.22	79	6.79	6.72	6.76	18
97.	Rape	5.29	3.72	4.49	64	5.50	7.64	6.59	22
98.	Rim	4.17	3.44	3.80	106	3.46	1.64	2.53	130
99.	Screw	4.41	4.44	4.43	69	7.00	6.60	6.80	17
100.	Scrotum	5.12	3.80	4.45	67	3.67	3.08	3.37	114
101.	Semen	4.46	4.04	4.25	76	4.25	3.04	3.63	107

02.	Shit	3.58	2.94	3.25	131	7.75	8.36	8.06	3
03.	Shithead	5.58	4.48	5.02	41	6.71	6.24	6.47	23
04.	Sixty-nine	3.79	4.40	4.10	88	5.00	3.40	4.18	91
05.	Slut	5.88	5.48	5.67	23	5.83	5.96	5.90	38
06.	Sodomy	4.58	4.72	4.65	56	3.04	1.48	2.25	136
07.	Son of a bitch	4.29	3.44	3.86	101	7.96	7.72	7.84	7
08.	Spic	5.12	5.36	5.25	34	4.92	4.68	4.80	71
109.	Suck	4.96	4.68	4.82	49	6.54	6.36	6.45	24
110.	Sweathog	3.21	2.88	3.04	138	4.62	4.64	4.63	74
111.	Tail	2.96	3.16	3.06	136	3.92	3.84	3.88	104
112.	Testicles	4.92	3.52	4.20	80	3.42	3.40	3.41	111
113.	Tit	3.58	5.44	4.53	62	6.71	5.16	5.92	37
114.	Twat	5.38	4.88	5.12	35	5.50	2.36	3.90	102
115.	Urination	3.75	1.64	2.67	142	3.79	4.56	4.18	92
116.	Vagina	4.21	2.84	3.51	121	5.54	4.40	4.96	67
117.	Whore	5.79	5.12	5.45	28	6.12	6.36	6.25	30

	Witnessing	Taboooness				Frequency			
		Male	Female	Mean	R-O	Male	Female	Mean	R-C
1.	A french kiss	3.00	2.84	2.92	139	5.42	5.60	5.51	47
2.	A homosexual	6.42	6.00	6.20	13	2.79	2.24	2.51	131
3.	Acts of child abuse	7.46	7.68	7.57	3	2.29	2.04	2.16	140
4.	Anal sex	5.92	7.76	6.86	7	2.38	1.24	1.80	146
5.	Belching	3.83	4.20	4.02	94	6.00	6.00	6.00	35
6.	Defecation	5.83	6.52	6.18	14	3.04	2.12	2.57	128
7.	Drunkeness	3.37	2.16	2.75	140	7.25	8.12	7.69	10
8.	Extreme violence	6.38	7.40	6.90	6	4.08	2.56	3.31	117
9.	Farting	4.83	4.32	4.57	58	6.92	6.36	6.63	19
10.	Goosing	4.46	4.64	4.55	59	3.21	3.44	3.33	115
11.	Heavy petting	3.75	6.12	4.96	45	3.71	3.08	3.39	112
12.	Intercourse	4.75	6.72	5.76	20	3.58	2.20	2.88	122
13.	Masturbation	6.63	7.32	6.98	4	2.50	1.72	2.10	142
14.	Murder	8.08	8.64	8.37	1	2.12	1.16	1.63	148
15.	Nudity	3.13	4.24	3.69	114	5.67	4.40	5.02	64
16.	One exposing self	4.75	6.60	5.69	22	4.29	2.88	3.57	108
17.	Oral sex	5.29	7.64	6.49	11	4.00	1.68	2.82	124
18.	Person picking nose	4.71	5.28	5.00	43	4.17	5.28	4.74	73
19.	Pornography	4.12	5.88	5.02	40	4.88	3.00	3.92	101
20.	Rape	7.42	8.32	7.89	2	2.00	1.16	1.57	149
21.	Revealing clothes	2.67	4.08	3.39	124	5.75	4.76	5.25	58
22.	Shooting moons	3.58	3.64	3.61	117	5.25	3.92	4.57	76
23.	Sodomy	5.96	6.24	6.10	16	2.63	1.40	2.00	144
24.	Spitting	3.58	3.96	3.78	107	5.67	7.00	6.35	29
25.	Sticking out tongue	2.79	1.80	2.29	146	4.92	6.68	5.82	39
26.	Stripping off clothes	3.88	5.20	4.55	60	4.67	3.16	3.90	103
27.	Streaking	3.54	3.76	3.65	116	3.63	2.16	2.88	121
28.	Swearing	2.88	2.20	2.53	143	7.75	8.48	8.12	1
29.	Touching genitals of the opposite sex	4.67	6.00	5.35	31	4.17	2.24	3.18	118

0.	The finger	3.83	3.16	3.49	123	6.08	6.72	6.41	27
1.	Urination	4.54	5.00	4.78	51	5.75	3.44	4.57	77
2.	Vomiting	4.25	4.64	4.45	68	5.00	5.84	5.43	48

Note - R-O refers to rank-order from 1 (first) to 149 (last).
One word was repeated for control purposes, but data were averaged in table.

A Matter of Semantics

Looking at frequency ratings in Table 4, it is clear there exists a great number of comparisons that can be made. One point to be made is that different words for the same concept are used with different frequencies. It is interesting to note that the vulgar or taboo forms of a concept, in many cases, are used more often than are clinical or nontaboo forms. Here are some examples with ratings of frequency in parentheses.

Table 5a. *Concepts and Frequency.*

---

boobs (6.04), *tit* (5.92), *breast* (5.55), *knockers* (4.25)
pussy (6.2), *vagina* (4.96), *cunt* (4.9), *twat* (3.9),
      furburger (2.53), *poontang* (2.18), *hairpie* (2.06)
piss (6.41), *urination* (4.18)
shit (8.06), *crap* (6.35), *defecate* (2.65)
prick (5.63), *pecker* (5.25), *penis* (5.24), *cock* (5.2),
      dick (4.96), *peter* (3.51), *pud* (3.31), *dong* (2.98)
jerk off (4.76), *beat off* (4.2), *masturbation* (4.12),
      hand job (3.84)
fuck (7.63), *screw* (6.8), *lay* (6.43), *intercourse* (5.55),
      hump (4.63), *copulation* (2.67), *coitus* (2.47)
orgasm (5.59), *come* (5.14), *climax* (4.29), *ejaculate* (3.94)

If these taboo words are more common in reality than nontaboo counterparts, one must rethink some assumptions about the nature of the lexicon and how adults communicate about taboo. These data also must be considered in broadcasting education, law and other concerns involving emotion-laden language.

Of Words and Deeds

There are also many possible comparisons across both words and deeds that are suggested by Table 5. Below are the top ten words and the top ten behaviors used to make the following chart (Words are in italics, behaviors are not. Ratings are in parentheses). Rank-order within the list of 148 items is also given. These data also support the notion that swearing is very, very common.

Table 5b. *Frequency of Words and Deeds.*

swearing (8.12)	rank	1
hell (8.06)		2
shit (8.06)		3
ass (8.00)		4
asshole (8.00)		5
bullshit (7.88)		6
son of a bitch (7.84)		7
damn (7.76)		8
goddamn (7.74)		9
drunkenness (7.69)		10
jesus christ (7.67)		11
farting (6.63)		19
the finger (6.41)		27
spitting (6.35)		29
belching (6.00)		35
stick out tongue (5.82)		39
french kiss (5.51)		47
vomiting (5.43)		48
revealing clothes (5.25)		58

In the minds of college students there is a great deal of swearing in our society and as a behavior it occurs commonly with other highly frequent behavior such as being drunk, spitting, farting, sticking out the tongue, and wearing revealing clothing. While these behaviors are considered crude in American culture, they do occur frequently and are part of American life. Just because these words and deeds are offensive is no reason for social scientists to exclude these items from frequency and offensiveness rating studies.

The comparison of words and deeds would have been very difficult to do outside of laboratory ratings because these behaviors are offensive, embarrassing, illegal, or infrequent. Further, some of these words (e.g., *copulation*) may never have been observed in public because they are low frequency words or too clinical in nature. The rating procedure gives a method of relative comparison between the use of these words and the occurrence of these behaviors as they exist in the judgments of our subjects.

Conclusion

The main point of these frequency studies is to establish the relative frequency of the phenomenon of dirty word usage. This was achieved by both laboratory and field studies. No one could deny that people use dirty words in the real world. The field study captured some portion of that truth. From the new data reported here, dirty words occur at a moderately high rate relative to some nontaboo words in our language. There are no estimates of how a particular individual uses this language throughout the day. The data only refer to average language use and not specific people in specific places. The goal was to indicate at what rate dirty words do occur in our culture... and the answer is frequently.

The reason these data are needed is because traditional methods and traditional word counts, as reviewed in the introduction, give the impression that Americans do not swear. The tables listed here now give researchers and those interested in human communication a new outlook on colloquial American speech.

There are additional lines of support for the high frequency conclusion. Age of acquisition is generally a good indicator of the importance of linguistic concepts and of frequency of usage. Words that are learned early are used frequently. The durability of language when threatened by old age, brain damage, or other insults to the brain, is another line of support. High frequency words and important concepts, e.g., those learned in childhood, are the last to disappear during traumatic decline. Dirty words are both learned early and remain late, another sign of high frequency. These physiological variables are explored elsewhere (Jay, 1985).

That words occur at different rates in itself is not an important finding. The next question to ask is *why* do words occur at different rates? To answer that question with regard to dirty words requires a look at the underlying dynamics of language usage. It is the meaning of the individual word, the purpose that it serves, and the relation between the speaker and listener that determines absolute frequency. In short communication context accounts for the use of a given word. Communication context is the subject of several chapters in this book and represents the "bottom line" for dirty words.

It is clear in field studies of both adults and children that males use dirty words more often than females. In the rating studies, these sex differences may disappear. Because subjects are using a criterion of the "average speaker" and not personalizing these ratings, it may be that women and men are thinking of the same speaker or model when making their judgments. That prototypical swearer may differ from what occurs in specific locations with specific speakers. What this means is that women may swear a great deal in private places (dorm rooms, parties, etc) and not in public. These speaker differences are examined in chapter 5.

Chapter 5

The Offensiveness of Words: Sex and Semantics

What language offends Americans? What words and deeds are so vile that we must be protected from them by laws? What events in our lives are so powerful and anxiety-provoking that we hesitate to speak about them with others? What terms and concepts have been tabooed for generations and will continue to be taboo for our children? What is the worst insult you can give to a member of the opposite sex? These are some of the challenging thoughts that arise when people consider the power behind dirty words and obscene language.

In this chapter some of the underlying semantic domains of offensive language are explored from a psychological point of view. The topic of taboo or obscenity is not limited to psychological analysis, of course, and other disciplines and points of view are considered. One needs to look at legal, religious, anthropological, and linguistic data to get a complete picture of obscenity. The main focus will be on a psychological perspective of the phenomenon. Most of the literature cited comes predominantly from the social sciences and the remainder from law, linguistics, and sociology. As has been stated elsewhere in the book, there is very little empirical literature in the social sciences on the dirty word phenomenon.

A second factor included here is the dynamics of communicating with taboo words between speaker and listener. One of the goals of this research is to look at how people communicate with each other in the real world. This picture of natural communication shows the distinct mentality of the American male and the American female, who communicate differently about taboo information.

There has been a great deal of effort in psychology to scrutinize the differences cited in the literature that distinguish males from females. The interpretation of dirty word usage is unchanged by that effort. Reported differences in cognition, mathematical abilities, aggression, personality, intelligence, and social roles are being erased in current publications. But little, if any, research shows that males and females swear at people in the same fashion.

At the end of the chapter are presented the results of a role-playing experiment, where males act like females and females act as males. Because "offensiveness" changes under different roles, we are left with the conclusion that much of producing and reacting to dirty words is based on the roles which are acquired during early years. The differences in dirty word usage are due to our attempts to present ourselves as congruent with the expected behavior for our position in society. To do otherwise is to run the risk of being labeled as a role-deviant to some degree.

Gender differences in offendedness is not the only issue. Speaker-listener differences based on age, race, ethnic background, or degree of friendship are factors contributing to verbal aggression. As such these differences bring up the topics of racial slurs, religious expression, sexual harassment, verbal abuse, and insults in general. One benefit of knowing the semantics of offensiveness is to decrease the frequency of these occurrences in future conversations. It is assumed that speakers can become more sensitive to another person's state of mind, adjusting language accordingly. Offensiveness data contribute to the awareness that other people may be offended by certain words that one originally (due to ignorance) thought were harmless. The more one knows about how other groups think and speak, the more sensitive we become to their likes and dislikes.

Purpose of the Chapter

The purpose of this chapter is to describe the semantics underlying offensiveness. It will be shown that men and women are offended by different words. It will be shown that although the field of psychology does not know a great deal about how words offend us, that verbal aggression and insult do exist and underly our concept of sexual harassment. The literature shows again that women and men use dirty words differently and, with respect to sexual harassment, are harassed by different types of behavior and language. One cannot describe the semantics of offensiveness of dirty words without describing gender differences in dirty word usage; thus, this chapter is about gender *and* semantics.

Offensiveness versus Offendedness

There is one distinction that needs to be made when talking about how words affect us. *Offensiveness* is a term used to denote the degree to which a certain word or concept possesses negative or aversive properties. Offensiveness is related to the concept of taboo in that the more offensive a word is the more likely it is to be taboo. Taboo represents our inhibitions about using a word because of its offensiveness. *Offendedness* is a reaction to a word by a person who hears or reads the word. Offendedness is a property of humans in response to words that vary in negative content. Dirty words can be measured as stimulus items for offensiveness. Peoples' reactions to the words can indicate how offended they are to a given word.

In chapter 4 on Frequency, there are several tables of data displaying the ratings of word frequency and ratings of tabooness or offensiveness. Offensiveness ratings provide the starting point to examine the semantics underlying obscene speech. In general most of what we know about peoples' reactions to the offensiveness of speech in psychology comes from laboratory-type ratings. Many of these studies use paper-and-pencil surveys or interviews to provide data. Very little is known about the physiology of being offended by a word alone. We will look at several different empirical methods that have been used to measure both offensiveness and offendedness.

First, a little background. Graduate students at Kent State University were designing some of the first word-rating studies. For a pilot study to test materials and instructions, it was necessary to determine how long the experiment would take and obtain some initial impressions about how college students would perceive dirty words as stimuli. A small group of subjects were assembled in a small room. Word lists were handed out and the subjects were asked to rate each word on the computer forms with a number from one to nine. The number was to indicate to what degree the subject was offended by the word; the higher the number, the greater the offense. "You mean how much I am *personally* offended?", one subject asked. Without much thought, he was told, "yes", to his question. At the end of the experiment, he returned the computer sheet and every word was rated "1." A few other subjects answered similarly.

The point of the story is simple. Researchers were not getting data about the properties of words, but instead were getting data about the personalities of college students. Offendedness is a personal reaction to a stimulus; it is not a quality of a word *per se*. Offendedness is different than offensiveness because offendedness tells one about personality factors not semantics. Granted, being offended is in part a function of the word presented to a person, some people "act" as if they are not offended by anything...expecially college students at Kent State University in the early 1970's, the scene of student protest and death. To find offensiveness data, the method had to be depersonalized, which was done to obtain the ratings in the Frequency Chapter and here on offensiveness. A recent example follows.

The Massachusetts 1978 Ratings

This experiment (see chapter 4 on Frequency) presented students with a 155 item list of words and behaviors to be rated for frequency of usage and degree of offensiveness to the general public. Table 1 lists the top 20 items from that list with mean ratings (1= not offensive at all, 9= most offensive imaginable).

Table 1. *Twenty Most Offensive Items.*

witnessing murder	8.36
witnessing rape	7.88
witnessing acts of child abuse	7.57
witnessing masturbation	6.98
motherfucker	6.93
witnessing extreme violence	6.90
witnessing anal sex	6.86
cunt	6.80
cocksucker	6.53
cockteaser	6.53
witnessing oral sex	6.49
fuck	6.38
witnessing a homosexual	6.20
witnessing defecation	6.18
blow job	6.10
witnessing sodomy	6.10
douche bag	5.86
cock	5.81
pussy	5.77
witnessing intercourse	5.76

These words were selected from dictionaries of slang and colloquial usage and from previous rating studies. They were randomized in booklet format and following the words were a list of behaviors that the subject was to rate on the same offensiveness scale (1 to 9). Additional details and controls appear in the Frequency chapter.

These are ratings of offensiveness. Subjects were instructed to estimate the degree to which each of the items were offensive to the general public. We were not interested in an individual subject's ideas or personality. We were only interested in how words and behaviors could be measured with an offensiveness "measuring stick" and ranked relative to one another. The numbers are average values of the degree to which one of the words (in italics) or acts (denoted by the prompt "witnessing") possesses offensive features or content.

Here is a summary of the major semantic features or properties that make words or acts offensive in America. They include: sexual content, aggression, body functions, body parts, race, and religion.

Aggressive Content

It is clear that the most offensive items on the list are witnessing acts of violence with ratings of 7 or 8 (5 is mid-point on the scale). Of the first 16 items with ratings of 6 or more, 10 involve observing behavior rather than a spoken word. In fact half of the list of "witnessing" items have ratings greater than 5. Violence is separate from speech and more offensive. If we apply this finding to the movies, it would seem that for a motion picture depicting stereotypical "sex and violence", it would be the behaviors rather than the speech which would be most objectionable. Such a dichotomy between behavior and language brings into question the nature of ratings given to motion pictures. While the rating systems look at violence, nudity, explicit sexual acts and explicit language, it seems that the depiction of behaviors involved with murder and abuse are more objectionable than speech itself.

Experimenters need to pay attention to the possibility of multiple interpretations of words in their studies. In the future, studies should be designed to gather data on how the subjects are interpreting dirty word stimuli or we could tell subjects how to think of the words as in Driscoll's study (1981). His subjects were told to consider the words presented as epithets, eliminating the interpretation of *bitch* as "female dog." Otherwise, when a subject is asked to rate a word such as *shit* and the meaning is not given, it is not clear which grammatical class or functional category forms the basis of the decision. *Shit* could be a noun meaning feces, a noun meaning a dislikeable person, a verb, an exclamation or an expletive. Each of these uses has a different level of aggression. Many dirty words (*asshole*, *bitch*, *dumb ass*, or *whore*) were rated as used frequently in an aggressive or angry manner. Also these word ratings represent or cover a wide range of aggressiveness.

Were these ratings tapping an aggressiveness dimension? *Massachusetts* ratings were correlated with the 22 words that appeared on Driscoll's list. The end result, r= .37, indicated a moderate degree of relationship between offensiveness and aggressiveness. The point of the comparison and relation between the ratings is that offensiveness is not merely a matter of sexual semantics in these dirty words. The fact that they are used aggressively to express anger or violence is equally important.

Sexual Content

Offensive language includes words denoting body parts and sexual acts. Those words which point out deviant or derogatory features of sex (*motherfucker*, *cunt*, *cocksucker*, *cockteaser*, and *blow job*) are atop the list along with *fuck*, which also obtained a rating in the 6 range. In fact most of the words on the "offensive" side of the scale have something to do with sexual conduct to some extent.

American society is very concerned with regulating sexual acts. There are laws and sanctions that control age, location, manner, and intensity of sexual relations between humans. What is not controlled legally has been sanctioned by religious customs, parental consent, and traditional mores within the American way of life. The control of the language about sex and communication of sexual messages is one extension of these formal regulations.

Regardless of what caused Americans to place a taboo on sex, the offensiveness of "sex" is obvious. Words that describe sex acts, sexual anatomy, sexually transmitted disease, sexual health practices, sexual appliances, and deviant sexuality have all achieved some degree of offensiveness.

Body Functions and Body Products

Words that are associated with bodily waste products and the acts of elimination of those products are offensive to most Americans. In childhood parents regularly use euphemisms for these products and acts, such as *pee pee, doody, number 1* and *number 2, poop, wee wee* or *tinkle.* Later, the child will hear siblings or peers using more offensive words, such as *shit, crap, turd, fart* and *piss.* The child's early use of these words as insults contains the euphemisms, like *poophead,* but words are later replaced by the more offensive insults that adults and older children use, like *shithead.*

Speech using bodily products and processes as referents changes with time, as does one's concept of self. We develop a concept of what is "my body" and what is not body. For example, phlegm, snot, earwax, perspiration, urine, feces, or saliva sooner or later are associated with the reaction of disgust. Some of these words and their referents which evoke the disgust response occur in many languages and cultures.

Feces represents one of the most universal elements of disgust. Some people may regard semen, menses and vaginal secretions with equal disgust. It is the product itself that is taboo but the *word* associated with the product becomes offensive. To call someone a body product name is to reduce the person to the product. So, the word takes on the semantic properties of the product and the name of the body product or process becomes a form of insult.

It is interesting that while some taboo words can be used as both insults and terms of endearment, such as *old son-of-a-bitch,* these body product and body process terms are more unidimensional in their meaning. Body products and processes are rarely used in a flattering or positive manner and perhaps the degree of offensiveness of these body parts and products is indicated by the number of obscene and insulting words associated with them.

The point here is that certain body functions, body parts, and body products become a tabooed subject and evoke a reaction of disgust. Emotions and revulsions about food and oral incorporation were recently examined by Rozin and Fallon (1987). To the degree that the words and concepts surrounding food-related emotion are associated with insults, offensiveness, and cursing, these data merit attention. It is not just that the basis of disgust is interesting. The process of disgust is a very potent emotion in American culture. Food aversions resulting in vomiting are quickly learned and rarely forgotten. It is not surprising that the products of disgust becomes a form of insults in almost every culture.

Racial Slurs

Since the era of civil rights legislation in the mid-1960's Americans have been more attentive to the use of racial slurs and epithets. Most of the words that are based on racial or ethnic semantics ended up in the upper half of the ratings. These words include, *chink*, *coon*, *hebe*, *kike*, *nigger*, and *spic*. While these high ratings portray the degree of offensiveness as words, we still have a lot to learn about how words affect their targets. From a legal point of view it is interesting to note that in hearings involving pornography, obscenity, *and* racial discrimination psychiatrists have been used as expert witnesses. Psychiatrists testify as to how the stimuli (words, pictures, insults) affect the people in question. The testimony generally focuses on one person's response to the stimuli. But what the courts really need are general data on the offensiveness of swastikas, racial epithets and the like. The courts also need data indicating how the average person on the street reacts to "fighting language" and language that constitutes disorderly conduct or disturbing the peace.

Obviously a word alone cannot harm a person's body. The physiological impact of the word gains its strength by some association stored in memory. Racial slurs may be associated with other episodes of prejudice, stereotyping, and perhaps threats of physical violence. These expressions may be in some way a violation of a person's civil rights, in the same manner we conclude that sexual innuendo is sexual harassment. The important feature of racial slurs is that when speakers use slurs, we assume that such speech is correlated with underlying prejudice, bigotry, narrow-mindedness and racism. It is not the word *per se* that is feared so much as the potentially undesirable behavior that goes along with the talk. Minorities are justified in being suspicious of verbal bigotry to the degree that the talk may be correlated with harassment, denial of civil rights, aggression or other improper or illegal conduct.

The use of racial slurs must also be considered in context. It may be a problem of losing face or honor. If one is called a *nigger* as opposed to *African-American*, the target is being treated at a lower level than the speaker. The language not only degrades the listener but also depersonalizes him/her as well.

Such a degrading reference may lead to or instigate further verbal or physical retaliation from the target to the speaker.

A line of research suggested by the racism argument would be to determine empirically how language is related to attitudes and/or behavior. Does a certain kind of language mean that the speaker is disposed to act in certain ways or are words and deeds two unrelated responses?

God is Dead: Have Religious Terms Lost Their Clout?

It is interesting to see that terms based on *religious* meanings and those which use animal imagery as a basis for insults are not on the "offensive" side of the scale. While some of these religious terms are highly offensive (profane and blasphemous) to the devout, college students judge them to be quite mild.

In chapter 3 on Anger Expression, the evolution from religious-based swearing to obscenity-based terms was discussed. These offensiveness data merely confirm the notion that religious taboos, relative to other taboos, are not offensive. It should be noted that contemporary laws used to control the sale, distribution, production, or use of sexually explicit materials were derived from earlier control of blasphemous and profane material.

Validity of The Ratings

As with the ratings and estimates of word frequency, it is important to establish the validity and reliability of the ratings by correlating them with other measures of word offensiveness. We need to be assured that what we are measuring and calling "tabooness" or offensiveness is similar to what other researchers have found in the past.

The Jay 1977 tabooness ratings (Table 3) were compared with Baudhuin's (1973) ratings of word favorableness (derived from a semantic differential technique). The correlation of $r = -.66$ between those two measures was interpreted as: the more taboo a word is, the less favorable it is in general. In a related study, Driscoll (1981) had college students rate epithets for aggressiveness and for frequency of aggressive use. Current data were correlated with Driscoll's data. The relation was in the expected direction, $r = .37$, indicating a moderate correlation of offensiveness and aggression. This last statistic also means that not only semantic meaning but also pragmatic use of a word (to aggress) determines a word's level of offensiveness.

Another validity check was made by comparing the ratings from the Jay 1977 study with the offensiveness ratings in the Massachusetts Study (Table 5). With the deletion of one of the ambiguous words (*blow*), the remaining 27 taboo words were correlated with the later study, r= .79. This is an impressive degree of stability in light of the fact that these two studies were run in the Midwest versus New England and that they were done several years apart. College students, thus, would seem to have a fair amount of agreement on what constitutes offensive language in America today. Equally encouraging is the high degree of generality in the rating method and the replication of the results in different laboratory settings at different times.

The Relation Between Frequency and Offensiveness

What would one expect the general relation to be between a word's degree-of-offensiveness and how often it is used in public? It would make sense that as words increase in general offensiveness that they should be used less. After all, if tabooness is the degree to which a word is inhibited and offensiveness is related to tabooness, then the correlations between ratings of tabooness or offensiveness and ratings of frequency should be negative. Two correlations support this conclusion. The correlation between tabooness and frequency ratings in the Jay 1977 study was r= -.31. Here the religious and body part words were the least taboo but the most frequent. Stronger taboo words were rated as being heard less and mild taboos were heard more. A correlation of offensiveness and frequency from the Massachusetts Study indicates a similar mild negative relation, r= -.11, for the 117 word items used there.

Results of these two studies suggest that offensive words are those which are heard less frequently. One paradox is that *fuck* and *shit* account for some 50% of actual swearing in public. While *fuck* is frequently used it is also considered to be very taboo. Maybe subjects in the laboratory and the people on the street have a different criterion for tabooness. Maybe speakers just want to use a very strong word when they are upset or angry. The second hypothesis for the person on the street is supported by the model of Anger proposed earlier. A person who is going to publicly cry out in anger or frustration must be experiencing a high degree of pain. Choosing a very strong word such as *fuck* is appropriate, as anything milder (*poop*) would not serve the purpose of letting off enough steam.

Gender, Research and Word Ratings

It would be redundant to pursue others' findings about word ratings here. All the word rating studies of offensiveness (see bibliographies by Jay, 1979; or Jay, 1985) come to the same conclusions, which may be summarized as follows. Males use more offensive language than females. Males use more and different words than do females. Males and females both use more offensive language around members of the same sex, than around members of the opposite sex. Finally, as might be expected, the sex of the person conducting the experiment influences the results, as males disclose more to male experimenters than to female experimenters and female subjects are more open with female than male experimenters. The last point is no minor detail. Language researchers must be careful to balance sex of experimenter with sex of subjects or risk obtaining biased results.

All these rating studies certainly are important for purposes of replication, generality of findings, and comparison of different word lists, subject samples, time of testing, and geographic locale. However, all rating studies are limited to one method of establishing a person's sense of how offensive a word is, that is, a paper-and-pencil reaction. We need to examine different types of reactions and consider differences in methodology. It is this question of methodology that will reappear when we look at gender differences, not to reaffirm the validity of offensiveness ratings, but to confirm the hypothesis that males and females use dirty words differently.

Conclusions About the Semantics of Offensiveness

There is general agreement that American taboos are those stemming from terms for body parts, body products, body processes, religious, animal, and ethnic terms, as well as social deviations and ancestral allusions. These categories are typical of adult patterns. Children focus more on physical, mental, and visible differences in their early insulting and name-calling rituals. According to current studies, no researcher has found any other semantic domain to be considered, such as ear lobe length or astrological sign. The agreement on semantics is not grounds for stopping the search for underlying dimensions of insults, sexuality, or other types of verbal aggression. It is possible in the future that people could insult each other based on factors of DNA structure or behaviors that are not known currently in American science.   Advances in genetics, space exploration, brain physiology, and cross-cultural comparisons may unearth new ways for people to curse each other.

Offendedness

Offendedness is also a very interesting psychological variable. How do Americans react to different language? What do their bodies do physiologically? How do they respond verbally? What personality factors cause one person to overreact and another not to react at all?   These are some of the questions that require answers within the individual subject or within a specific group of subjects. They are questions of offendedness.

Below is some of the literature on perceptual defense, physiological reaction, and the influence of personality. These make up the little information we have on offendedness. *Note*: It is important from here to the end of the chapter that offendedness depends on the *gender* of the offendee. From here on, the specific gender or sex-of-subject effects in the reported research deserve special attention.

Perceptual Defense & Gender

The most famous piece of research in experimental psychology involving dirty word reactions was from a study designed to explore the question of "perceptual defense." In fact this is the only time experimental psychologists were preoccupied by the effect of dirty words on humans.   These experiments began roughly with McGinnies' now famous study in 1949 and continued through the 1950s and early 1960s.

McGinnies had presented neutral and emotionally charged (taboo) words to subjects with a tachistiscope. The "T-scope" is a device which presents visual material very rapidly (100th of second) to viewers looking at the screen. It is like a high-speed slide projector. As the subjects were viewing the words and trying to figure out what word appeared on the screen, McGinnies recorded their galvanic skin response (GSR) and the duration of time the word had to be on the screen (visual threshold) before it was recognized. A high GSR reading is indicative of a strong emotional reaction and elevated visual threshold times means difficulty in perception.

The major finding, which generated hundreds of subsequent studies, was that the taboo words took longer to perceive and that the subjects had higher GSR levels, relative to those levels for neutral words. The subjects were assumed to be "defending" against the taboo words or threatening stimuli, since they took longer to recognize them. McGinnies also reported that the males had lower thresholds than the females for both the taboo and the neutral words. Thus, a sex of subject factor was also a possible explanation.

McGinnies' experiment was later found to contain many flaws with respect to response bias, perceptual bias, and the particular words selected for the study. There are two good reviews of the area of perceptual defense by Dixon (1971) and Erdelyi (1974). But for this discussion of offendedness, we will look at some of the research that focused on subjects' reactions to dirty words.

Postman, Bronson, and Gropper (1953) wanted to examine the sex differences in offendedness reported by McGinnies (1949). They required subjects to *write* down their guesses at the words rather than say them, when testing visual thresholds (Imagine having to say a word like *bitch* or *kotex* in a psychology experiment in 1949!). Postman et al. also took care to equate all the words on frequency of occurrence, too. (It could be that taboo words had different frequencies than neutral words, which caused them to be recognized at higher thresholds.) They found that with the written format that females had higher recognition thresholds than males when the dirty words were presented.

Very few studies after Postman's actually used taboo words to test sex differences in visual thresholds. Nothman (1962) examined the strategies used by both McGinnies and Postman et al. by testing differences in words and how subjects had to respond. Visual recognition thresholds were again used as was the oral versus written mode of response to compare male and female subjects. Under these constraints females showed significantly greater mean differences between taboo and neutral word recognition times compared to males. Oral reporting had a significantly higher mean difference between taboo and neutral words than did the written method. Thus Nothman confirmed the previously found sex differences in response mode using dirty words.

What about the sex of the person conducting the experiment? Miller and Solkoff (1965) designed an experiment to test both the response mode and experimenter sex on visual recognition thresholds for dirty words. They found that males who had to respond orally had significantly higher thresholds for dirty words for both male and female experimenters. When the males had to write their responses there was no difference due to the type of word reported. Females showed no significant word or experimenter effects. Miller and Solkoff concluded that perceptual defense existed only in the males and only when the males had to respond orally. The male effect of perceptual defense was a contrast to all the previous studies on the use of dirty words. The perceptual defense studies became increasingly confusing and it seemed that methodological flaws were at the root of defensive cognition and not some moral guardian in the brain.

Following this brief examination of how humans perceive taboo words under the perceptual defense paradigm, psychologists became preoccupied with other theoretical questions about perception and gave up their concentrated research on dirty words. There are other studies that used taboo word reactions to show us about how people perceive dirty words. The conclusion from the research designed to show that the body protects the mind from threatening stimuli was unclear. The attempts to show that the way a person had to *report* the dirty words was the cause of perceptual defense were countered by an equal number of studies that found *No* report effect (Erdelyi, 1974). Other studies tried to prove that the offendedness effect was to be found in physiological responses of the body. With these physiological measures one gains a different perspective on the concept of offendedness.

Physiological Reactions - Pupillary Response. Several people in the social sciences have studied how aversive stimuli affect the human body. People interested in stress, emotion, arousal, attention, perception, and physiology have tried to establish a relation between events outside the body and the physiological reactions to and awareness of these events. In general, humans are not acutely aware of changes in heart rate, blood pressure, pupil dilation, brain wave activity or other bodily changes. The physiological changes must be detected with machines, rather than relying on subjects' inaccurate self-reports. One attempt to relate stimulus qualities to bodily reaction involved pupillary dilation (Hess, 1965). The pleasantness of a stimulus is associated with increased dilation. The pupillary response had been used with taboo words as stimuli. The thinking was that when one sees something we want or we think is pleasant, the pupil dilates; when one sees something aversive or unpleasant the pupil constricts.

Stelmack and Mandelzys (1975) measured pupillary response to sets of taboo and nontaboo words but also added another personality variable. They divided subjects into introverts, extraverts, and ambiverts (sometimes extraverted, then introverted). The hypothesis was that since introverts were more susceptible to fear and punishment than extraverts, their higher level of arousal (introverts) would be related to greater pupillary size. Subjects were presented with words via tape recorder and pupillary response was recorded. Results confirmed the personality hypothesis that introverts showed the greatest average pupil size *but* the effect of word type was not confirmed. Taboo words caused no more physiological arousal than nontaboo words.

The words were rated at different levels of pleasantness, however. The experimenters had all three groups rate the word types. Taboo were rated significantly more unpleasant than nontaboo words. The effect was *not* due to the words alone. The explanation lies in the notion that introverts formed a conditioned fear reaction more readily to these words, than did the extraverts. These fear differences were maintained despite the differences in ratings of the words by both extraverts and introverts. No evidence was found to support the idea that the pupil constricts to unpleasant stimuli. Pupillary response is not an automatic response to an aversive word; it is a function of the person hearing the word and his or her history of fear reactions.

Did Researchers Forget "Context"?

Neither the perceptual defense literature nor research that tried to put a dirty word detector in the eyes, or other parts of the body have succeeded. Why? Because one's reaction to dirty words is not a simple process. The reason is context. The personality of the subject, the environment of the experiment, the type of words selected, the sex of the subject, the sex of the experimenter are all contextual variables that cannot be separated one by one to provide a simple answer. The way one is offended by insults, racial slurs, or dirty words is not known in specific terms. It seems that the field of psychology replaced the idea of perceptual vigilance, perceptual defense, repression, and response bias questions with a different theory. Now the field prefers to think of humans as processors of information at different levels of awareness. The role of context in processing stimuli is of course very important. Where this leaves present work is with a new set of metaphors to explain how people perceive and remember words -- but no new "hard data" about how the human body responds when offended by dirty words! Maybe scientists should just go back to *asking* people what offends them personally or look at what *type* of people are offended, that is, at personality and gender types.

Personality, Gender & Dirty Word Reactions

Psychologists have a number of different personality tests that can be used to see if different personality types use or react to dirty words in different manners. Some of these personality dimensions are examined next. Without describing these personality tests in detail here, the people who have high scores on sexual repression or religiosity are prime candidates for dirty word experiments, as will be seen.

   Sexual Repression. Schill, Emanuel, Pederson, Schneider, and Wachowiak (1970) studied the personality factors of repression, sensitization, and defensiveness in relation to males' free association to sexual double entendres (e.g., *screw* or *cherry*). The free association test is one where the subject says the first word that comes to mind, after hearing the stimulus word (*screw*). Subjects were tested by either a male or a female experimenter. Subjects showed the greatest sexual responsiveness to the male and greatest inhibition with the female; which is not surprising. Personality differences were not found for the female experimenter. But, for those tested by the male, the subjects with low sensitivity yielded the greatest sexual responsiveness, relative to subjects with defensive personalities.

   Milner and Moses (1972) noticed that since females were not looked at in the Schill et al. study, no general comments about sex of subject would be possible. Milner and Moses re-ran the free association experiment with both male and female subjects. They found no differences when subjects were run by the same-sex experimenter. However, when tested by the opposite sex, males' sexual responsivity was inhibited by the female experimenter. Female subjects tested by the male experimenter showed the least sexual responsivity of any of the experimental groups.

Religion. Kutner and Brogan (1974) asked groups of college students to list slang expressions for a list of sex-related words. They found that males listed more words than females. For females they found that religious involvement and traditional sex role orientation were inversely related to extensiveness of sexual slang. Sanders and Robinson (1979) found a similar pattern of gender differences in the use of sexual language, as men and women clearly preferred to use different types of sexual terminology in different contexts. They suggested that public or social norms exist for how we are to engage in private communication about sex.

Mabry (1975) used a factor analysis technique to determine what semantic factors of profane language (abrasive, technical, expletive, euphemistic or latent) accounted for subjects' ratings of how likely they were to use these words. He then used sex of subject and strength of religious belief scores to see if these subject variables were related to probability of use ratings. He found that males with strong religious beliefs had lower use ratings than other males or females. Strongly religious males and females were also more reserved in their projected use of sexual and excretory words than other subjects.

Grosser and his colleagues (Grosser & Laczek, 1963; Grosser & Walsh, 1966) conducted research into the perceptual defense phenomenon but used religious training as another variable. In the first study they used male and female college students with either secular or parochial secondary school backgrounds. They studied the utterance latencies (pause or hesitation in speech) related to taboo, aggressive and neutral words. They found slower responses to the taboo words and that the effect was most pronounced in the parochial females relative to any other group. The later study did not include an examination of religious background but did confirm the earlier sex effects for the perceptual defense researchers.

In the broadcasting business, one assumes that when the viewers or listeners do not complain, they accept or like what they are receiving. But when people complain about program content, broadcasters take notice. A study in England showed that viewers were most offended by bad language on television, relative to sex or violence. Interestingly, over half of those completing the questionnaire for the Independent Broadcasting Authority (Wober, 1980) noted that they were religious. Again, another link of religiosity to one's offendedness by foul language.

Religious belief and one's need to repress sexual thoughts and language seem to be natural candidates for dirty word studies. These studies do not really report any surprising results but they do go beyond stereotypical impressions to offer proof of how some personality types use words differently than do others.

Offendedness: A Few Conclusions

Psychologists have not provided convincing evidence from laboratory studies about how taboo words affect people. Perceptual defense literature is fraught with methodological problems. There is insufficient physiological data about how the body reacts to dirty words. If ethical problems with laboratory exposure to taboo stimuli can be overcome, now is the time to obtain EEG, heart rate, pulse rate, pupillary reactions, and other correlates of arousal for dirty words. Granted, these laboratory studies are artificial, but they would provide some correlative data for what is obtained on the street. Those interested in offendedness are left with very little empirical research to prove that words cause harmful effects on people. Personality, religion, and repression are highly likely correlates of offendedess, as is the gender of the receiver. In fact by examining gender differences in insulting rituals, one can gain more insight into both offensiveness and offendedness.

Gender-Related Insults

The insult ritual is part offensiveness and part offendedness. The speaker must choose a word that fits the occasion and the target of the insult. Making the target feel offended is the goal of the insult in most cases. If we did not expect the target to react to the language, we might choose a different method, replacing insulting, to change the target's behavior. Insulting is a language of negative persuasion. The language of love is a positive persuasion. American culture has its own language of love and that of insult. As with the case for love, men and women do it (insulting) differently.

When men and women insult each other, they employ different concepts of sexuality, deviance, and characteristics of gender appropriate behavior. There are several sources of evidence that men and women choose different types of words to insult each other. We find that men and women are offended by different words, depending on the semantics of the word. Following are some examples of the differences in semantics that males and females use to insult and offend each other.

Of Friends and Strangers

An interesting factor that needs to be considered is that most of the insult rituals occur in a speech setting in which it is *strangers* that verbally assault each other. When a friendship or familiarity exists between speakers, a more qualified set of terms is probably selected. The pool would be more restricted because previous communications pointed out sensitive terms and pet names. Words which would normally be perceived as endearing, such as, *dear, sweetie, honey,* or *baby* can also used with an ironic tone in order to derogate or annoy friends or acquaintances. If the relationship between speakers is an employer/employee relation, some of these pet terms and gender specific referents may border on the phenomenon of verbal sexual harassment, for example, if an employer called his secretary *sweetie.*

The ironic use of pet names for insults works in a different manner than with harsher words. Words such as *motherfucker, nigger, son of a bitch,* or *bastard* are frequently used between close male friends, functionally, as terms of endearment. As with pet names the manner of pronounciation, intonation, and accentuation are the cues as to whether the specific word is meant as an insult or not. There are no extensive data on either the endearment effect or the irony effect of these words and this irony phenomenon deserves more attention. The voice (prosody) issue means that a word in isolation does not provide enough information about whether it will or will not have a damaging effect on the listener. We must also know about the context in which the word was used, how it was pronounced, and the relation between the speaker and listener.

A recent study by Bell, Buerkel-Rothfuss, and Gore (1987) examined the nature of idiomatic expressions used between romantically involved heterosexual couples. In general, the more closeness or love between the couples, the greater the number of idioms they used for affection, sexual encounters, and other sexual matters. Their personal idioms were used for labeling outsiders, sexual invitations, expressions of affection, expressing displeasure, terms for genitals or body parts and teasing insults. The insults were idioms that were used to derogate one's partner in a spirit of play. For example, *fat piggy* or *hogmo* for poor table manners; or *wimpatus* to refer to a mate who was afraid of doing something. These data verify the notion that the relation between a speaker and a listener affects the type of insult selected. Close couples develop idiosyncratic and private idioms or insults to express displeasure or to derogate a partner, thereby cutting off other listners from the true degree of emotion being expressed.

A Short Dictionary of Gender-Specific Insults

These are common terms that exhibit some specificity of who can say the insult o who will be the target of the insult. They are terms that are not idiosyncratic, are used all over the country, and are not limited to one race or minority. These terms are part of a ritual or routine that Americans employ to insult others and are based on: assumed personality flaws, social interaction, or physical appearance. To understand the insult ritual, one must be able to take the point of view of the speaker: why would you call me that? Insults are categorized by the target's sex and cause for the insult. The lexicon is not exhaustive or extensive; there are several slang dictionaries listed in the bibliography to give the reader more verbal ammunition, if necessary.

Words That Will Insult Males

Motherfucker. This word stands alone as the most offensive in American English. It conjures up allusions to sexual deviance, sex behavior, ancestry, and taboo. The word found its origin in inner-city life in the early part of this century and became widespread following World War I. It is a commonly used insult between inner-city males but less common among female speakers.

It is probably the multiple violations in this word that make it stronger than a simple, one syllable word. This word contains offense against sex, society, and family. What more could a speaker want in an insult?

Queer, Fag, Homo, Wimp, Pussy, Wussy, Gay, Cocksucker. One of the most offensive insults to a male is to suggest that he is sexually inadequate or a homosexual. The most offensive of this lot is *cocksucker.* These words are targeted almost exclusively at males and focus on lack of potency or female-like qualities such as, *pussy, sissy, wussy, douche bag* or *dildo.*

Effeminate insults occur more frequently from male speakers than from female speakers, to insult other males with these words. The terms are almost exclusively used to target a male in either case. Females use these words to describe and/or insult effeminate males, socially inept men or undesirable men. These words are rarely used against women, although we have recorded some women calling each other *pussies.*

Word counts of children's insults indicate that this category of social-sexual deviations is acquired early, along with physical and mental insults. The conclusion is that as with other sex-appropriate behavior, there is more pressure on little boys to act like men than pressure on girls to act like women. Words denoting female deviance (*dyke*) appear at a later point in children's insulting speech.

Bastard, Prick, Asshole, Son of a Bitch, Cock. These insults focus on the social ineptness, non-caring, self-centered, harmful, or mean qualities of the target. We see below that women, who have similar underlying behaviors are also targeted but with a different set of terms. The male insulted is told that he has done something socially wrong or has not come through when he was expected to. Notice how the words are based on either social deviations or body parts. *Bastard* and *prick* are deemed very offensive insults by female speakers and are targeted at stupid, unresponsive self-centered males. Is *prick* the functional equivalent of *cunt* for females? The last question is posed because both terms are body parts used by the opposite sex to insult the other.

Turkey, Nerd, Jerk. These insults mainly target a person who is socially inept. In addition they indicate that the male is probably physically unattractive and exhibits no strong sexual identity, one way or the other. Thus, these males are more neutral than *homos* or *wimps* and their sexuality is not directly attacked. These males are ugly weaklings, ineffective, unlikeable and obnoxious toward females.

Macho, Stud, Playboy, Wolf. From a women's point of view these are men who exploit women. They are not unattractive or inept. Their problem behavior is that they do not give any compassion or intimacy. They also provide no sense of future commitment.

Men and women have different definitions of love and what behaviors constitute the basis of a loving relationship. The male values qualities of physical attractiveness and sexual intimacy. The female is looking for the sense of commitment and caring or personal friendship. The lack of these qualities in males' actions is a cause for these insults from female speakers.

These are not strong insults in as much as they are used to indicate that a male is selfish, horny, deceitful, but also friendly. These males are probably physically attractive but their unusual sexual desire and lack of respect for women make them less than desirable for a long-term relationship.

Words That Will Insult Females

Cunt. One rarely hears women say this word in public. It is one of the most offensive insults that can be hurled at a woman. Along with *slut* and *whore*, these terms are based on sexual looseness. Notice that there is no equivalent for masculine looseness. It is only when men exploit women that we generate insults toward him. A woman's sexual looseness gets insulted, but a man's does not.

Since the female finds the word *cunt* to be one of the most offensive in our language, it is not surprising that she chooses the word *prick*, as an indication of being highly offended by a male. Both male and female insults *cunt* and *prick* are metonymies wherein the person is represented metaphorically as a body part. They have no brains, no heart -- only genitals.

Tease, Prickteaser, Dickteaser, Cockteaser. These terms are used by men to insult women who initially are perceived as if they are promising sexual intimacy to males. In the end she does not fulfill the promise. The major focus in these insults is the discrepancy between appearance and reality. What he sees is not what he gets, so he feels cheated. He feels slighted; she gets insulted.

These women are sexually stimulating and physically attractive. The male wants sexual intimacy in a relationship; he wants to be able to express a sexuality with a mate. When she will not become sexually intimate with him, he views this as a game, as teasing. He notifies her of his feeling offended by calling her a name.

Bitch. She is the socially harmful woman or a social deviant. The one who does not do what is expected. *Bitch* is offensive when used by both women and men speakers. Males may also use *bitch* to indicate that the woman wants too much from him or is smothering him. His use of the word may also mean that she is overly demanding or mean to him. The term *bitch* implies that a woman has a social or personal problem: her sexual behavior is not in question.

Scag, Witch, Dog. These terms focus on the social ineptness and physical unattractiveness of the female in question. The sexual preference of the target is assumed to be neutral.

These are the female equivalents of *nerds*, etc. Accordingly, males view this category of females as having qualities such as being obnoxious, unattractive and totally without sexual appeal.

Dyke, Butch, Lesbian. These are words for female homosexuality. In the general population they are not frequently used by females to insult other females but are used to denote female homosexuality. They are more likely to be used by males as insults to females. Notice that they rely on the powerful fear about homosexuality in a male's conception of the world. A male assumes that because homosexuality is insulting to him that it will be an insult to a female, too. He uses these words to insult women who he perceives exhibit masculine behavior or attitudes.

Conclusions

Women and men view the world differently. As much as the field of psychology would like to present a more balanced picture, the dirty word literature shows that we are different. These differences are based on different underlying cognitive models and metaphors for sexual and interpersonal behavior. The language of insults and name calling supports the view that we are operating on different assumptions about what makes our hearts and minds tick. The data in this study suggest that women seem to operate in a world concerned with intimacy, social desirability and security; while men's concerns seem to be sex, power, and physical attractiveness.

A supporting piece of research was conducted by Preston and Stanley (1987), who tried to determine what was "the worst thing" one could call another person. Overall they did not find differences as a function of sex of subject. Subjects generally agreed on what was insulting. What they did find, however, is that insults do depend on the sex of the speaker and the sex of the target of the insult. Insults based on sexual looseness (*cunt*, *slut*, or *whore*) were directed only to women. Homosexual insults (*gay* or *faggot*) were directed only to men by other men. The worst insult a man could call a woman was *cunt*. The worst thing a woman would call a man was either *bastard* or *prick*; while the worst insult, woman to woman, was the word *bitch*.

These findings confirm and support the dictionary of insults listed above and the notion that men and women insult each other with a different set of semantics and cognitions about the world.

One helpful general book on the nature of our differences based either on sex or culture is edited by Holland and Quinn, *Cultural Models in Language and Thought* (1987). This book of readings offers both methodology and data on a variety of differences in cognition and language.

The section above on gender differences in insults supports the idea that women and men swear in different fashions. We also think about the world in different terms and value different qualities of social and interpersonal interaction. The next section is designed to provide additional research on linguistic differences and gender differences with speech acts that use dirty words.

Other Studies Reporting Gender Differences

There are several linguistic routines that are used differently by males and females. Whether these differences will continue to be replicated in future years is questionable. These routines are reported only briefly here, as these factors have already been reviewed (See Jay, 1980b and Jay, 1985). The reader is advised to consult the reviews for specific gender differences in word usage, or investigate the original literature cited below.

Jokes

Coser (1960) reported evidence that males tend to take authority over telling jokes in social settings involving groups of males and females. Females take on the recipient role. Studies by Chapman and Foot (1976; 1977), and McGhee (1979) have also reported sex differences in the use of humor and joke telling. These authors go into great detail, explicitly studying the material used in sexual jokes.

Story Telling

Sutton-Smith and Abrams (1978) studied the spontaneously reported narrative fiction stories from 5- to 11-year-old kids. They were looking for differences in psychosexual content of the stories. They found that boys selected psychosexual or obscene stories, while girls were more likely to tell "romance" stories. Their study is important because of the early emergence of sex difference in language that it shows and because the children's stories were spontaneously, rather than manipulatively, reported.

The Dozens

Abrahams (1962) recorded instances of verbal dueling also known in the ghetto as "sounding" or "playing the dozens" in Philadelphia over a period of two years. These games of throwing insults back and forth between participants about each other or members of other's families occurred in groups of only boys. Females did not participate in these games. In a similar setting, Lerman (1967) reported male dominance in the use of argot, slang, and swearing when he examined the records of juvenile delinquents. The differences in language of slang and argot brings up the question of vocabulary in general. Another source of general differences between black and white English, and men and women is Dillard's (1977) book on black English.

Hostile and Aggressive Vocabulary

Gilley and Summers (1970) asked subjects to complete a set of one hundred sentences. Males used significantly more hostile verbs (*stabbed*) than did females which the authors went on to explain in terms of general hostile tendencies. Whether males are always more aggressive than females has been questioned (Frodi, Macaulay, & Thome, 1977). The particular design of the experiment under review must always be examined carefully. Those experiments which are most natural provide a clearer look at the real world than those which use elaborate machinery or deception. Sometimes the amount of verbal aggression depends on the target of aggression, as we would expect. Golin and Romanowski (1977) found that verbal aggression was inhibited toward a female, when she did not provoke the subject. When provoked the female target elicited the same amount of aggression as male targets. Greenberg (1976) was careful to note that the type of verbal aggression (sarcasm, derogation, profanity, and threat of attack) affect the way a person perceives the speaker's aggressiveness. The low intensity attacks (criticism or sarcasm) were found to elicit lower aggressiveness ratings than did higher levels (threats). While these situations were somewhat contrived in the laboratory, they may still be indicative of how aggressiveness is perceived on the street, allowing one to speculate about how verbal aggression may be related to physical violence. Aggression is more carefully addressed in the chapter on the First Amendment and

Free Speech because aggression is the issue involved in the "fighting words" doctrine.

Taboo Vocabulary

One of the earliest articles that established sex differences in taboo word usage was Steadman's 1935 compilation of college students' lists of various types of taboo speech. He reported that males provided more examples of coarse or obscene speech than females. Later, Hunter and Gaines (1938) asked college students and faculty to provide word ratings of a list of words derived from Steadman (1935). They found that females were more restrained in usage than males and that freshmen showed more restraint than seniors or faculty. Foote and Woodward (1973) using an open-ended response technique with college students as subjects asked for a report of examples of obscene speech either in writing or orally on a tape recorder. Males produced more examples of dirty words than females, a tendency which was more pronounced on the tape recorder method versus writing. Kutner and Brogan (1974) obtained similar results when they asked college student subjects for a list of slang expressions. Walsh and Leonard (1974) asked their subjects to list words for the term "sexual intercourse". They found that males listed more terms than females; females listed a higher percentage of technical terms (e.g., *coitus*) than males; females were more likely than males to list euphemisms (e.g., *make love*); and finally, both males and females reported that they used more dirty words more often with members of the same-sex than with mixed company.

An interesting parallel in taboo language usage can be seen in sexual graffiti. A study by Arluke, Kutakoff, and Levin (1987) recently examined gender differences in bathrooms of five colleges and universities in 1972 and 1984. In both studies, female graffiti, relative to males', made fewer sexual references. Female graffiti were more socially acceptable with respect to the language used and content of the message. There were no significant differences over time to suggest changes in gender differences from the 1970's to the 1980's.

Attitudes about Using Taboo Words

Halaby and Long (1979) surveyed college students about their attitudes toward using dirty words in a variety of contexts. Their data indicate that males tended to use more profane language in the same-sex crowds relative to mixed company. Similarly females used these words more often around other females. However, freshmen males were more inhibited than either freshmen or sophomore females in some contexts. Fine and Johnson (1984; Johnson & Fine, 1985) also examined college students' perceptions about the use of obscenity. They found that females were less likely to use anatomy words than males and that for females, these anatomical references were still taboo. Males and females had different motives for using obscenity. The main reasons to use dirty language is to express anger or to express feelings. The purpose of using this type of language was to gain psychological release, while the linguistic habits of using words automatically were less important. In their recent study, Johnson and Fine focused more on how males and females see each other and themselves using taboo words. Males perceived that females use obscenity less frequently than females' estimates. Females also think their own use of obscenity is equally important as a male's reason for using it. Both males and females agree that males use obscene speech more than females. And both males and females believe that younger people use obscenity more than older speakers. In a study of men's and women's expletive usage, Bailey and Timm (1976) replicated the finding that, overall, men use stronger language than women *but* that age was an important factor for women. Women in this study over the age of 43 refrained almost entirely from using strong expletives, but those from 19 to 34 reported using them frequently.

It is certainly true that the college campus and the four years spent there offer a unique speech community. Obscenity on campus is perhaps a linguistic marker of the college student that separates him or her from the rest of the public. These attitudes and perceptions about the use and appropriateness of using obscenity are very important background for the next topic, sexual harassment. Once again the questions of appropriateness and sex of company become crucial elements in the legal argument.

Sex Roles, Sex Differences and Dirty Word Usage

There is ample literature, as cited above, indicating that men and women use different types of dirty words and that what they find offensive and insulting is based on somewhat different semantic domains. Support for sex differences in taboo language usage comes from both laboratory surveys and experiments and from field studies of actual usage. One of the questions remaining is, to what extent are males and females aware of the ways they differ in language use? The next experiment was designed to look at that question.

The research was designed to assess the degree to which people know that the use of dirty words is part of a role they must play to appear as typical males and typical females (whatever those stereotypes may be). The hypothesis was that men and women in public use language according to social norms that they have acquired and that if one asked men to act like women and women to act like men, they could appropriately respond as members of the opposite sex. We wanted to know if men know how to swear like women and if women know how to swear like men, at least with the words presented. These data may bear some information on the question of verbal sexual harassment covered later.

The next section includes an abstract of the role playing research. These data were presented at the 1979 Meeting of the Midwestern Psychological Association in Chicago.

Several decades of research indicate that females, compared to males, are more offended by dirty words and further, using production measures, females are less likely to say them. Since methodological problems abound in this area (Rumenik, Capasso, & Hendrick, 1977), one is not sure if previous data are accurate or artifactual. Currently, psycholinguists are developing word usage models based on contextual factors such as speaker-listener relationships; sex role would emerge as one dimension of this factor. Following the contextual trend, the research below was designed to (a) investigate how speaker-listener gender influences dirty word offensiveness and (b) bring into question previous interpretations.

Procedure

The rationale was to examine word offensiveness when speaker-listener sex roles are crossed, not confounded as in previous studies. Role playing was used to ndicate intragender sensitivity to dirty words. From previous research, four factors were suggested: (a) sex of speaker (a hypothetical male or female), (b) sex role played by the listener-subject (appropriate sex, opposite sex, or no role manipulation), (c) actual sex of the listener-subject, and (d) words used (28 dirty words, 32 non-dirty words used in previous research). A subject (45 male and 45 female undergraduates enrolled in introductory psychology courses) was given instructions to play one of three roles (male - female - not explicit) when rating a randomized list of the 60 words in booklet format. Subjects, as listeners, rated each word individually on a 9-point offensiveness scale (1= not offensive at all, 9= most offensive imaginable) depending on the Speaker and Role portrayed. Three separate sets of ratings were obtained. First, subjects were given a practice run with the list with no Speaker mentioned (these data are not reported); next they were asked to rate the offensiveness of the words for each Speaker (male/female) separately; the order of speaker was counterbalanced. The design was: Role (3) x Speaker (2) x Listener (2) x Word (28, only the dirty words were of interest). An analysis of variance was conducted on the scale values.

The predicted result of interest is the interaction of Role, Listener, and Speaker. When role is not explicit, a replication of previous research findings is anticipated and role playing will provide a picture of intragender sensitivity. The main effects of Speaker and of Role are of interest; however, Sex of Listener is not interpretable apart from the interaction. Effects at the level of Words are expected, but are of secondary interest.

Results

With the exception of effects for Sex, Sex x Speaker, and Sex x Word, all remaining effects were significant (p< .01). Mean offensiveness ratings for the Role x Speaker x Listener interaction are presented in Table 2. A Neuman-Keuls analysis was used for cell comparisons. When Listener Role was not explicit, results replicate traditional findings: the male speaker-male listener communication is less offensive than any other combination (macho effect). With role playing, the fact that males and females are aware of each other's reactions is indicated: when asked to play opposite roles, females accurately portray the macho effect. When asked to play appropriate roles, female listeners no longer portray the typical overreactive part, but indicate less offensiveness to female speakers, the female counterpart to the macho effect. The main effect of Speaker indicates that females using dirty words are perceived as more offensive than males. The effect of Role playing indicates, interestingly, that with no explicit role instructions, offensiveness ratings are higher than Opposite, or Appropriate role instruction Ratings, which implicates a "response bias" to be offended (give high ratings) in previous experiments. In other words, subjects shift their ratings as a function of the role the experimenter tells them to play. They are generally biased toward giving higher ratings of offensiveness, unless one tells subjects what role to play.

Table 2. *Mean Offensiveness Ratings as a Function of Speaker Sex, Listener Sex, and Listener Role.*

Role: Respond as APPROPRIATE Sex

	Sex of Speaker		Sex of Listener
	MALE	FEMALE	
	3.90	4.07	MALE (as male)
	4.43	3.59	FEMALE (as female)

Role: NO EXPLICIT Instruction to Listener

	Sex of Speaker		Sex of Listener
	MALE	FEMALE	
	4.23	5.27	MALE (not explicit)
	5.15	5.87	FEMALE (not explicit)

Role: Respond as OPPOSITE sex

	Sex of Speaker		Sex of Listener
	MALE	FEMALE	
	5.38	4.72	MALE (as female)
	3.11	4.95	FEMALE (as male)

Note - Scale values are: 1= not offensive at all,
                                9= most offensive imaginable

Discussion

Because speaker-listener sex previously has been confounded, it is not clear if females actually are more offended than males by dirty words. With role playing instructions, data indicate that females may not always overreact or males underreact to the perception of dirty words. The research presented in the brief abstract and in preceding sections (e. g., Johnson & Fine, 1985) demonstrate that males and females have different perceptions of the offensiveness of dirty words but to some degree are sensitive to the nature of the opinions of the opposite sex. A speaker's sensitivity to how a listener will comprehend and react to the use of dirty words is not perfect. Males and females differ in their notions of what constitutes offensive speech. This difference of opinion may be in part responsible for differences in sensitivity to verbal sexual harassment, the next topic of discussion.

Verbal Sexual Harassment

Men and women have different concepts of love, insult, and aggression. The words they use to express these emotions or feelings are different. To the degree that a speaker lives in his or her sex-egocentric world, unaware of the other's sensitivity, he or she runs the risk of offending, harassing, insulting, or at least confusing the opposite sex without knowing it. One of the most problematic areas occurs with the topic of sexual harassment, especially those episodes involving language. Several reports were reviewed, indicating sex differences with regard to the language and semantics underlying insults. These data along with previous data reported in this book, may provide some insight into a language or gender-based predictor of sexual harassment. Now that we know how men and women talk about each other, we should not be surprised that what women perceive as harassing is different that what men perceive. The result -- trouble at work!

What constitutes sexual harassment? The legal definition of the term seems quite specific. According to EEOC Rules and Regulations (U.S. Equal Employment Opportunity Commission, 1980) it is:

> Unwelcome sexual advances, requests for sexual favors, and other verbal or physical conduct of a sexual nature constitute unlawful sexual harassment when (a) submission to such conduct is made either explicitly or implicitly a term or condition of an individual's employment, (b) submission to or rejection of such conduct by an

individual is used as the basis for employment decisions affecting such individual, or (c) such conduct has the purpose or effect of unreasonably interfering with an individual's work performance or creating an intimidating, hostile, or offensive working environment. An employer is responsible for sexual harassment by its agents or supervisory employees regardless of whether the employer knew or should have known of their occurrence. An employer is responsible for acts of sexual harassment in the workplace committed by "nonsupervisory employees" where the employer knows or should have known of the conduct and no immediate and appropriate corrective action was taken.

(cited in Masters, Johnson, & Kolodny, 1988, p 490)

In reality what *verbal* sexual harassment means is less clear than what a physical form of harassment means. Pinching, slapping, touching, or hugging are obvious to the observer when they occur. What is verbal harassment? These cases amount to unwanted jokes or explicit sexual references or suggestions, sex-based insults, or written or oral comments. Included here would be the use of cartoons or graffiti, pet names, sexual gestures, comments about sexual performance, virginity, or preference, staring or leering, commenting about body parts, or using sexually derogatory labels. These verbal forms are more problematic for employers and workers alike. In a recent study on the topic, for example, Hemphill and Pfeiffer (1986) found that not only do males find many of these verbal acts less offensive than do females but the location of the occurrence of the act (office, business lunch, or party) can affect the offensiveness of the act. Females are more offended by these acts than are males and acts are rated more offensive in formal business settings than in those settings which are socially-relaxed.

In a recent survey of over 8,000 federal employees (Saltzman, 1988) the differences in the perception of behavior that constitutes harassment between males and females is clear. In all categories the percentage of females who felt the behavior in question was sexual harassment is greater than the percentage of males. Both females and males agree that "pressure for sexual favors" is a form of harassment, with 98% and 90% respectively. However, the rest of the categories show a wider (more than 10%) discrepancy:

deliberate touching	92% versus 82%
letters and calls	84% versus 67%
pressure for dates	76% versus 66%
suggestive looks	76% versus 60%
sexual remarks	64% versus 47%

In fact it is the category of sexual remarks that shows one of the greatest differences in perception. These sexual remarks may come in the form of swearing or in sexual jokes, especially jokes with women as the butt of the joke. It may also be the case that most of these situations, as they are perceived by the employees, portray the victim as a woman and the perpetrator as a male. In any case it is clear that women in this study have a lower threshold for sexual harassment than do men.

Another question about harassment deals with context. The workers above were federal employees. What type of results would be obtained for construction workers, college students, the elderly? It may be that the preponderance of office-type jobs at the federal level is a context that breeds sexual innuendo and harassment. There is apparently a great deal of interpersonal contact in many offices and admittedly, people get bored at their desks. Whether we can extrapolate from this federal sample to other occupations and age ranges remains to be demonstrated.

Harassment and Power

Harassment is a type of sexual coercion. A common scenario is for a woman to be asked by her boss for sexual favors as a means of securing or advancing her position in the firm. The person doing the coercion has economic power over the employee and uses this power to get the worker to cooperate sexually. Therefore, harassment is probable in virtually any setting where there exists a hierarchy or chain of command. Nurses, law students, college students, military personnel, and medical students have high rates of reported instances of sexual harassment. Most commonly the instigator is a supervisor or owner of the business. The overwhelming majority of the victims are female. Unfortunately, we know very little about the impact of such experiences on the victims (Masters, Johnson, & Kolodny, 1988).

Harassing the Boss

Verbal sexual harassment is instigated usually by a boss or supervisor and less often by a co-worker. What happens when workers swear or use obscene and profane speech directed toward management? Do bosses have the right to fire that employee? What are the grounds for releasing workers? What are the rights of workers to use vulgar speech or shop talk? These questions direct the question of obscenity on the job *up* the power hierarchy rather than *down* it.

A recent review by Graham (1986), who practices law in the area of labor and employment litigation, has some of the answers about swearing at the boss or at the "company." As with other areas of free versus restricted speech, the answers lie in the context: when and where the use of obscenity occurred, the precise nature of the symbols, words, or gestures selected, and the target of the abusive language. Essentially, it is a question of the worker's right to expression versus the employer's right to maintain order and respect in the workplace.

Protected Speech

The National Labor Relations Board has made many judgments about the rights of workers to use vulgar speech. Below are the general factors where obscenity is protected under the National Labor Relations Act. First, the speech is an outburst related to a formal grievance proceeding or during contract negotions. Speech provoked by equally offensive management remarks is protected. The language must occur in a private rather than public space; i.e., not on the shop floor in front of many other employees. Comments about the company as a whole or those comments that are in general political in nature are acceptable. The speaker's rights are thus protected under these conditions.

Unprotected Speech

The speech that is unprotected and can lead to suspension or discontinuation of employment is as follows. Personal attacks directed at management on the shop floor or in the presence of other workers is not protected. If the employee has been warned to stop using profanity and the speech is repeated and has a negative impact on employees, this speech may be punished. Both speech that is so abusive that it causes workers to engage in violent and disruptive acts and speech which is a threat to discipline can be punished. Interestingly, in relation to verbal sexual harassment, the management is responsible for controlling obscenity, sexual remarks, and racial epithets; otherwise the management is held liable if these comments go unchecked.

The worker has the right to talk dirty, but the speech cannot be malicious, openly public, inflamatory, or insubordinate. Therefore, both the employee and the management have to control their tongues on the job.

Summary and Conclusion

Americans are offended by a variety of different types of words. However, most of these terms involve a limited number of semantic domains. Referents to sex organs and sex acts, especially deviant ones, are highly offensive. Terms for body parts, products and processes are offensive and also related to the emotion of disgust. Americans are also offended by profane and blasphemous speech but not as much as years past. Racial slurs and epithets, social deviations and insults based on animal names or referents account for the remainder of offensive speech terms. Being offended also depends on the gender of the speaker and the gender of the target, as many studies have reported sex differences in production and reaction to different types of dirty language. Some types of language are so offensive and unwanted that laws about sexual and verbal harassment have been enacted to protect people on the job.

Chapter 6

Free Speech and Censorship

What are Americans' rights to say and write what they please? At what point can one's speech be curtailed? The purpose of this material is to show how one's speech is or can be affected by obscene language and restrictions upon it. The movies watched, the records listened to, the conversations engaged in on the phone, and even some of the words used on the street are subject to restriction, censorship, and other controls.

The word "obscenity" is a legal term, commonly misused by the person on the street to describe any profane or taboo language. A more specific meaning of the term can be determined by reading through the Supreme Court decisions and rulings on that speech which is not free and is not protected by the First Amendment of the American Constitution. The definition of obscenity is not fixed but dynamic because the law of the land is an organic document which grows, changes, or evolves over time in response to changes in society and the courts' decisions. It is the goal of this chapter to outline the nature of restrictions put on our otherwise free speech. It begins with the language of the First Amendment and follows with issues related to it. A case of disorderly conduct, i.e., fighting words is examined. The other topics include the evolution of self-censorship in the motion picture industry and constraints in other entertainment and communication media. These media are motion pictures, video recordings, audio recordings, cable television, computer networks, and dial-it phone services. These media were selected to examine restrictions on the spoken or recorded word. Printed material, literature, pornography, and other visual sexual material have been studied extensively elsewhere. Here, it is the specific language or verbal references that are in question.

First consider the First Amendment:

> Congress shall make no law respecting an establishment of religion, or prohibiting the free exercise thereof; or abridging the freedom of speech, or of the press or the right of the people peaceably to assemble, and to petition the government for a redress of grievances.

An absolutist position on the Constitution would say that all speech is free and there are to be no restrictions at all. However, the decisions made by the Supreme Court over the last 100 years have restricted four types of speech acts, which are:

obscene speech
defaming or libelous speech
fighting words
that which poses an imminent danger

Each of these categories is examined briefly to establish its legal history. Finally, the focus is on the concept of obscene speech and its current interpretation and applications. It should be noted that people commonly associate the term obscenity with pornography, as they associate sex with violence. While the legal decisions affecting free speech, that is language, also affect other types of communication, such as photography, movies, magazines, or live performances, speech and pornography are two different categories of "speech." Pornography *per se* is not discussed here and the arguments are confined to language.

Imminent danger. The court case which established the notion of imminent danger was *Schenck v. US*, decided by the Supreme Court in 1919. This case tested the legality of the 1917 Espionage Act, regarding the limiting of dissident anti-war opinions. Justice Holmes' criterion was "whether the words used are used in such circumstances and are of such a nature as to create a clear and present danger was that they will bring about the substantive evils that Congress has a right to prevent." Holmes continued that "no man in falsely shouting fire in a theater and causing a panic" shall have his speech protected.

Because speech is a powerful and suggestive means of communicating it must not be used in a harmful or dangerous manner. The notion behind imminent danger is to protect the innocent or unsuspecting person from powerful words and thoughts. Originally the concept was applied to subversive political points of view, but the opinion that words can cause danger was also applied to disorderly conduct and fighting words.

Defaming Speech and Libel. These are rulings that take place in a court of civil law or tort law, as opposed to contractual laws and rulings. They involve cases where one person seeks damages, that is usually an amount of money, from another person, who has been accused of a non-contractual wrongdoing.

One tends to hear about cases of libel when a famous person or public figure has been defamed or libeled by a newspaper or magazine story. The target of the speech would seek damages to restore the harm to reputation and mental health.

Fighting Words.   The fighting words doctrine began with the case *Chaplinsky v. New Hampshire.* Chaplinsky was handing out literature for Jehovah's Witnesses in Rochester, New Hampshire, in 1942, when citizens complained that he was denouncing religion as a "racket" and they wanted him stopped. Later, following a disturbance, he was warned by police to stop leafletting. Chaplinsky refused, was arrested, thereupon calling the arresting officer, "you are a damned Fascist and the whole government of Rochester are Fascists." He was found guilty of a New Hampshire law making it illegal to "address in offensive, derisive, or annoying word to any other person lawfully in a street or public place." The court later referred to these words and expressions as fighting words and this doctrine was more recently used to arrest anti-war protesters during the Vietnam era, who called policemen "pigs" (see Gard, 1980; or Haiman, 1972).

We will return to the subject of fighting words by examining a real world case below.

Obscene Speech.   The definition of obscene speech did not appear until recently in legal decisions. While there have been numerous local and State rulings, there are three landmark cases in Supreme Court actions; these are *Roth*, *Miller*, and *Pacifica.* Prior to Roth, American obscenity laws were similar to those which developed in England several centuries ago and were more religious in their basis, as opposed to suppressing purely sexual material or sexual behavior.

As a crime, obscenity in America and in England started with sexual material which attacked religion and religious beliefs. Many of these rulings today would seem more fitting to the classification of profanity or blasphemy. In the American colonies there was no common-law tradition of the use of an obscenity against religion during the 1700's. Massachusetts was the only colony where there were obscenity statutes. Offenses against religion, such as blasphemy, were punishable by death until 1697. Another punishment was boring through the tongue with a hot iron. A strict censorship system was created in 1662 but it did not focus on sexual matters. There were no recorded cases in Massachusetts until the famous *Fanny Hill* prosecution in 1821, whereby the publisher was found guilty.

The first obscenity case in the United States was in Pennsylvania in 1815 and Vermont was the first state to pass an obscenity statute. During most of the

1800's there was little enforcement of either state or federal laws regarding obscenity. However, when Anthony Comstock started a campaign against distributing obscene literature in the mails, Congress responded and federal laws were strictly enforced.

America's notion of obscenity stemmed from a 19th century English case known as *Regina v. Hicklin.* This definition was used as the basis of the 1873 federal enactment, which was followed by some 30 state laws. The Hicklin test for obscenity was as follows:

> whether the tendency of the matter charged as obscenity is to deprave and corrupt those whose minds are open to such immoral influences, and into whose hands a publication of this sort may fall.
>
> *(The Report of the Commission on Obscenity and Pornography,* 1970).

Most of the current obscenity laws in the United States are based on a definition rendered in 1957 in *Roth v. United States.* Here the attempt was to narrowly define obscenity for adults in order to remain constitutionally valid.

The *Roth* case (appealed along with the *Alberts* case in 1957) had the Supreme Court first set out a three-part test of obscenity. These tests were further stated in a 1966 case known as *Memoirs.* The *Memoirs* case is notable because it originally was tried in the state of Massachusetts. Note that much of the recent field data and rating studies by the author were conducted there.

The three-part test following *Roth* is that, for a work to be considered obscene, it must be established that:
1. the dominant theme of the material taken as a whole appeals to a prurient interest in sex,
2. the material is patently offensive as it affronts contemporary standards relating to descriptions of sexual matters, and
3. the material is utterly without redeeming social importance.

Following the *Roth* decision, there were several major court cases dealing with obscenity, one of which was the *Memoirs* case previously mentioned. These cases indicated that obscenity standards based on terms like "prurient interest", "patently offensive", or "community standards" were too vague and elusive to guide judicial decisions. People would not know when they were producing, marketing, or purchasing a work that was clearly obscene.

In 1969 in the case *Stanley v. Georgia* the court offered a doubt about the underlying premises of the *Roth* decision which was that the First Amendment values could broadly prohibit the dissemination of "obscene" materials. In *Stanley* the Court decided that the First and the Fourteenth Amendments prohibit making the mere possession of obscene materials a criminal offense. It decided that even if the material met the narrow standards put forth in *Roth*, the private possession of the materials was not constitutionally prohibited. In other words, an individual has a right to read or look at what s/he pleases, a right to satisfy one's needs, emotional or intellectual, in the privacy of one's own home, even if the materials are without social value or "obscene." A ruling in the spring of 1990 excluded a class of pornography involving children.

In 1973, the Supreme Court tried to develop a more workable and uniform standard for obscenity in the *Miller* case. The three-part test from *Roth* was changed because it was indeed not workable. The end result was that community standards of prurient interest need not be based on national standards, but rather on state or even local definitions. The specific acts that were deemed potentially obscene were to be spelled out by state or by federal legislatures and the term "utterly without redeeming social value" was replaced by "serious literary, artistic, political, or scientific value." The result of the *Miller* case was that all three of these criteria must now be met:

1. The average person, applying contemporary community standards, would find the work, taken as a whole, appeals to the prurient interest in sex; and

2. The work depicts or describes, in a patently offensive way, sexual conduct specifically defined by the applicable state (or federal) law; and

3. The work, taken as a whole, lacks serious literary, artistic, political, or scientific value.

Further, in *Smith v. US* (1977) the frame of reference for 3 above must in all cases be national in scope. In other words, the Court declined to adopt a state's definitions of community standards in federal obscenity decisions. Rather, the Court held that, though community standards could be applied, the doctrine of supremacy made the state laws not binding if in opposition to federal law.

The final case which affects what can be broadcast in the electronic media is *FCC v. Pacifica*. This is a case involving a radio station in New York, WBAI, one of the Pacifica stations, that played George Carlin's "Seven Dirty Words" routine over the radio during the daytime hours. Here, the court upheld the FCC's right to regulate the content of speech over the radio. *Pacifica* recognizes the

pervasiveness of media and its impact on minors. Notice that the *Pacifica* ruling
is not on obscenity but on the FCC's indecency standards for broadcasting. By
supporting the regulation of an "indecent" but not obscene program, the Court has
extended the government's censorship of expression beyond those limits set forth
in *Miller v. California*.

     What can be concluded about the right of Americans to free speech? They
do enjoy a great deal of freedom to express any number of ideas. However, they
do not have the right to use speech that will incite others to violence (fighting
words). They cannot make false statements about others that damage their
reputations (libel). They are not free to tell an audience ideas that would create an
imminent danger to the lives of others, especially that which would disturb the
peace and security offered to them by the government. And finally, they are not
free to use sexually explicit speech or obscene speech. Further, the speech that is
produced for and on public electronic or other communication channels is not
totally free. One must take into account the age of the potential audience and the
time of day. And where entertainment is involved, these industries of film,
recordings, television, music, and other businesses have generally developed a
method of self control, as is made clear later in the chapter.

A Case of "Fighting Words"

In many states the classification of swearing, cursing, insulting, verbal abuse, or
fighting words is defined within the doctrine of disorderly conduct. The author
became involved with a case that allows several points to be made about swearing
in public and the rights guaranteed under the First Amendment.

The Doctrine of Fighting Words

Since the original definition of the fighting words concept in the *Chaplinsky* case,
the Supreme Court has delineated conditions that must be met before a court can
find that a speaker's language or words constituted fighting words and are beyond
First Amendment protection. According to a review by Gard (1980), there are four
primary elements to the fighting words doctrine:

1. The utterance must constitute an extremely provocative personal insult, a factor which requires an analysis of the content of the expression in question (see *Norwell v. City of Cincinnati*; *Cantwell v. Connecticut*).

2. The words must have a direct tendency to cause immediate violent response by the average recipient (see *Gooding v. Wilson*).

3. The words must be uttered face-to-face to the addressee (see *Gooding v. Wilson*).

4. The utterance must be directed to an individual and not to a group of people (see *Gooding v. Wilson*).

Like many of the decisions we must make about obscenity and the use of taboo language, fighting words are by nature contextually determined. The court must examine the circumstances in which the words are uttered. If any of these four factors are not present, the language may not be denied protection guaranteed by the constitution. These decisions about the contextual influences on language are both judicial and psychological in nature. Further, the requirement that the words be extremely provocative personal insults has not been given a thorough examination by the courts to date.

The Buffkins v. City of Omaha Case

The *Buffkins* case involved a woman from Denver who was flying to Nebraska to visit her family. Local police had received a tip that a "black" person on her flight was carrying drugs. The officers stopped Buffkins, told her that they had received the tip and took her to an office. She was not permitted to use the phone, and she was questioned for over an hour about her trip to the area. She did not allow them to search her bags but told them where she was staying in the area as she was accompanied by her sister at that time. Finally, she was released.

The officers finally decided they had no grounds to detain Buffkins and released her, telling her to "have a nice day". She was picking up her bags and used the word "asshole", in reference to the "system", she claimed. She did not direct the insult to the officers, she maintained. The officers testified that Buffkins had used "asshole" as a vulgar name to refer to one of them. She was arrested and taken to police headquarters, charged with disorderly conduct. She was fingerprinted and booked. Her luggage was examined and no drugs were found.

Her attorneys were interested in the nature of swearing by the average person and the concept of fighting words or disorderly conduct, as defined by the Omaha code. They wanted to know about the psychological factors involved in the specific case before them.

Buffkins was acquitted of the criminal charges of disorderly conduct. She and her attorneys decided to bring forth a civil suit based on a violation of Buffkins' First, Fourth and Fourteenth Amendment rights. They sought expert testimony about the nature of the word *asshole* and how people react to the word. The case provided a valuable window on the use of dirty words in America.

The following analysis was submitted as a written deposition in the case of *Buffkins v. City of Omaha* in the summer of 1989. The pertinent information has been excerpted and condensed below. First is a presentation of the legal background from both federal and Nebraska rulings. The final part of the deposition includes relevant psychological and psycholinguistic data, much of which came from the author's research.

It was intended here that the social science data and opinions would, 1) stick to the relevant facts, 2) not wander into judgments concerning mainly legal issues (e. g., vagueness or overbroad interpretation), and 3) be directed to the attorneys and not to the client in the case. Courts have a difficult time with expert witnesses, especially those from psychology and psychiatry backgrounds because the courts lack knowledge of social science methods. Nonetheless, decisions about the average person, reasonableness of behavior, and whether (any) language automatically incites violence are the province of social science research and theory.

Previous Federal Court Cases

What are the legal precedents to Buffkins' situation? The deposition required a psychologist to interpret legal decisions. Lawyers and judges may form a different opinion. What is interesting here is the situation as a whole, in which a person used "fighting words." The interesting question are what are the precipitating events, additional violent or provoking behavior, the needs of the speaker and listener, the role of weapons, and the reasons that the police officers were confronting Buffkins, as a speaker, in the first place?

Excerpts from the Deposition

1. *Chaplinsky v. New Hampshire*

Here it was ruled that a person did not have the right to use "fighting words" or words that were "likely to cause an average addressee to fight...." The court also said that the words were used "without a disarming smile...", recognizing that it was not a word alone that could influence the addressee's behavior.

2. *Cohen v. California*

This is a case where a draft protester was arrested for wearing a jacket that said "Fuck the draft". In the opinion written by Justice Harlan he noted that Cohen's statement contained no "conduct" --only words. *Cohen* is cited here in order to bring up two additional cases that support the notion that the words must be directed to another person and that the words must incite acts of violence.

3. *Cantwell v. Connecticut*

Here the point of the fighting words doctrine is that the words must be "directed to the person of the hearer". The case concerned a person who verbally attacked two listeners on the street about the subject of organized religion but did not use strong epithets or personal abuse. The ruling held that the speech must attack or incite directly not merely offend an innocent bystander or overhearer.

One question for the *Buffkins* case is whether she made an impersonal attack on "the system", as claimed, or did she direct the word toward one of the arresting officers?

4. *Gooding v. Wilson*

The case involved some pretty violent conduct and offensive language. In an appeal on a decision of the Georgia courts, which let the assault and battery charges stand, the notion of abusive language and opprobrious words were the focus. Justice Brennan's opinion in overruling the state court again stated that the words must "have a direct tendency to cause acts of violence".

Racial and Gender Headcount

The majority of the fighting words cases involve male speakers. Many of these incidents involve black speakers. The cases that involve women speakers are also predominantly black women. It is less clear from the law reports what the racial background of the arresting officers are in these cases. It would certainly be worthy of merit to further examine the doctrine of fighting words on the basis of racial and gender biases. Stereotypical attitudes or reactions on the part of law enforcement officials or on the part of the speakers may play a more significant role than the language *per se*. It may also be worthy of note that many of the situations or contexts involve suspicious behavior, violence, or weapons that are the most threatening element in the arrest rather than the language alone.

The topic of race is another possible contextual variable that has not been studied widely with respect to language offensiveness. It would seem that we know little about cross-racial offensiveness and/or what might provoke one race to violence but not another. Maybe racial stereotyping or misunderstanding is a potent element in the *Buffkins* case. If not (if the stereotyping is not an element), the racial and gender factors underlying the concept of provocation to violence via language must be made more clear. What offends one sex or race may not necessarily offend white, male police officers, and vice versa. The answer to the question may also affect our definition of the "average person".

The Laws of the City of Omaha and State of Nebraska

A further avenue of insight into the case is the nature of the Omaha code and legal cases in Nebraska involving fighting words.

1. The Omaha municipal code
    Article III. Offenses against the public peace
    Sec. 20-41. Definition.

For the purpose of this article "obstruct" shall mean to render impassable without causing unreasonable inconvenience of hazard.

Sec. 20-42 Disorderly Conduct.

It shall be unlawful for any person purposefully or knowingly to cause inconvenience, annoyance or alarm or to create the risk thereof to any person by:
(a) Engaging in fighting, threatening of violent conduct; or
(b) Using abusive, threatening or other fighting language or   gestures; or
(c) Making unreasonable noise.

2. *State v. Groves*

In 1985, the Nebraska Supreme Court declared *motherfucker* and *fuckhead* to be "fighting words." They also declared that the section 20-42 of the Omaha code to not be overbroad or vague.

The *Groves* case involved a police officer who observed Groves in a parking lot with what appeared to the officer to be a bolt cutter. After what was described as "menacing" behavior following the officer's display of his badge, the officer drew his revolver and summoned backup assistance. At this point Groves called the officer a *motherfucker* and a *pig* and challenged the officer to arrest him. Groves called one of the backup officers a *fuckhead* and was then forcibly handcuffed and arrested for disorderly conduct.

In this present context, it is important to note that both participants were armed (Groves was seen with a knife shield under his coat). Given the time of night and the location of the incident the behavior (not the language) was certainly suspicious. It is not clear, however, that the language alone constituted fighting words.

3. *State v. Boss*

The first case of *fighting words* in Nebraska where a defendant was arrested for abusing an officer was *Boss*. Boss was pulled over by an officer for driving too fast on icy streets. He got out of his car and grabbed the officer by the wrist and said, "you dirty son-of-a-bitch." They struggled and Boss hit the officer, knocking off his glasses.

Again, the behavior or conduct was what appeared threatening not the words, *son of a bitch*, alone.

4. *State v. Dreifurst*

Here the State used the ruling in *Boss* to define both abuse and fighting words. One of the defendants called the arresting officers, "fucking pigs", "son-of-a-bitch", "fucking cops", and "bastard". The court held that the words did constitute *fighting words* and abuse of an officer.

There is a recent review of the Nebraska rulings by Osthus (1986) pointing out that the circumstances behind *Groves* and other fighting words/abuse cases are questionable. While the words used are offensive and insulting, the words in themselves are not those that were narrowly defined in the *Chaplinsky* case, as those which would immediately incite violence or breach of peace. One additional review of fighting words as free speech was offered by Gard (1980). Gard goes beyond the Nebraska courts and examines the general ineffectiveness of the doctrine up to 1980.

(Note - Attorneys for both sides asked very few questions regarding the legal background of fighting words in the oral deposition phase and in the courtroom testimony. Most of the questions focused on the psychological and linguistic analysis of the case.)

Psychological and Psycholinguistic Background

The remainder of the deposition involves the psychological and psycholinguistic research bearing on the case and the opinions of the author.

1. Men are less offended by vulgar speech than women.

Research on sex differences in language usage supports the cultural stereotype that: a) males are less responsive to dirty words than females, or b) that females are more responsive to dirty words, or c) both are true. Although variation across individual words does exist, overall male ratings of taboo word stimuli are lower than females (Jay, 1977).

Support for these differences come from word rating studies in laboratory settings, Galvanic Skin Response (the lie detector apparatus), and the issue of sexual harassment. In the field of psychology and other social sciences, many of the previously held views about gender differences are currently being reversed. What were held as facts separating males from females are no longer taken for granted but are gaining objective scrutiny. It is in the area of language comprehension and usage that a difference does exist, especially with taboo words (Jay, 1980b).

The point of sex differences in reaction to dirty words is that the average male is less offended or more callous about hearing and using this type of speech than females. Police officers are expected to be more callous about vulgar speech than civilians due to their specific training about verbal abuse.

If males have a higher threshold for being offended by dirty language than females, a speaker might expect less reactivity from a male than a female. Perhaps, the notion that words immediately provoke violence is different for males than females. Additionally, a trained officer would be expected to be more tolerant and less reactive than a civilian in the same circumstances. One wonders what specific training the City of Omaha or the State of Nebraska provides trainees on the topic of verbal abuse and fighting language.

2. Men hear and use vulgar speech more than women.

When one listens to people swearing on the street, males outswear females by a ratio of 2 to 1 (Jay, 1986). The same holds true for children (Jay, 1989; Hall & Jay, 1988). Males use a larger vocabulary of dirty words and they use more offensive words than females use.

One particular question of interest here is the degree to which the officers have heard and used the word *asshole* in the past. How often do they use/hear the word at leisure or on the job? What are their responses when they do hear the word? Violence? One would get the impression that these officers had experienced a history of either observing or being involved in tumultuous or violent reactions to hearing the word *asshole*. The data would indicate that men certainly have more experience hearing and using these words than women, at least in public.

3. The semantic meaning of "asshole."

It is common in these cases to present dictionary-type definitions of word usage. Six different slang dictionaries were used to provide definitions of *asshole*, referring to a thoughtless or foolish person. These definitions need not be detailed here.

4. The pragmatic usage of "asshole."

Several pages of detailed information about how *asshole* is used "in the street" were taken from Jay (1977; 1986. Also see tables in Frequency chapter) in order to establish that dictionary definitions were insufficient to show actual usage. Briefly, the main points of the argument are:

   Asshole is used frequently by both males and females but more often by males than females.

   Asshole is rarely used to refer to a body part but in the overwhelming majority of cases is used as a marker of social deviation (foolish, thoughtless deviant act).

   The majority of the referents are males not females.

   Asshole is rarely used as an expletive without a target.

   Many dirty words that denote thoughtless behavior, call on the target, implicitly, to correct the behavior.

   This social corrective interpretation of verbal aggression is further supported by the writing of Averill (1983), who reported that most instances of anger followed by verbal aggression had the intent of changing the deviant behavior not provoking more aggression.

Acquisition of meaning.   It is worth mentioning that the word *asshole* does not appear in a child's vocabulary before the age of eight years. Many of their earlier insults are based on obvious physical or behavioral differences and the word *asshole* rarely appears in children's public speech, especially females.

   Semantic Usage in Field Confirmed by Laboratory Study.   One additional form of support for the social deviation meaning of the word *asshole* comes from another study (Jay and Burke, 1980). Here a group of subjects were given a list of taboo words and asked to use each in a sentence that typified the word's most common usage. For male subjects 81% of the sentences were based on social deviation and only 8% referred to body parts in the sentence. The effect is even more direct with females. All of the female sentences used the social deviance interpretation.

In the laboratory, subjects' impressions and reactions to language are considered real. Any speaker's intuitions about how he or she speaks is not necessarily a fact that he or she learned explicitly through training. Psycholinguists have a tradition of asking subjects to respond to language and examining the commonality of their responses in order to summarize how people use language.

5. The offensiveness of the word "asshole"

In general the data indicate that *asshole* is not a highly offensive word, not in league with *motherfucker*, *cocksucker*, or *cunt*. Any word could be intensified with additional taboo words, for example *fucking asshole* or *goddamned*, *motherfucking asshole* but it was not in the Buffkins case. Buffkins certainly could have chosen a number of more offensive words (not necessarily fighting words) or she could have intensified the word *asshole* with additional adjectives. She did neither.

In previous research (Jay, 1977) the word *asshole* received a mean rating of 5.88 on a 1-to-9 scale. The word was ranked 10 on a list of 28 taboo words. In a later study (Massachusetts Data, see Frequency Tables) similar results were obtained. The word obtained a 4.79 rating on a 1-to-7 scale and was ranked only 86th on a list of 149 items. In comparison to the rank of 86th for *asshole*, *cocksucker* was 10th, *fuck* was 12th, *motherfucker* was 5th, and *son of a bitch* was 101st. These relative rank orderings are to be considered in light of recent Nebraska cases of disorderly conduct involving some of these words.

There is one other pertinent psycholinguistic study of relative offensiveness or perceived verbal aggressiveness. Greenberg (1976) presented college students with a list of expressions that covered seven increasingly aggressive categories. The subjects rated the messages on a scale from 0= not at all aggressive to 9= extremely aggressive. The lowest category of aggressive messages was criticism (e.g., you do that too slow), second was stereotypic derogation (e.g., you're dishonest), third was stereotypic derogation with cursing (e.g., you act like an asshole), fourth was severe derogation (e.g., I see perverts come in here, but you're the worst), fifth was severe derogation with cursing (e.g., you act like a motherfucking idiot with shit for brains), sixth was stream of profanity (e.g., I don't give a motherfucking shit if you stick your ass out of the goddamned window), and finally threat of physical attack (e.g., I'm going to kick your ass). The phrase "you act like an asshole" received a mean rating of 4.64, the middle of the scale. All of the phrases from the fourth through seventh categories were rated higher. But none of the phrases was rated 9, that is "extremely aggressive".

The study makes two relevant points. Only low to moderate aggressiveness is perceived by the raters for the term *asshole*. Other language (*motherfucker*) and that combined with strings of profanities (*goddamned shithead son of a bitch*) were perceived as more threatening. None of these categories, even the most aggressive, provided a rating of either 8 or 9. These points reinforce the relative inoffensiveness of the word *asshole* and that the word is not categorized as a type of fighting word (i.e., threats of physical attack) by the subjects in this experiment.

6. Males are less offended by "asshole" than females

In one study (Jay, 1977) the word *asshole* had a mean rating of 5.88, as mentioned above. Males and females rated the word differently, however. Males only gave the word a 5.48 rating, while females gave it a 6.21. This difference amounts to over one-half of a scale point. Additional support for the stereotype that males are the users of dirty words comes from a study on expected usage of dirty words as a function of location, status, and dominance (Jay, 1978c). In this study college students rated a variety of campus locations, personnel, and the appropriateness of the person in the location (e.g., in your own room versus in the dean's room).

Ratings of likelihood of usage placed the male policeman third on the list of 14 occupations with a mean likelihood of 63%. Further when subjects rated various locations on a college campus where one would likely hear a dirty word, the police security office had a rating of 44% making it one of the highest non-student locations and 16th on a list of 45 campus locations. People expect men to swear, especially policemen.

Final Notes on the Buffkins Case

In courtroom testimony the author was asked questions about both laboratory and field data regarding the offensiveness of the word *asshole*. The final opinion was that the word was not the type of language which provoked immediate, violent response. At the present time (1991), the civil court ruling, which found the officers and the City innocent, is being appealed.

Restrictions on Media

Several types of communication and media channels are subject to censorship and regulation in America. Within each, what speakers may say and what listeners or viewers may hear has been constrained by governmental laws, industry policies or public pressure. Several of these media are outlined below and the chapter concludes with an extensive analysis of language restrictions and censorship in the motion picture industry.

Cable Television. A target of federal exploration of free speech is that of cable television. The Cable Communications Policy Act of 1984 attempted to regulate or prohibit the transmission of "any matter which is obscene or otherwise unprotected by the Constitution." It is not entirely clear today if the FCC has the power to regulate cable television in the same manner as it does radio and television media. Some confusion exists at to whether the medium is more like a newspaper purchased and used by individuals or more like television and radio, where the product is essentially free, if one owns a receiver. Sporn (1985) has written an extensive analysis of the content regulation of cable television with respect to the First Amendment issue.

Insider talk about the FCC indicates that with recent replacements on the commission during the Reagan years, the FCC is turning more conservative and will probably regulate the medium with tighter controls. Tighter controls mean a broader interpretation of what the FCC interprets as indecent. The FCC prohibits the transmission of obscene material, as defined by the Supreme Court. The indecency standard is a much broader concept and refers to sexually explicit conversations, violent and aggressive speech, and references to sex acts and sex organs. Recall that it was the indecency regulation that was in question in the *FCC v. Pacifica* case, as mentioned above in the discussion of fighting words.

Dial-a-porn. In the 1970's the Bell Telephone Company expanded its services to include sports results and dial-a-joke type services. In the early 1980's, FCC rulings combined with the de-regulation of dial-it services, led Bell to auction the dial-a-porn service to other providers. Now a customer can use a dial-a-porn number and carry on a live conversation or use a Mass Announcement Network Service to receive a pre-recorded sexually explicit message.

The Meese Commission on Pornography targeted the dial-it services, as they did cable television and computer networks. While these media seem innocuous enough for those adults who are willing to pay the expenses for passive (sexual?) charge, the problem is with their children. The Commission wanted to look closely at how different media offering sexually explicit materials affected children. When the use of these adult media services by children came under scrutiny, the owners were caused to develop more secure systems and stricter self-regulation.

The Party Line. Another of the services offered by large and small phone companies within the last decade is the party line service also referred to within the industry as "group-bridging services". The numbers of these services are advertised as a chance to participate in stimulating group discussions or play trivia games. The actual use appears to be something quite different (Leerhsen, 1988). There are two obvious problems with the party line service that will lead to changes in the future. First, at a dollar per minute for the privilege of talking to strangers, the monthly bills for some people are very high, on the order of $5000 to $6000. And once again many kids get on the phone without Mom or Dad knowing about it. The second problem is based on the widespread use of taboo speech. Most of the users are males apparently soliciting sexual favors via phone or at least talking about them. There is also a good deal of racial insults, abusive talk, and other hostility; for example,

> "If that eight-year old is still
> on the line, she can suck my dick".
> To which a girlish voice responded,
> "Fuck you".
> (Leerhsen, p 72).

Forces behind the Meese Commission report and other pressure groups like them will probably not let party line services go untouched.

In 1991 the prospect of public use of video phones is at hand. The picture phone is almost certain to create another problem with regard to obscene phone calls. With the capability of offering a picture with a voice, one needs little imagination to see how dial-a-porn or party sex talk will appear when picture phones reach the homestead.

Obscene Phone Calls. There are millions of reported cases of obscene or annoying phone calls per year in the United States and many more that go unreported. There are federal and state laws which prohibit these calls and those who own phones can find the phone company's advice for handling them in the front of their phone books. Calls are typically made by males who have difficulty in establishing interpersonal relationships with other adults. They usually know their victims and may call them repeatedly to enact their masturbatory fantasy on the phone without getting caught or confronting their victim. Generally, these calls fall into one of three categories: the caller boasts about himself and describes the masturbation action in detail (most common), or he tries to get the victim to make revealing comments about her sex life to him, maybe by telling her it is a "sex survey", and thirdly, threats to the victim, such as finding her, seeing her or getting to her. Clinically, the caller has a type of deviant sexual behavior that psychologists label "paraphilia", a class of behaviors which include voyeurism, exhibitionism, sadomachism, fetishes and other behaviors that include nonhuman objects or inappropriate partners (children or unwilling adults). Callers are most similar to exhibitionists, who regress into adolescent masturbation to fulfill their inadequacies by talking to and relating to women in a immature fashion. Their behavior persists and increases over time, as their thoughts and actions become more abnormal and compulsive and normal desires are displaced by the phone-calling fantasies. They are generally passive and introverted and not highly likely to physically harm the victim, although the psychological trauma can be severe and long-lasting. They are treated successfully, when caught, with a combination of aversive therapy, desensitization, orgasmic reconditioning and social skill learning.

Those victimized by these calls are told to hang up immediately and not willingly listen to any obscene words or become angry with the caller while on the phone. Answering machines and caller identification machines have been used to stop such annoying and obscene calls. There are currently, however, some questions in many states about the right to use caller identification machines on a broad scale.

Computer Networks. The computer service where a user can access a computer network using a phone, modem, and a home computer, are similar in content and nature to the phone dial-a-porn service. Computer users can read computer bulletin boards, send and receive messages with other users, or make conference calls involving several members. One of these networks is called *Sextex.* These computer networks are also popular as a form of dating service in both the United States and Europe.

Audio Recordings. In the mid-1980's a group of anti-rock and roll music people formed the Parents Music Resource Center to regulate the "blatant explicit lyric content" of popular recordings (Ward, Stokes, & Tucker, 1986). In September of 1985 that same group lobbied the Senate Commerce Committee, based on the clout of several prominent senators' wives. A hearing was conducted to examine the effect of rock and roll lyrics on its listeners. As one result, the Recording Industry Association of America agreed to place stickers on records which indicate "explicit lyrics -- parental advisory" in cases where member record companies deemed it appropriate.

Very recently local communities have taken an aggressive role, attacking record stores that market "obscene" material to pre-teens. In Alabama in the fall of 1989, a salesman was arrested but later acquitted for selling a copy of a 2 Live Crew record to a young teen. Later in the spring of 1990, a Florida man was also arrested for selling the same recording to another youth. The recording in question contained very explicit language describing sex acts and other offensive behaviors.

In another matter related to music, Vokey and Reed (1985) have examined the alleged subliminal messages in some of these recordings and found no significant impact of the lyrics on listeners. Parents had claimed that records contained subliminal messages calling for teenagers to engage in demon worship, suicide, drug usage, and deviant sex acts. It would seem that whatever the content or nature of these lyrics may be, the lyrics and the language in them should be compared to the language that normal adolescents already use. Many kids already know the dirty words before listening to them on recordings. On the topic of lyric content in rock and roll see Pattison (1987).

A recent study by Yee, Britton, and Thompson (1988) was designed to assess adolescents' (public high school students) attitudes and interpretations of popular rock and roll lyrics. The questionnaire administered focused on preferences, comprehension of lyrics, attitudes and values, and background material regarding self-behaviors. The results indicate that adolescents have great difficulty comprehending lyrics, even those of their favorite tunes.   Over half of the respondents when asked to interpret lyrics, gave an interpretation that was labeled incorrect by a group of expert raters. One student described the elaborate "Stairway to Heaven" by Led Zeppelin, as a story "about a lady who likes shiny jewelry." Interpretations of lyrics with strong sexual innuendo were equally puzzling to the teenagers.   With respect to self-reported behavior, some interesting positive correlations were found. Preference for heavy metal music, which emphasizes themes of violence and sex, was correlated with significantly more reported arrests. With pornography questions, similar results were found, as the heavy metal variable was also correlated with exposure to X-rated films and with exposure to nude photographs and magazines. The positive correlations, however, do *not* prove causal connection and the music preference factors account for a very small (10%) portion of the variance in scores. In other words preferences are not particularly strong predictors of attitudes.

So, the concerns on the part of groups such as the PMRC and the National Parent Teachers Association would seem to go unsubstantiated.

Conclusion

Language on the street and language in the media is subject to restrictions. With the creation of new media in the future, we are likely to see controls similar to those in the past. When the new video cassette market boomed in the 1980's, there was a need to either legally control the distribution of indecent or obscene tapes, or allow the producers and marketers to develop their own rating system. In order to understand how our language is restricted we need to understand how society and the law changes along with human expression. Furthermore, our concepts of taboo, obscenity and profanity must change to reflect the changes in laws and language.

The Evolution of Cursing in American Film

Most industries involved in the production and marketing of materials with questionable speech, such as television, radio, motion pictures, cable television, audio recordings and print media, have imposed self-restrictions and ratings to prevent legal sanctions by outside authorities. The film industry is a good example of self-regulation due to pressure from outside and inside the trade. The goal of this last section of the chapter is to examine the evolution of questionable language in the American motion picture industry. The subject is divided into two main topics, the nature of language restrictions in the industry and an empirical analysis of language in a sample of American films.

Language Restrictions in American Films

The motion picture industry emerged at the turn of the century and attempted to regulate its own productions without government intervention. Nevertheless, several groups such as the Catholic Church, kept a watchful eye on the content of motion pictures and at one time brought great pressure on motion picture producers to control explicit or questionable language and other content (sex). Several writers have plotted the evolution of law, language and motion pictures, including De Grazia and Newman (1982), Randall (1970), and Steinberg (1982). By examining the subjects and language that people have complained about or tried to censor and by looking at *who* did the complaining and *how* a response was made, one can see Americans' reactions to explicit language in film. Some questions about restrictions and ratings emerge: what words and phrases were suppressed? What changes in censorship of language occurred over time? What happened when the rating system was adopted? Below are the answers to these questions and a brief historical analysis.

The Church

The Catholic church has been from the beginning and still is a strong force against liberal sexual behavior and coarse language. The church had a film banned as early as 1916 and has from that time made classificatory judgments dividing films between those recommended for viewing versus those films which are objectionable. The church became directly involved in the drafting of the Motion Picture Production Code which sought to establish restrictions on film content in order to obtain approval by the industry. The most obvious involvement was the formation of the Legion of Decency in 1934. Catholics, based on the Legion's decisions and recommendations, were to promise to refrain from seeing objectionable films.   The church still remains active in reviewing and recommending films today.

The Film Industry

Following is a brief history of the industry's side of the story. In 1915 a National Board of Review of Motion Pictures was established, not as a form of censorship *but* as a classifier of films. This is an important form of review that has emerged most recently in both the film and audio recording industry. The National Board as constituted had no authority to direct which films could be shown or distributed. It had no legal relation with the producers or distributors of motion pictures. However, one of its policies was to prohibit the use or appearance of obscenity or vulgarity, when these offend, or the use of blasphemy in film content. During the same time period of religious and industry controls, state and local governments also established motion picture censorship boards, especially in big cities (e.g., New York or Boston). So, we see forces outside and inside the medium interested in content.

In 1921 the Motion Picture Producers and Distributors Association asked the Postmaster General of the United States, Will Hays, to be the President of the MPPDA, which was to be organized formally in 1922.   Hays accepted and remained in that position, "The Hays Office", until his retirement at the end of World War II in 1945. During that period, of course, many events occurred that changed the nature of the motion picture industry and its art. One very significant event was the appearance of sound in film in 1927. The use of sound energized the industry and altered the shape of the art form. The industry was attentive to its potential for offending viewers and sought internal control of content. Similar to an earlier form of restrictions set forth by the then defunct National Association of Motion Picture Industry, a set of eleven guidelines for things *not* to appear in film was re-established. Thus, in 1927 the MPPDA offered some guidelines referred to as the "Don'ts and Be Carefuls." The words banned were the following:

god, *lord*, *jesus*, *christ*, *hell*, *damn*, *gawd*, and "every other profane and vulgar expression however it may be spelled."
(Steinberg, p 391).

These words, according to the censors, were those that would have fairly universal impact on English-speaking audiences at home and abroad and would result in lack of distribution or banning, either of which would cost the producers dearly.

By 1929 sound was universally used in motion pictures and new methods of strengthening the power of the Hays Office were considered. Hays was bothered by coarse language and "cuss" words like *damn*. So in 1930 we find the Production Code, similar but more elaborate than the 1927 "Don'ts and Be Carefuls" and more precise in nature. The 1927 rules are almost humorous by today's standards, and so are the standards initiated by the 1930 Production Code. Here, no approval was given to the use of such words in motion pictures:

> ...Obscenity. Obscenity in word, gesture, reference, song, joke or by suggestion (even when likely to be understood only by part of an audience) is forbidden.

> Profanity. Pointed profanity and every other profane or vulgar expression, however used, is forbidden. No approval by the Production Code Administration shall be given to the use of words and phrases in motion pictures including, but not limited to, the following:
> *alley cat* (applied to a woman), *bat* (applied to a woman), *broad* (applied to a woman), *bronx cheer* (the sound), *chippie, cocotte, god, lord, jesus, christ* (unless used reverently), *cripes, fanny, fairy* (in a vulgar sense), *finger* (the), *fire* (cries of), *gawd, goose* (in a vulgar sense), *"hold your hat"* or *"hats", hot* (applied to a woman), *"in your hat", louse, lousy, madam* (relating to prostitution), *nance, nerts, nuts* (except when meaning crazy), *pansy, raspberry* (the sound), *slut* (applied to a woman), *s.o.b., son of a tart,* toilet gags, *tom cat* (applied to a man), travelling salesman and farmer's daughter jokes, *whore, damn, hell* (excepting when the use of said last two words shall be essential and required for portrayal, in proper historical context, of any scene or dialogue based upon historical fact or folklore, or for the presentation in proper literary context of a Biblical, or otherwise religious quotation, or a quotation from a literary work provided that no such use shall be permitted which is intrinsically objectionable or offends good taste).

In the same section on "profanity" the Production Code Administration also noted:

> the following words and phrases are obviously offensive to the patrons of motion pictures in the United States and more particularly to the patrons of motion pictures in foreign countries: *chink, dago, frog, greaser, hunkie, kike, nigger, spic, wop, yid.*
> (see Steinberg, pp 392-393)

The areas of Obscenity and Profanity were two of the 11 areas of concern of the Code. It may seem puzzling why the Code went into such detail on the use of *damn* and *hell*. Well, the story lies in the making and selling of *Gone With The Wind (GWTW)*.

The story of GWTW has many fascinating twists and turns and makes several points about language, morality, censorship and the film industry. Certainly GWTW is a great piece of craftsmanship that on the whole could never be slighted by the use of one word or one questionable sentence. The quality of the film allowed its producers to tackle head on the moral arbiters in Hollywood and cause the Code as originally written to be amended.

The infamous line in the movie was Clark Gable's, "Frankly, my dear, I don't give a damn." The line was not in the original script but David Selznick added *damn*, knowing that the Code forbade its use. The original version was "I don't care", and had been approved by the Code Administration. The altered version caused objection from the Hays office, with which Selznick fought for approval on the grounds that the word was not a profanity but merely a colloquialism which expressed a force of drama that was essential to the film. Selznick argued that allowing the proper use of the forceful word would not only be harmless but the use would be remembered by the audience and further allow the Code Administration the power to allow some otherwise objectionable oaths and phrases. Hays finally approved the use of *damn* but fined Selznick $5,000 for violating the Code. One week later the MPPDA added the exception to the use of *hell* and *damn*.

Hays resigned in 1945 from the MMPDA and a new administration developed during difficult times. The House Un-American Activities Committee was conducting hearings involving Hollywood figures. The new office was taken over by Johnston, who, in order to signal a change of leadership, changed the MMPDA to the current title of Motion Picture Association of America. Later in the 1950's, Supreme Court rulings would begin to undermine the authority of the Production Code Administration and cases which would ultimately begin to define "obscenity" (*Roth*) were taking place. The Administration would face a challenge to its Profanity clause in the 1960's.

Several films in the decade prior to film ratings were banned for language use. Notable were *The Moon Is Blue* for the use of "virgin" and other sexy words (1953) and the *Anatomy of a Murder* (1959) for the use of "rape" and "contraceptive". In 1962 *The Connection* was banned in New York solely on the use of "shit" as a slang term for heroin. Much of these censorship activities on the state level would soon come to an end, at least on a fine level of scrutiny of film language.

In 1966 the sophisticated film *Who's Afraid of Virginia Woolf?* was granted approval, making an exception to the language used therein. This exception recognized that the industry could not stand as a moral guardian against films with such merit. Specifically, *Virginia Woolf* used a script change from "screw you" to "goddamn you", much in the same manner as GWTW. From this point on it became obvious to the Code Administration that the language of the Code needed to be streamlined. Under Jack Valenti and in response to Supreme Court rulings regarding the need to protect children from pornography, the MPAA moved to a classification system for movies. The classification of "suggested for mature audiences" or SMA began to warn potential viewers of film content. These classification schemes have continued until the present day.

Two Supreme Court decisions in 1968 (*Ginsberg v. New York* and *Interstate Circuit v. Dallas*) indicated that a system of classifying films could be declared constitutional, if the guidelines for the classifications were well defined. These rulings also stated that material that was not considered obscene for adults could be deemed obscene for children (*Ginsberg*). Shortly following these rulings, the Motion Picture Association of America announced its new regulatory code, which included G, M, R, and X ratings. In March of 1970, the R and X ratings raised admission age limits to 17 years. The M category was changed to GP. In 1972 the GP was changed to PG to emphasize parental guidance in film selections. Later, in 1984, the PG category was expanded by adding PG-13 in response to the violence in *Indiana Jones and the Temple of Doom*. In 1990 the film *Henry & June* was given the new category rating of NC-17, category between R and X ratings, allowing explicit but non-pornographic films to obtain wider distribution.

The particular interest in all of these restrictions, guidelines, and rating systems is on the issue of language in film. Regardless of the behavior or acts depicted in any film, what type of language will be restricted? With attention to the language used in films, Jack Valenti, from MPAA, testified to the Meese Commission on Pornography (*Final Report*, 1986) that:

> G rated movies may go beyond polite conversation
> PG can have some profanity

The film's use of stronger sexually derived words used only as expletives, require the PG-13 rating

A sexually derived word in a sexually explicit context gets an R and more han one expletive results in an R rating

X rated films contain brutal or sexually related language

It should also be mentioned that the XXX rating is not awarded by the MPAA but is a promotional category for sexually explicit unrated films.

Video Movies. Throughout the recent history of the motion picture industry the MPAA provided the rating system that parents and programmers used to distribute and promote movies. However, with the rapid growth of the video cassette recorder market in the 1980's a different type of motion picture has emerged and escaped the MPAA rating scheme. Movies for TV, made-for-video movies, and movies that were not released for the theater market are the problem. Getting a rating from MPAA may cost several thousand dollars and the new programmers and distributors can market their wares without MPAA approval; so why bother? The problem is that video retailers and rental outlets are coming under pressure from state and local legislatures and from parents for adequate ratings of video products. In January of 1988 a group of small video companies, the Independent Video Programmers Association sought a solution through the Film Advisory Board. The rating scheme is applicable to the growing field of unrated movies and is designed to head off governmental intervention and parental complaints. The rating system looked like this:

L language	EL extreme language	V violence
EV extreme violence	EPS explicit sex	S sex
N nudity	EN extreme nudity	SA substance abuse
M mature		

An example of the MPAA system versus the FAB design can be made with the 1987 Oscar nominee for best picture *Fatal Attraction* starring Michael Douglas and Glenn Close. It carries the MPAA rating of R. The new video industry rating would have scored it: MMM/EL/EV/EPS/N/SA. Translated the latter means that the picture is extremely mature, and contains extreme language, extreme violence, explicit sex, nudity, and substance abuse.

In the spring of 1990 the FAB revised its rating system to the following categories:

C = Children, ages 7 and under.

F = Family, some violence and fight scenes.

M = Mature, some sex scenes.

VM = Very Mature, extreme language and nudity.

EM = Extremely Mature, extreme language, sex/nudity, extreme violence and substance abuse.

AO = Adults Only, ages 18 and over, frontal nudity/erotica.

Here, the system is a bit more descriptive than the MPAA system with regard to objectionable content (e.g., substance abuse or frontal nudity). However, neither system makes the language description very clear.

I attempted to determine the nature of the language codings, in relation to the MPAA code and to find out what was classified as "extreme" language. Unfortunately, as with the MPAA, the objective definition of these categories has not been put into writing, at least from the materials forwarded by Elayne Blythe, the President of the FAB.

Most of the FAB materials point out that the intent of the rating system is to inform the public of the contents of films but not to censor. The FAB believes in freedom of choice and their motto is: "Accentuate the Positive." The Board also offers further distinction through an "FAB Award Winner" seal featured on motion pictures.

The classification of films on the basis of language content without a clear description of those restrictions leaves many questions unanswered. What words and phrases are all right for children? Teenagers? Are there limits to the number of dirty words that are used within more restrictive categories? How has the nature and scope of dirty language changed over the history of restrictions and rating systems?

A Study of Cursing in American Films 1939-1989

The study was designed to examine language restrictions and restrictions in general in the film industry. These included: change from religious taboos to aggressive and sexual language, gender differences in language use and the emergence of the ating system in the motion picture industry. Would films mirror changes in offensiveness and gender differences? Would language before the rating system be more restricted than after the system was employed? The analysis was designed to answer these specific questions.

To a great degree the present research is an extension of an earlier interest in stereotyping in film. The previous analysis measured the extent to which beer drinking, a male dominated activity, was represented in American films (Jay, 1988). Here it was seen that gender, class and age stereotypes were supported by contemporary film. It was also noted that many of the bar scenes, drinking scenes and those involving physical violence were also highly likely to contain verbal aggression, insulting and cursing. The present study has been set up to continue the analysis of stereotypes with respect to language use in film imagery.

The evolution of film ratings and restrictions along with differences in American cursing, as a function of time and gender lead to the following set of hypotheses of interest.

Experimental Hypotheses

The specific hypotheses to be tested are as follows. First, that there has been a progressive increase in the amount of swearing in motion pictures over time. These increments in incidents of swearing should be related to changes in restrictions and rating systems in the film industry, so that the total number of curse words used in a film increases over time. Second, the gender stereotype of men swearing more frequently in public than females is supported by film characters portraying Americans. The number of curse words used by males per film is greater than curse words used by female characters. Finally with respect to semantics, films should reflect a shift from religious cursing to sexual and aggressive cursing over time. The use of *damn* and *hell* should decrease with time, while the use of words like *fuck* and *shit* should increase over the years. The pattern of film language content should follow language shifts within American society. These changes in explicit language use should also appear in response to the relaxation of film censorship and restrictions from earlier periods.

Method

Film Sample. A preliminary set of 120 films, which were used in a variety of media and communication courses were selected from the film library at North Adams State College (Massachusetts). Most were assumed to represent popular and important American films, as many had received awards and other forms of recognition. Several films from the 1980's were rented from local stores, as they were not catalogued at the college. All films were in videotape format to allow for controlled analysis and review. While over 100 films were analyzed (See Appendix 1), only 73 were selected for initial analyses: twelve from the period 1939 to 1960 ten from 1960 to 1970, twenty from 1970 to 1980 and thirty-one from the 1980's.

The periods of the 1970's and 80's were overrepresented so as to concentrate on films with mainly female leads or mainly male leads in order to compare gender differences after the present day rating system was adopted. Almost all of the films were produced primarily for adult audiences.

After the initial analysis was conducted, a second analysis was carried out to further clarify the use of language in recent films. Many of the earlier films were dropped from the secondary analysis along with several which presented a bias in light of the second set of questions (for example, the film did not contain enough dialogue from female characters or had dialogue limited only to male characters).

Film Reviewers. Film reviewers were volunteers from a college psychology course on the topic of human communication. They were given course credit for conducting the reviews. Additional reviews were conducted by the author. All reviewers were given a training session which consisted of watching a five-minute segment of Eddie Murphy's *Raw* and counting the number of taboo or obscene words. All subjects reached the criterion level of proficiency during the session. Only one reviewer omitted one word in the entire training sequence. Reviewers were assigned one of the following: pre-1960's; 1960's; 1970's; films from the 1980's with mainly Male lead characters; or those with mainly Female lead characters. Each reviewer (except the author) analyzed films from only one of these periods. Each student reviewer watched 10-12 films and the author reviewed the rest.

Inter-reviewer recording reliability was measured by correlating two analyses of the same film by different raters. The mean interjudge reliability correlation was r= .94, indicating a very consistent recording method.

Content Analysis. Each reviewer was given a pre-printed recording sheet to note language use. The sheet indicated whether a male or female was speaking. Twenty-seven frequently used taboo words, based on previous research (Jay, 1977) were listed. The reviewer was instructed to place a check beside each word when it was used and words not appearing on the list were to be listed and tabulated, as a function of sex of speaker. Reviewers were told to be as inclusive as possible with regard to insults and questionable comments, as the author would make the decision about the final tabulation of words to be included or rejected. The preprinted word list ranged from very offensive language (*motherfucker*) to mild insults (*pig*). The words pre-listed on the tally sheet were: *fuck, shit, jesus/christ, hell, damn, ass, asshole, goddamn/god, bitch, piss, pig, bastard, bullshit, son of a bitch, whore, slut, cock, cocksucker, motherfucker, queer, fag, dick, cunt, pussy, prick, screw,* and *crap.* A common occurrence was the additional listing of offensive words not prelisted, for example, *tits, shithead, pecker, scumbag,* or *dago,* to name a few.

For each of the films the following were tabulated: total number of words, words from males, words from females and the number of times *fuck* and *shit* were used. These were the dependent variables subjected to statistical analysis.

It should be mentioned that although the use of *hell* and *damn* (H&D) were not subjected to the original analysis of variance, the frequency data were collected and are reported separately below.

Results and Discussion

An analysis of variance using a computer program (BMD) was conducted on the following variables: Decade of film release (four levels), total number of curse words, words from Males, words from Females and total number of *fuck* and *shit* (F&S) per film. This analysis revealed the following significant results, which are summarized in Table 1.

Decade of Film Release. There is a significant increase in the use of cursing over time, $F=7.35$ ($p < .001$). The mean number of words for the pre-60's, 60's, 70's and 80's (with standard deviations in parentheses) were: 1.58 (3.87), 24.8 (31.88), 84.1 (62.1) and 81.03 (73.77), respectively. It is obvious that before the film rating system allowed more explicit language in the late 1960's, there was very little cursing relative to modern films.

It should be noted that there is a great deal of variance in the amount of swearing in films, especially in more modern ones. This is evident by the size of the standard deviations reported above. In other words, while cursing has increased over the years, it is still possible to watch contemporary films with infrequent cursing. It seems as if the average modern film has about 70 to 80 swear words but in general the amount of swearing in films depends on the date of release. Older films still have episodes of verbal aggression and insulting, they just employ more euphemisms and acceptable language than modern films. It should also be noted that the variability (standard deviations) has increased over time. This is to say that not only was there was very little swearing several decades ago, but there was little variation in the amount of swearing from one film to another.

It appears that the great transition occurred at the end of the 1960's, that films prior to that time constrained strong language and that films of the 1970's to the present have reached a certain plateau. After all there are only so many swear words that can be uttered in a 90-minute popular film.

Gender of Speaker. Over the decades reported above both male and female characters have produced significantly more explicit language, F=4.54 (p< .006) and F=4.86 (p< .004), respectively. Over the four time periods males have increased according to the following means, 1.5, 22.6, 71.75 and 61.55. Females have increased over the same period from .08, 2.2, 12.25 to 19.48. The average over all time periods for males and females were 49.13 and 11.94, respectively, showing males outswearing females by a ratio of over 4 to 1. A more direct comparison of males versus females, however, appears below (Analysis Two). These data are summarized in Table 2.

The hypothesis of gender differences was supported and the comparison of the mean number of words also supports the language and gender stereotypes in American culture. While on the street, males use twice as many taboo words as do females, the situation in films is probably a bit overblown. Many popular films are based on action, sex and violence and more films rely on popular male actors than on females to make a profit.

Semantics. The amount of times swear words *fuck* and *shit* are used has increased significantly over time, F=4.13 (p<.009). The mean number of times F&S appeared per film over the four time periods was, 0, .4, 21.3 and 34.71, respectively. Here a steady increase in strong language, as measured by the use of *fuck* and *shit*, is evident.

The hypothesis regarding the evolution of the semantics of swearing was also supported. As American culture has shifted to a different form of insult and taboo, the American motion picture industry has generally done the same. Probably the hallmark of this shift was the evolution of the rating system in the late 1960's, which directed film producers and others away from the censorship of specific words used.

Analysis Two

A second analysis of variance was conducted to test more directly the nature of gender differences in recent films. For this analysis the 12 films with predominantly female leads were compared with 15 films from the same period (1979-1988) having mainly male leads. Films from the earlier decades were eliminated because of the lack of swearing in the pre-rating system era. It was assumed that a concentration on more recent pictures would provide a more realistic view of female swearing in contemporary America. Five films were eliminated from the previous analysis of variance: *Scarface*, *Streamers*, *Splash*, *E.T.* and *Wish You Were Here*; the first two because of the lack of or low number of female characters, the next two because of the PG ratings and the last because it was a British release. The major independent variable is Sex of leading characters and the dependent variables are Total number of swears, Male swears, Female swears and number of F&S per film.

Results

Total Number of Swear Words. The total number of swear words in Male lead films was an average of 80.66 per film versus 49.41 total swear words for Female lead films. This difference of an average of 30 swear words was only marginally significant (p= .10). Note that there is a large standard deviation of swear words, 56 for Male films and 35 for Female Lead films. However, the means are in the predicted direction, with more swearing in Male versus Female Lead films.

Language Explicitness. The number of times *fuck* and *shit* were used was not a function of the types of leading characters. Male films use F&S an average of 29.4 times and Female films use F&S an average of 21.83 times. Recall that these two words alone account for some 43% of all the curse words used in modern films.

While the proportion of *hell* and *damn* (H&D) was not subjected to statistical analysis, the data can be reported, as the trend is obviously very strong. If one looks at the proportion of cursing in a film that is H&D versus F&S, an interesting reversal appears. In the 1960's H&D accounted for 53% of all the curse words sampled, while F&S was less than 1%. By the 1980's F&S accounted for 37% of the curse words in Male lead films and 36% of the words in Female lead films. Conversely, H&D in the 1980's only account for 10% of the swearing in Male films and 15% of the words in Female films. So, not only is there more cursing in modern films, it is more sexually explicit than the mild religious-based cursing (from today's standards) of earlier times.

Speakers and Film Leads. There is an interesting difference in swearing patterns, as a function of the sex of speaker and the type of film viewed. Male speakers swear an average of 69.46 times in Male Lead films but only 23.58 times in Female Lead films. Thus there is significantly more Male words in Male films, $F=8.15$, ($p <.008$).

The trend repeats itself for Female speakers. Female speakers swear an average of 11.2 words in Male Lead films but 25.83 words in Female Lead pictures. This is a significant difference, $F=4.37$, ($p <.05$). Thus women swear more in films with predominately female characters.

General Discussion

The major goal of the present project may seem like proving the obvious to some readers. However, the nature of language use in motion pictures lends itself to objective analysis and empirical investigation. It would seem pointless to speculate about or engage in anecdotal evidence when one's hypotheses can be tested and proven. Perhaps it is the magnitude of the popular importance of the motion picture industry in American society that makes film analysis necessary. So many of us spend a great deal of time, effort and money watching motion pictures and they are certain to affect viewers in many different ways.

The question of censorship and rating schemes is an ongoing problem for motion picture producers. The evidence presented here shows that as the industry standards have relaxed, the type of language in modern films has become more like everyday speech with respect to taboo and obscene speech usage. Whether the evolution of explicit speech in film is good or bad is not the point. The point is that modern films are more realistic than those of only a few decades past. It must seem odd to watch an old World War 2 film such as *Wake Island* where soldiers call each other "thick headed clunk" relative to the hundreds of F&S's in *Platoon*. Soldiers did swear in the second World War, did they not? One wonders if the normal lay person notices the difference in these war films.

While the rating systems provide general guidelines for categorizing films based on behavior and language, the systems do not make definitive statements about particular words, as censorship schemes did in the past. As language is almost devoid of meaning without context, it makes some sense to base ratings of individual films on their contents without general restrictions. It may be the case that by examining the language used in films that are already rated, one could establish some general correlations between words and ratings. Maybe a fruitful question to ask would focus on the total number of curse words or the types of words used in PG categories and X categories. These categories should in many ways have different language than that in typical adult or R-rated films. How does the type of film or genre influence language use? Do comedies have more explicit language than action films, for example? It would be interesting to contrast films within one subject matter such as war, sports or westerns, and plot the language differences over time. One would suspect that all of these subject matters have increased the use of taboo language at the same rate, but some categories may have increased faster than others.

Methodological Issues

What is the reality of strong language? When one walks out on the street one hears men out-cursing women at a ratio of about 2 to 1 and the words men use are more offensive than women use (Jay, 1986). In the present study, films from the recent past generally portray this stereotype. One word of caution is that the type of language stereotype presented depends on the nature of the film whether female or male characters have the leads. A more detailed analysis of language use would count the actual number of lines or words each character had to determine the overall proportion of strong language to nontaboo speech. It is clear that taboo words are among the most frequently used in English and they are used liberally in contemporary motion pictures. The accuracy of female swearing both in the real world and the film world is a topic worthy of further analysis.

The issue of an accurate metric for language stereotypes in film raises two additional concerns. What constitutes a Male film versus a Female film, and, secondly, were the "right" words counted? Other researchers may define film types with different criteria. Those chosen here are not well-established categorizations used in the film industry, if any exist. The language issue is less problematic. Establishing more conservative or liberal rating schemes would in all probability not alter the general significant findings above. However, by limiting the analysis to common individual words, something is missed. Consider the phrase, "I'm going to kill you", or "I am going to have sex with you". Neither would have been counted or reported above; yet each of these have an impact like individual words studied above. These sentences are about sex and violence but they do not contain obscene words. Conversely, consider the phrase "you big fag", which is very hurtful to a six-year old or perhaps a gay male adult but would not be too offensive to adult women or heterosexual males. In analyzing films for children, a different criterion may be needed to speak about offensive insults.

Appendix 1

Films from 1939-1960

Title	Date	Total Number of Bad Words
Bedtime for Bonzo	(1951)	0
Rebel without a Cause	(1955)	1
Casablanca	(1943)	0
Gone with the Wind	(1939)	5
All Quiet on the Western Front	(1958)	0
High Noon	(1952)	0
North by Northwest	(1959)	0
Ruby Gentry	(1952)	0
It's a Wonderful Life	(1947)	0
Gung Ho	(1943)	13
Psycho	(1960)	0
Dial M for Murder	(1955)	0

Films from 1960-1969

A Raisin in the Sun	(1961)	7
Bonnie and Clyde	(1967)	9
Easy Rider	(1969)	12
Fail Safe	(1964)	10
In Cold Blood	(1967)	33
Midnight Cowboy	(1969)	107
Take the Money and Run	(1969)	1
The Graduate	(1969)	13
The Odd Couple	(1967)	10
Who's Afraid of Virginia Woolf	(1966)	46

Films from 1970-1979

Alice Doesn't Live Here Anymore	(1975)	69
Alien	(1979)	58
All that Jazz	(1979)	67
Blazing Saddles	(1974)	105
Coming Home	(1978)	121
Days of Heaven	(1979)	6
Diary of a Mad Housewife	(1970)	69
Great Santini	(1979)	73
M. A. S. H.	(1970)	92
Mean Streets	(1973)	166
North Dallas Forty	(1979)	234
Interiors	(1978)	17
Klute	(1971)	17
Five Easy Pieces	(1970)	61
Rocky	(1976)	36
Portnoy's Complaint	(1972)	93
Carnal Knowledge	(1971)	93
Last Detail	(1973)	221
Woodstock	(1970)	30
One Flew Over the Cukoo's Nest	(1975)	54

Films with Female Leads-1980s

Witches of Eastwick	(1987)	38
9 to 5	(1980)	28
Moonstruck	(1989)	10
Fatal Attraction	(1987)	35
Silkwood	(1983)	28
The Rose	(1979)	92
The Morning After	(1986)	26
Aliens	(1986)	72

Norma Rae	(1979)	38
Liquid Sky	(1983)	138
Extremities	(1986)	40
Frances	(1982)	48

Films with Male Leads-1980's

Breathless	(1983)	25
Color of Money	(1986)	86
Return of the Secaucus 7	(1981)	60
Bull Durham	(1988)	153
Terminator	(1984)	29
Lethal Weapon	(1987)	149
The Verdict	(1982)	26
Atlantic City	(1981)	37
Repo Man	(1984)	184
Big Chill	(1984)	49
Ordinary People	(1980)	69
Blade Runner	(1982)	8
On Golden Pond	(1981)	80
Stakeout	(1987)	96
Spike of Bensonhurst	(1987)	159

Other Films from the 1980's

Streamers	(1983)	280
E. T.	(1982)	13
Wish You Were Here	(1987)	117
Scarface	(1983)	299
Splash	(1984)	29

Table 1. *Curse Words, Film Type and Film Date.*

	Pre 1960	1960's	1970's	1980's	Mean
Sample #	12	10	20	31	
Mean Words	1.58	24.8	84.1	81.03	61.10
Males	1.5	22.6	71.75	61.55	4.14
Females	.08	2.2	12.25	19.48	1.95
F&S	0	.4	21.3	34.71	20.63
H&D		53%		12%	

Table 2. *Male and Female Lead Films 1980's.*

	Male Lead Film		Female Lead Film
Mean Total Words	80.66	>	49.41
F&S	29.4	=	21.83
H&D	10%		15%
Male Speaker	69.46	>	23.58
Female Speaker	11.2	<	25.83

Note - The material on cursing in American film were adapted from a paper originally presented at the meeting of the Popular Culture Association in March of 1990 at Toronto, Canada.

Chapter 7

Unfinished Business and Future Research with Dirty Words

There is much more to the story of how dirty words are used in American English than the previous few chapters have revealed. A reading of the literature recorded into the bibliography shows that much of the material listed there was not included in the discussions above. While all of the research in the bibliography is important, some of it did not fit into the organization of the chapter subjects. Other research remains too preliminary to offer conclusions at the present time. The purpose of this final discussion is to consider several fruitful areas for future research on the topic of dirty word use in America.

Some Unfinished Business

There are many loose ends and unanswered questions stemming from the research in the preceding chapters. Of present concern are those issues related to criminal and civil law and those regarding the content of entertainment and news media because these factors have a wide and immediate impact on a large segment of the American population who consume them. The questions and comments about research with media and legal (and all other) issues are meant to spur potential research agenda. They are not meant to be exhaustive or, if answered, conclusive with regard to the topic. Some of these are follow-up questions to previous research, some are new directions on old topics.

Verbal Sexual Harassment. Lawyers, employers, labor union leaders personnel managers and employees need a clearer definition of what words and phrases constitute verbal sexual harassment. Terms such as "sexual innuendo" and "unwanted sexual remarks" are too vague and broad. Workers and managers need to know where boundaries of acceptable behavior are. More research utilizing the work force population as subjects is suggested. These samples would logically include government and military personnel. Research on verbal sexual harassment may be related to sexual humor and joking, gender related insults and the powerful influence of social-physical setting on use of dirty language. Another source of data can be the court records and proceedings of cases involving verbal sexual harassment. Labor and civil actions in these cases may specify the language in question.

Fighting Words and Disorderly Conduct. Law enforcement personnel, judges, and lawyers, as well as citizens, need a clearer definition of what language constitutes a violation of disorderly conduct or fighting words statutes. While these criminal laws differ by community and by state, the people involved with these decisions would benefit from good psychological or social science data regarding Americans' impressions and perceptions of fighting language. There is also a need for the legal concept of fighting language to separate the use of dirty or insulting words from a verbal threat of a physical attack. Threats are more likely to provoke a retaliation than the use of a dirty word alone, but research should be conducted to demonstrate the causative factor(s) of fighting behavior because many of these court cases include both threats to physical harm and dirty language, and it is not clear whether threats or language should be the basis for judgment.

The line between First Amendment rights and criminal conduct must be made clearer. This is true with respect to cases of obscenity and those where language use is considered to be a form of racial discrimination. As American culture becomes more diverse and minority populations increase, the issue of racial discrimination and racial slurs becomes more important. Is a slur the basis of a discrimination suit or a violation of a fighting words statute? The answer in part depends on the listener's reaction to and interpretation of the language used. Further research on Americans' reactions to language would help the courts decide the nature of "the average person" in question. What language is considered discriminatory by the average American? Another more long term project should examine how a persistent exposure to racial slurs, ethnic derogation and language stereotyping affects minority group children over the course of development.

Media Content, Restrictions and Impact. Here is a broad and diverse class of language material. Initial research projects could be limited to one medium. In the text, a project examining language in motion pictures was presented. This method could be adopted for content analyses in television, cable television, radio and print media. The purpose of these analyses would be to describe the frequency and offensiveness of the language used in widely consumed media. A later study would examine the impact of this language on users. One has to wonder about how dirty language affects populations such as children, non-native speakers or other subgroups of the American population.

As for the issue of obscene speech and media content, the year 1990 marked increased public pressure to further control the production of recordings and motion pictures through labeling and classification. The motion picture industry created a new label for films that appear artistically violent and sexual in nature but not X-rated; thus emerged the rating NC-17. It would be informative to compare language differences in NC-17 and X-rated films. It is still not clear what words and phrases constitute "explicit" lyrics to the music recording industry. Several cases in 1990 focused on the content of recordings as "obscene" speech, while the boundaries between obscene and non-obscene words are not clear in court rulings. Another line of research would examine the interpretation that children and young adults give to the words and phrases they perceive in the songs they hear. Does the average teenager hear the sexual innuendo and figurative language and interpret it as sexual or violent in nature? What is the impact of such figurative language on personality: thought or behavior? Further, how are the dirty words and phrases of black street language interpreted by black speakers versus those who do not know this slang and jargon? Is it appropriate for white speakers to make judgments about how black language may influence non-black children?

Aggression and Deviance. The model of aggression specified in chapter 3 needs to be validated in the laboratory and in more natural settings. A simple question involves the pragmatic value of using dirty language to vent frustration and aggression: why do speakers use these words instead of others? Another line of research should compare physical and verbal aggression, especially in samples that do not consist solely of college psychology students. There is research to indicate that undereducated people have poorer coping skills than educated people. Poor coping strategies may result in more extreme verbal and physical reactions to frustration or threat of harm. While the role of alcohol consumption with verbal and physical aggression has been documented, how dirty word use is affected by alcohol consumption is not known.

Studies of verbal aggression should be expanded to include deviant subgroups, such as street gangs, psychopaths, violent criminals and sex abusers. The purpose here is to compare how these nonnormal people use dirty language relative to normal speakers. It may be that some quality of deviants' language use is different and that the difference could be exploited to help identify members of deviant groups. As a related issue consider the following. It may be the case that sexually abused children are exposed to a lexicon about body parts, products and processes at an earlier age and to a greater extent than are nonabused children. The appearance of language differences in young children, as such, could be used to indicate the potential threat to a young child's life. Another reason to sample these populations is to determine the pragmatic function that dirty language plays in the group, e.g., aggression, humor, dominance or racial hatred.

Humor and Comic Strips. Although the topic of humor appreciation was mentioned in relation to children's acquisition of dirty language, the role of dirty words in humor appreciation by children and adults has not been explained by psycholinguists. It is true that several books and journals have explored the nature of humor in general terms but humor appreciation with dirty language in natural settings (e.g., bars, concerts, or parties) has not gained the attention of those interested in language processes. Some interesting questions might involve the use of taboo versus nontaboo words in the same joke frame: which is funnier and why? What gender and personality variables underlie humor appreciation for aggressive, neutral or dirty jokes? How does social economic status or education contribute to the appreciation of dirty jokes?

Another line of questions involves the nature and impact of comic strip humor. There have been several studies on the nature of comic strips with regard to sexism, gender stereotyping and aggression (Brabant & Mooney, 1986; Mooney & Brabant, 1990), however content analyses and impact studies of comics with dirty words remain to be conducted and published. Preliminary work in this laboratory indicated that the use of insults, profanity and other dirty words is widespread in large, regional newspapers. One has to wonder how this language is perceived by children and adults and further, what is the impact of this language on those who read the comics. Another question of interest to the author is: at what age do children know that people in the comics are insulting each other? And, when do children know what the cursing symbols, "@#&*!", mean?

Humor in other media, such as television, videotaped movies and audio recordings may also be examined. The point of these studies would be to document the type of dirty words used in these media and how extensively such language appears. Psychologists could then examine the influence of dirty language humor on the consumer. Perhaps the development of a large database is the first step.

The Relation between Spoken Language and Other Forms of Expression

How are dirty words related to other forms of emotional expression? In particular, it would be informative to relate the material on spoken language to the use of graffiti and nonverbal, dirty gestures.

Graffiti. The nature of the lexicon used in speech versus graffiti should be compared. Gender differences, age of acquisition and the function of such language could be studied. The role of emotional expression in adolescence and deviant subcultures and gangs would seem to be important.

Nonverbal Gestures. The nature and scope of "obscene" gestures should be compared to spoken language counterparts, where identified. The relative frequencies and offensiveness of some of these have been estimated but no field studies clarifying the pragmatics of gestures have been found. The function of such communication and acquisition have not been addressed by current research. It might be necessary at some point to indicate how gestures are related to stages of sentence production and compare non-obscene gesturing with the obscene types.

Race and Ethnicity

Within the borders of the United States there are rapidly growing Hispanic and Asian populations, along with others from all over the globe. Two immediate questions arise, how will these non-native speakers acquire dirty language and what terms from their languages will become included in American English? Some Hispanic terms have already been employed in American motion pictures, along with those of Italian and French origin. A logical follow-up would be to address the interpretation and impact of these episodes on American listeners. Do Americans recognize the swearing frames from other cultures and make assumptions about what is being said, or do these foreign language episodes attract minimal attention and memory from listeners?

Minority groups in America have been the target of racial slurs and verbal abuse from competing social groups in contact with them. It would seem that social workers and public officials would benefit from understanding the nature of cursing and insults among minority groups. Any Americans in contact with non-native speakers should be interested in the nature of taboos and offensiveness of language in order to reduce abusive or offensive communication.

Language of the Elderly

The population of the American elderly will continue to grow into the next century. The use of dirty language in this segment has been ignored. Emotional expression, senile decline and Alzheimer's disease are areas directly related to the use of dirty words. Researchers in the author's laboratory are collecting data from a population of elderly in nursing homes but a much broader sample of healthy adults is needed also. These data would provide information for families of the elderly with reasons for and descriptions of the kinds of language they hear from their older relatives with aging problems accompanied by frequent dirty language use.

Neurological and Physiological Issues

Several brain syndromes have been associated with the use of taboo speech but no comprehensive explanation has emerged to indicate the neurological background of the episodes. The most well-known studies are on the nature of Tourette's Syndrome (TS), the disease associated with chronic use of obscene speech and other unusual forms of expression. It would be interesting to compare the lexicon of TS patients with more normal forms of swearing. Several reports have shown the use of obscene speech following brain surgery and after a stroke. The type of language used and the neurological causes need to be specified. After surgery, where is the point that normal language is limited by brain dysfunction but obscene language remains intact? Another issue related to neurological health is the use of obscene language in a "retarded" adult population. One wonders how these speakers learned the language, how the obscene lexicon compares with their other channels of communication and what social or pragmatic functions obscene speech plays in their daily lives. As psychologists are turning more and more to physiological bases to explain human behavior, there appears to be a great deal to be found in studies relating the brain and obscenity.

Health and Communication

Because dirty language has been around for several hundred years, we can conclude it must fulfill some useful function in human communication. The commonplace expression "letting off steam" would seem to indicate that dirty words have some cathartic effect for users in relieving anxiety, tension or frustration. There have appeared in psychological literature on stress many papers regarding physical methods of stress release but not much attention has been paid to the "getting it off your chest" through the use of dirty words. It may be useful to use Type A and Type B personality classifications to examine how such people use obscenity to deal with anger. It has been reported that Type A's have difficulty with hostility and frequently use obscene speech.

In much of the literature on sexual behavior, dirty words are viewed negatively. For example, obscene phone calls, pornography, sexual harassment, coprolalia and verbal child abuse are all harmful in some way to users and/or listeners. Are there any sexual behaviors that are enhanced positively by the use of dirty words? Why are obscene words used during sexual intercourse? How are dirty words used in intimate relationships, as terms of endearment or enticement? Research in this area would attempt to show the positive use of dirty language in human sexual behavior.

A related issue is the role of dirty language in doctor and patient conversations. First, to what degree are taboo words used in psychotherapy and, secondly, what is the effect of patient versus counselor use? Does cursing help patients express anger and frustration or does it provide a poor channel of expression? Are doctors who curse more or less credible, more or less effective, as a result of such use? In another setting, how does the family physician use dirty language in routine examination? Do child or adult patients use euphemisms or dirty words for body parts, processes and products? Are there certain parts of the country or certain social, economic factors that are related to the use of dirty language? Do military doctors use a different and more vulgar language than those in private practice? What vulgar and slang terms are used by gynecologists and their patients? Is the use of slang necessary to give sexual advice to the young or undereducated patients? The answers to these medical questions would not only advance the field of psycholinguistics but may influence the way patients are treated in the United States.

Cognitive Psychology and Linguistic Disciplines

Although there has been rapid growth in the fields of cognitive psychology (human information processing) and linguistic theory in the last 30 years, the role of dirty language in these disciplines has been ignored. The present text provides ample evidence that dirty language is woven into the fabric of American language and thought and to ignore the frequent phenomenon is to give an incomplete picture of the higher mental processes of human beings. Psychologists have no idea of the effect of dirty language on memory, perception, attention, vigilance, discourse processing or "normal" communication.

In the field of linguistics, there has been no serious attempt to specify how taboo words relate to nontaboo counterparts. Where do taboo words fit in a model of language competence or syntactic structure? The interpretation of taboo language has a great deal to do with prosody, another area of study for linguists. Our knowledge about metaphors, figurative language and cliches should be expanded to include the very common use of taboo language in these types of speech. One would also think that the quest for language universals should include taboos, insults and obscene speech types. Finding such language universals would make cross-language comparisons necessary.

What about the use of dirty language in populations with speech disorders? What is the role of taboo speech in the hearing impaired? What is the nature and scope of dirty language use among those who use sign language? How are dirty words signed in American Sign Language? There have been very few papers related to these groups with speaking and hearing difficulty. Likewise the use of taboo speech among the blind may also provide an interesting area of study.

Social Forces

Social sciences have always been interested in the differences between individual behavior and behavior under the influence of social forces or in a setting with bystanders. There are many possibilities for research and these data would be important for those interested in mass communication, teleconferencing, persuasion, advertising, marketing, management and government. Are people who use taboo speech more or less credible or persuasive? How are dirty words used to intimidate people? What ritualistic functions do they provide for social groups in terms of religious, athletic, fraternal, law enforcement, military and government groups? How is the use of power or superordinate/subordinate relationships related to the use of dirty words or dirty jokes? How does one's use of dirty language influence the perceptions or impressions one forms about a speaker? How does the relationship between speakers/listeners affect the production and comprehension of dirty words? In what way do the media define or promote stereotyping through the use of taboo words? Does the use of dirty words provide a type of bonding or cohesion for speakers in a group setting? These are just some of the questions that need to be addressed at the social or group level.

Improved Methodology

The last area covered for future consideration is the use of better methodology. The issues here involve sampling, materials, control and setting.

Sampling. Too much of the information accumulated on the use of dirty words is limited to white, middle class, American college students. Younger and older, less educated, minority, non-native speakers and more working class groups need to be surveyed. These data should include both laboratory and natural setting research. The inclusion of religiousness and geographic location has also been all but ignored except in a few cases. Besides different types of subjects in experiments, additional dependent measures used in testing should be considered. There have been recent advances in methods and equipment used to study brain functioning, perhaps these methods used to study normal and abnormal language brain patterns could be used to monitor obscene language patterns. Also the polygraph device used in "perceptual defense" studies should be re-employed to correlate with offensiveness and frequency ratings. Physiological changes during obscene language use in conversations should also be recorded.

Materials. The advent of film and videotape technology must be exploited to provide more naturalistic and complex materials to be used as stimuli in research. Subjects could be shown videotaped scenes and asked to evaluate their feelings, the materials, the language used or to role-play along with one of the characters in the film. Videotape or audiotape recordings should be employed to obtain language samples in more natural settings. Researchers must bring the issue of ecological validity to the study of dirty words to avoid such invalid and unnatural studies, as were generated under the perceptual defense debate. Many of the motion pictures, music recordings or print media that contain obscene language should be used as stimuli in research. Audience reactions and judgments could also be made in the real settings, i.e., cinema complex or music concert.

Setting. The use of broader samples and more realistic materials will bring the researcher into more natural settings. The role of dirty word use in frustration can be studied at a busy street corner, in a traffic jam, during the lunch hour rush, waiting in line at retail businesses or during telephone conversations. Video and audio tape equipment can be used to examine sporting events, nightclub and bar environments and other settings that are associated with the use of dirty words.

Conclusion

There is plenty of research yet to be done on the topic of dirty words in America. This common and extensive phenomenon deserves the attention of psychologists, linguists and others interested in language and communication. To ignore it is to be ignorant of the totality of human expression.

Bibliography

Summary

   A literature search in psychology and related areas resulted in a compilation of 400+ resources concerned with mental, behavioral, and contextual aspects of the phenomenon of the use of taboo or dirty words. These sources include those previously published in an earlier version of the bibliography (Jay, 1979; 1987). Despite the pervasiveness of this verbal process, little substantive or programmatic research has evolved on the topic. References herein were located by topic, title, subject area, and cross-referencing. A search in 1979 of both *Psychological Abstracts* and *Index Medicus* was conducted. In 1987 a *DIALOG* search was made in the social and related sciences. The guiding principle for reference selection was to identify sources related to mental, behavioral, and sociolinguistic correlates of the verbal phenomenon. The represented areas within the discipline of psychology include psycholinguistics, perception, and methodological literature. Related areas outside of psychology concerned topics dealing with sociology, anthropology, linguistics, medicine, psychiatry, mass communication, humor, folklore, law, homosexuality, women's studies, and culture. Ultimately, these references serve to identify a potentially fruitful, viable, and interesting area of research for psychologists and others interested in verbal aggression, obscenity, free speech, gender differences, and taboo.

Bibliography

Aarons, Z.A. (1958). Notes on a case of maladie des tics. *Psychoanalytic Quarterly*, 27, 194-204.

Abrahams, R.D. (1962). Playing the dozens. *Journal of American Folklore*, 75, 209-220.

Abu-Zahra, N.M., & Antoun, R. (1970). On the modesty of Arab Muslim villages: A reply. *American Anthropologist*, 72(5), 1079-1092.

Alajouanine, T. (1956). Verbal realization in aphasia. *Brain*, 79(1), 1-28.

Alford, Finnegan, & Alford, Richard. (1981). A holo-cultural study of humor. *Ethos*, 9(2), 149-164.

Allen, I.L. (1983). Personal names that became ethnic epithets. *Names*, 31(4), 307-317.

Allen, I.L. (1984). Male sex roles and epithets for ethnic women in American slang. *Sex Roles*, 11(1/2), 43-50.

Aman, R. (1982). Interlingual taboos in advertising: How not to name your product. In R. J. Di Pietro (Ed.), *Linguistics and the professions*. Proceedings of the second annual Delaware symposium on language studies. Norwood, NJ: Ablex Pub. Co. 215-224.

Anisfeld, M., & Lambert, W.E. (1966). When are pleasant words learned faster than unpleasant words? *Journal of Verbal Learning and Verbal Behavior*, 5, 132-141.

Anshen, Frank. (1973). Sex and obscenity at Stony Brook. Unpublished manuscript, State University of New York at Stony Brook.

Archer, J., & Westman, K. (1981). Sex differences in aggressive behavior of schoolchildren. *British Journal of Social Psychology*, 20, 31-36.

Arluke, A., Kutakoff, L., & Levin, J. (1987). Are the times changing? An analysis of gender differences in sexual graffiti. *Sex Roles*, 16 (1/2), 1-7.

Ascher, E. (1948). Psychodynamic consideration in Gilles de la Tourette's disease (Maladie des tics). *American Journal of Psychiatry*, 105, 267-276.

Averill, J.R. (1983). Studies on anger and aggression: Implications for theories of emotion. *American Psychologist*, 38(11), 1145-1160.

Ayoub, M. R., & Barnett, S. A. (1965). Ritualized verbal insult in white high school culture. *Journal of American Folklore*, 78(310), 337-344.

Bailey, L. A., & Timm, L. A. (1976). More on women's--and men's--expletives. *Anthropological Linguistics*, 18(9), 438-449.

Balkanyi, C. (1968). Language, verbalization and superego: Some thoughts on the development of the sense of rules. *International Journal of Psycho-Analysis*, 49(4), 712-718.

Barron, Nancy. (1971). Sex-typed language: The production of grammatical cases. *Acta Sociologica*, 14(1-2), 24-42.

Baudhuin, E.S. (1973). Obscene language and evaluative response: An empirical study. *Psychological Reports*, 32, 399-402.

Bauman, R. (1977). Linguistics, anthropology, and verbal art: Toward a unified perspective, with a special discussion of children's folklore. In M. Saville-Troike (Ed.) *Georgetown University Round Table on Languages and Linguistics*, Washington, D.C.: Georgetown University Press, 13-36.

Bell, R.A., Buerkel-Rothfuss, N.L., & Gore, K. (1987). "Did you bring the yarmulke for the Cabbage Patch Kid?" The idiomatic communication of young lovers. *Human Communication Research*, 14(1), 47-67.

Bennett-Kastor, T. (1988). *Analyzing children's language*. New York: Basil Blackwell.

Berger, A. Swearing and society. (1970). *ETC.: A Review of General Semantics*, 30(3), 283-286.

Berger, K. Conversational English of university students. (1968). *Speech Monographs*, 34, 65-73.

Berges, E.T., Neiderbach, S., Rubin, B., Sharpe, E.F., & Tesler, R.W. (1983). *Children & sex: The parents speak*. New York: Facts on File, 460 Park Ave South, New York, NY, 10016.

Bergler, E. (1936). Obscene words. *Psychoanalytic Quarterly*, 5, 226-248.

Bergsland, Knut, & Vogt, Hans. (1962). On the validity of glottochronology. *Current Anthropology*, 3, 115-153.

Berkowitz, L. (1973). Words and symbols as stimuli to aggressive responses. In J.F. Knutson (Ed.) *The control of aggression*, Chicago: Aldine, 112-143.

Bernard, H. R. (1975). Otomi obscene humor. *Journal of American Folklore*, 88(350), 383-392.

Bersoff, D.N. (1987). Social science data and the Supreme Court: *Lockhart* as a case in point. *American Psychologist*, 42(1), 52-58.

Black, J.W., Stratton, C.S., Nichols, A.C., & Chavez, M.A. (1985). *The use of words in context: The vocabulary of college students*. New York: Plenum.

Blanchard, I. (1966). Socially unacceptable language in a hospital for the mentally retarded. *MR: Mental Retardation*, 4, 10-12.

Bloomfield, L. (1933). *Language*. New York: Holt, Rinehart & Winston.

Bock, D.G., Butler, J.L.P., & Bock, E.H. (1984). The impact of sex of the speaker, sex of the rater and profanity type of language trait errors in speech evaluation: A test of the rating error paradigm. *The Southern Speech Communication Journal*, 49, 177-186.

Boggs, S.T., & Watson-Gegeo, K.A. (1978). Interweaving routines: Strategies for encompassing a social situation. *Language in Society*, 7, 375-392.

Bostrom, R. N., Baseheart, J. R., & Rossiter, C. M.,Jr. (1973). The effects of three types of profane language in persuasive messages. *The Journal of Communication*, 23, 461-475.

Brabant, S., & Mooney, L. (1986). Sexrole stereotyping in the Sunday comics: Ten years later. *Sex Roles*, 14 (3/4), 141-148.

Bronner, S. J. (1978). "Who says?": A further investigation of ritual insults among white American adolescents. *Midwestern Journal of Language and Folklore* 4(2), 53-69.

Bronner, S. J. (1981). Saturday night in Greenville: An interracial tale-and-music session in context. *Folklore Forum*, 14(2), 85-120.

Brown, R. (1973). *A first language: The early stages*. Cambridge, MA: Harvard University Press.

Brown, R.G.B. (1961). Comments on Ross's "Patterns of swearing". *Discovery The Popular Journal of Knowledge*, January, 40.

Brownell, H.H., Potter, H.H., Michelow, D., & Gardner, H. (1984). Sensitivity to lexical denotation and connotation in brain damaged patients: A double dissociation? *Brain and Language* 22(2), 253-264.

Bruce, L. (1963). *How to talk dirty and influence people*. Chicago: HMH.

Burke, J.A. (1983). *The X-rated book: Sex and obscenity in the Bible*. Houston, TX: J.A.B. Press.

Buss, D. M. (1989). Conflict between the sexes: Strategic interference and the evocation of anger and upset. *Journal of Personality and Social Psychology*, 56(5), 735-747.

Butterfield, G. B., & Butterfield, E. C. (1977). Lexical codability and age. *Journal of Verbal Learning and Verbal Behavior*, 16, 113-118.

Cameron, P. (1969). Frequency and kinds of words in various social settings, or what the hell is going on? *Pacific Sociological Review*, 12, 101-104.

Cameron, P. (1970). The words college students use and what they talk about. *Journal of Communication Disorders*, 3, 36-46.

Carroll, J. B., Davies, P., & Richman, B. (1971). *The American heritage word frequency book*. New York: Houghton Mifflin.

Carroll, J. B., & White, M. (1973a). Age-of-acquisition norms for 220 picturable nouns. *Journal of Verbal Learning and Verbal Behavior*, 12, 563-576.

Carroll, J. B., & White, M. (1973b). Word frequency and age of acquisition as determiners of picture and naming frequency. *Quarterly Journal of Experimental Psychology*, 25, 85-95.

Cashman, P. H. (1980). Learning to talk about sex. *SIECUS Report*, 9(1). also appears in *Sexual Medicine Today*, (1981). February, 18-21.

Chapman, A. J., & Foot, H. (Eds.). (1976). *Humor and laughter: Theory, research and applications*. New York: Wiley.

Chapman, A. J., & Foot, H. (Eds.). (1977). *It's a funny thing, humour*. New York: Pergamon.

Chase, R. A., Cullen, J. K., Niedermeyer, E.F.L., Stark, R. E., & Blumer, D. P. (1967). Ictal speech automatisms and swearing: Studies on the auditory feedback control of speech. *The Journal of Nervous and Mental Disease*, 144(5), 406-420.

Chomsky, N. (1968). *Language and mind*. New York: Harcourt, Brace and World.

Closer to understanding what makes Tourette tic. (1981). *Medical Tribune*, July 8, 8.

Coates, J. (1986). *Women, men and language: A sociolinguistic account of sex differences in language*. New York: Longman.

Cohen, M. M., & Saine, T. J. (1977). The role of profanity and sex variables in interpersonal impression formation. *Journal of Applied Communication Research*, 5, 45-51.

Condon, W. S., & Sander, L. W. (1974). Neonate movement is synchronized with adult speech: Interactional participation and language acquisition. *Science*, 183, 99-101.

Cornog, M. (1986). Naming sexual body parts: Preliminary patterns and implications. *The Journal of Sex Research*, 22(3), 393-398.

Cornog, M. (1987). Names for sexual body parts: Regularities in "personal" naming behavior. In L. E. Seits (Ed.), *Festshrift in honor of Allen Walker Read* (number 2), (pp.132-151). Sugar Grove, IL: North Central Name Society.

Coser, Rose Laub. (1960). Laughter among colleagues: A study of the social functions of humor among the staff of a mental hospital. *Psychiatry*, 23, 81-95.

Coyne, J. C., Sherman, R. C., & O'Brien, K. (1978). Expletives and woman's place. *Sex Roles*, 4(6), 827-835.

Crest, Denali. (1974). Those four-letter words of love: Why we use them. *Sexology*, 41(1), 15-18.

Crystal, D. (1971). *Linguistics*. Baltimore: Penguin.

Dawe, H. C. (1934). An analysis of two hundred quarrels of preschool children. *Child Development*, 5, 139-157.

De Grazia, E., & Newman, R.K. (1982). *Banned films: Movies, censors and the First Amendment*. New York: R.R. Bowker.

Devereux, George. (1951). Mohave Indian verbal and motor profanity. *Psychoanalysis and the Social Sciences*, 3, 99-127.

Dictionary of American regional English. (1985). Cambridge, MA: The Belknap Press of Harvard University Press. Vol. 1, A-C.

A dictionary of contemporary and colloquial usage. (1972). New York: Avenel Books. Forward by R. Copperud.

Dictionary of slang and unconventional English by Eric Partridge (1984). P. Beale (Ed.). New York: Macmillan.

Dillard, J. L. (1977). *Lexicon of Black English*. New York: Seabury.

Dirty words and dirty politics: Cognitive dissonance in the first amendment. (1967). *University of Chicago Law Review*, 34, 367-386.

Dixon, N. F. (1971). *Subliminal perception: The nature of a controversy*. London: McGraw-Hill.

Donnerstein, E., Linz, D., & Penrod, S. (1987). *The question of pornography*. New York: The Free Press.

Dreizen, F., & Priestly, T. (1982). A systematic approach to Russian obscene language. *Russian Linguistics*, 6, 233-249.

Driscoll, James, M. (1981). Aggressiveness and frequency-of-aggressive-use ratings for pejorative epithets by Americans. *The Journal of Social Psychology*, 114, 111-126.

Dumas, B.K., & Lighter, J. (1978). Is slang a word for linguists? *American Speech*, 53(1), 5-17.

Dundes, A. (1985). The J.A.P. and the J.A.M. in American jokelore. *Journal of American Folklore*, 98, 456-475.

Durmuller, U. (1988). Sociolinguistic aspects of mural sprayscripts (Graffiti). *Sociolinguistics*, 17(1), 1-16.

Earle, H. H. (1973). *Police recruit training: Stress vs. non-stress*. Springfield, IL: Charles C. Thomas.

Edelsky, C. (1976). The acquisition of communication competence: Recognition of linguistic correlates of sex roles. *Merrill-Palmer Quarterly*, 22(1), 47-59.

Elmendorf, W.W. (1951). Word taboo and lexical change in Coast Salish. *International Journal of American Linguistics*, 17, 205-208.

Emeneau, M.B. (1948). Taboos on animal names. *Language*, 24, 56-63.

meneau, M.B.   (1937). Toda marriage regulations and taboos. *American Anthropologist*, 39, 103-112.

mmett, R. (1981). VNET or GRIPENET? *Datamation*, November, 48-58.

pstein, M.H., Repp, A.C., & Cullinan, D. (1978). *Psychology in the Schools*, 15(3), 419-423.

pstein, N., & Krakower, S. (1974). A measure of verbal aggression. *Perceptual and Motor Skills*, 39, 215-223.

rdelyi, M.H.   (1974). A new look at the new look: Perceptual defense and vigilance. *Psychological Review*, 81, 1-25.

Eriksen, C. W. (1963).   Perception and personality. In J. Wepman & R. Heine (Eds.), *Concepts of personality*. Chicago: Aldine.

Ernster, V.L.   (1975). American menstrual expressions. *Sex Roles*, 1(1), 3-13.

Estrich, R.M., & Sperber, H.   (1952). *Three keys to language*.   New York: Rinehart & Co.

ETC.: A Review of General Semantics. (1968). 25(2), 131-247.
    Special issue: Semantics and sexuality. Note - includes twelve articles on the topic.

Evans-Pritchard, E.E.   (1949). Nuer curses and ghostly vengeance. *Africa*, 19, 288-292.

Evans-Pritchard, E.E. (1929). Some collective expressions of obscenity in Africa. *Journal of the Royal Anthropological Institute of Great Britain and Ireland*, 59, 311-331.

Fain, T. C., & Anderton, D. L. (1987). Sexual harassment: Organizational context and diffuse status. *Sex Roles*, 16 (5/6), 291-311.

Fairbanks, H.   (1944). The quantitative differentiation of samples of spoken language. *Psychological Monographs*, 56, 19-38.

Family Violence Research Program. The Family Research Laboratory, University of New Hampshire, Durham, NH, 03824.   Program description and publications list available on request.

Farb, P. (1975). *Word play*. New York: Bantam.

Farrell, R. A. (1972). The argot of the homosexual subculture. *Anthropological Linguistics*, 14(3), 97-109.

Fay, A. (1977). Sexual problems related to poor communication. *Medical Aspects of Human Sexuality*, June, 48-62.

Feldman, M.J. (1955). The use of obscene words in the therapeutic relationship. *American Journal of Psychoanalysis*, 15(1), 45-49.

Ferenczi, Sandor. (1950). *Sex in psychoanalysis*. New York: Basic Books.

Final report of the Attorney General's commission on pornography. (1986) Nashville: Rutledge Hill Press.

Fine, G.A. (1976). Obscene joking across cultures. *Journal of Communication* Summer, 134-140.

Fine, G.A. (1979). Small groups and culture creation: The idioculture of little league baseball teams. *American Sociological Review*, 44(Oct), 733-745.

Fine, M. G. (1981). Soap opera conversations: The talk that binds. *Journal of Communication*, Summer, 97-107.

Fine, M.G., & Johnson, F.L. (1984). Female and male motives for using obscenity. *Journal of Language and Social Psychology*, 3(1), 59-74.

Fink, L.A. (1948). Our own taboos. *Journal of Sex Education*, 1(3), 100-101.

Fishbein, Morris. (1925). The misuse of medical terms. *American Speech I*, October, 23-25.

Flexner, S.B. (1967). Preface. In Wentworth, H. & Flexner, S.B. (Eds.), *Dictionary of American slang.* New York: Crowell

Flexner, S.B. (1976). *I hear America talking.* New York: Van Nostrand.

Flexner, S.B. (1982). *Listening to America.* New York: Simon & Schuster.

Flores, J. (1987, Fall). Rappin', writin,' & breakin'. *Dissent*, 34(4), 580-584.

Flynn, C.P. (1976). Sexuality and insult behavior. *The Journal of Sex Research*, (1), 1-13.

Foote, R., and Woodward, J. (1973). A preliminary investigation of obscene language. *The Journal of Psychology*, 83, 263-275.

Frank, Francine, & Anshen, Frank. (1984). *Language and the sexes.* Edison, NJ: State University of New York Press (300 Raritan Center Parkway).

French, N.R., Carter, C.W., Jr., Koenig, W., Jr. (1930). The words and sounds of telephone conversations. *Bell System Technical Journal*, 9, 290-324.

Freud, S. (1905). *Jokes and their relation to the unconscious.* London: Hogarth (1960 Edition).

Frodi, A., Macaulay, J., & Thome, P.R. (1977). Are women always less aggressive than men? A review of the experimental literature, *Psychological Bulletin*, 84(4), 634-660.

Fussell, P. (1983). *Class: A guide through the American status system.* New York: Summit.

Fussell, P. (1989). *Wartime: Understanding and behavior in the second world war.* New York: Oxford. Note - Especially Chapters 7 (Chickenshit, An Anatomy) and 9.

Gainotti, G. (1972). Emotional behavior and hemispheric side of the lesion. *Cortex*, 8, 41-55.

Galbraith, G., Hahn, K., & Leiberman, H. (1968). Personality correlates of free-associative sex responses to double-entendre words. *Journal of Consulting and Clinical Psychology*, 32(2), 193-197.

Gallahorn, G. E. (1971). The use of taboo words by psychiatric ward personnel. *Psychiatry*, 34, 309-321.

Gard, S. W. (1980). Fighting words as free speech. *Washington University Law Quarterly*, 58(3), 531-581.

Garner, T. (1983). Playing the dozens: Folklore as strategies for living. *Quarterly Journal of Speech*, 69, 47-57.

Gecas, V., & Libby, R. (1976). Sexual behavior as symbolic interaction. *The Journal of Sex Research*, 12(1), 33-49.

Geen, R. G., & Stonner, D. (1975). Primary associates to 20 verbs connoting violence. *Behavior Research Methods and Instrumentation*, 7(4), 391-392.

Gibson, H.B. (1963). A slang vocabulary test as an indicator of delinquent association. *British Journal of Social and Clinical Psychology*, 2, 50-55.

Gibson, H.B. (1966). The validation of a technique for measuring delinquent association by means of vocabulary. *British Journal of Social and Clinical Psychology*, 5, 190-195.

Gilley, H.M., & Summers, C.S. (1970). Sex differences in the use of hostile verbs. *The Journal of Psychology*, 76, 33-37.

Gilley, H.M., & Perkins, D.C. (1974). Hostile verb use by youthful male prisoners with single vs. multiple offenses. *The Journal of Psychology*, 87, 107-110.

Gold, R. (1957). The vernacular of the jazz world. *American Speech*, 32, 271-282.

Goldstein, K.S. (1967). Bowdlerization and expurgation: Academic and folk. *Journal of American Folklore*, 80(318), 374-386.

Goldstein, S.R., & Gee, E. G. (Eds.). (1980). *Law and public education: Cases and materials (2nd Edition)*. Indianapolis: Bobbs-Merrill, pp 88-111.

Golin, S., & Romanowski, M. A. (1977). Verbal aggression as a function of sex of subject and sex of target. *The Journal of Psychology*, 97, 141-149.

Gonzales-Reigosa, F. (1972). The anxiety-arousing effect of taboo words in bilinguals (Doctoral dissertation, The Florida State University) Dissertation Abstracts International, 33(07-B), 3303. (University Microfilms No. GAX73-00210)

Goodenough, F. L. (1931). *Anger in young children*. Westport, CT: Greenwood Press.

Gorman, W. (1964). Body words. *Psychoanalytic Review*, 51, 15-25.

Graham, M. A. (1986). Obscenity and profanity at work. *Employee Relations Law Journal*, 11, 662-677.

Grahn, Judy. (1984). *Another mother tongue: Gay words, gay worlds*. New York Harper (Beacon).

Greenberg, B. S. (1976). The effects of language intensity modification on perceived verbal aggressiveness. *Communication Monographs*, 43, 130-139.

Greene, D. R. (1988). Verbal abuse of teachers: The conflict between free expression and the orderly administration of the school. *Journal of Law and Education*, 17(3), 545-553.

Gregersen, E. A. (1979). Sexual linguistics. *Annals of New York Academy of Sciences*, 327, 3-19.

Grosser, G.S., & Laczek, W.J. (1963). Prior parochial vs. secular secondary education and utterance latencies to taboo words. *The Journal of Psychology*, 55, 263-277.

Grosser, G.S., & Walsh, A.A. (1966). Sex differences in the differential recall of taboo and neutral words. *The Journal of Psychology*, 63, 219-227.

Gui-sen, Tian (1987). A sociolinguistic analysis of linguistic taboos in Chinese. M.A. Thesis, Beijing Foreign Studies University, Beijing, China.

Haas, A. (1981). Partner influences on sex-associated spoken language of children. *Sex Roles*, 7(9),925-935.

Haas, A. (1979). Male and female spoken language differences: Stereotypes and evidence. *Psychological Bulletin*, 86(3), 616-626.

Haas, M.R. (1951). Interlingual word taboos. *American Anthropologist*, 53, 338-344.

Haertzen, C. A., Eisenberg, H. A., Hooks, N. T., Jr., Ross, F. E., & Pross, M. (1979). Estimating specificity of drug and alcohol subcultural groups with slang names for drugs. *Journal of Consulting and Clinical Psychology*, 47(3), 592-594.

Haertzen, C. A., & Ross, F. E. (1979). Does the frequency of definitions for a particular drug in slang dictionaries predict quality of knowledge of the slang? *Psychological Reports*, 44, 1031-1039.

Haertzen, C. A., Ross, F. E., & Hooks, N. T., Jr. (1979). Slang knowledge as an indicator of a general social deviancy subcultural factor. *Perceptual and Motor Skills*, 48, 1235-1240.

Haggerty, Laura C.G. (1930). What a two-and-one-half-year-old child said in one day. *Journal of Genetic Psychology*, 37, 75-101.

aiman, F.S. (1972). The fighting words doctrine: From Chaplinsky to Brown. *Iowa Journal of Speech*, 3(1), 3-31.

alaby, R., & Long, C. (1979). Future shout: Name calling in the future. *Maledicta*, 3, 61-68.

all, P., & Jay, T. B. (1988, March). Children's use of obscene speech. Presented at Popular Culture Association Meeting, New Orleans.

all, W.S., Nagy, W.E., & Linn, R. (1984). *Spoken words: Effects of situation and social group on oral word usage and frequency.* Hillsdale, NJ: Erlbaum.

ansen, C. H., & Hansen, R. D. (1990). Rock music videos and antisocial behavior. *Basic and Applied Social Psychology*, 11(4), 357-369.

arrell, W. A. (1981). Verbal aggressiveness in spectators at professional hockey games: The effects of tolerance of violence and amount of exposure to hockey. *Human Relations*, 34(8), 643-655.

Harris, M.B. (1973). Field studies of modeled aggression. *The Journal of Social Psychology*, 89, 131-139.

Harris, M.B. (1974). Aggressive reactions to a frustrating phone call. *The Journal of Social Psychology*, 92, 193-198.

Harris, M. B. (1974). Mediators between frustration and aggression in a field experiment. *Journal of Experimental Social Psychology*, 10, 561-571.

Harris, M.B., & Samerotte, G. (1975). The effects of aggressive and altruistic modeling on subsequent behavior. *The Journal of Social Psychology*, 95, 173-182.

Harrison, S.I., & Hinshaw, M.W. (1968). When children use obscene language. *Medical Aspects of Human Sexuality*, 2(12), 6-11.

Hartford, R. J. (1972). A social penetration model for obscene language (Doctoral dissertation, University of Maryland). Dissertation Abstracts International, 34(02-A), 861. (University Microfilms No. GAX73-18243)

Hartmann, L. (1975). Children's use of dirty words. *Medical Aspects of Human Sexuality*, 9, 111-112.

Hartmann, L. (1973). Some uses of dirty words by children. *Journal of the American Academy of Child Psychiatry*, 12(1), 108-122.

Hartup, W.H. (1974). Aggression in childhood: Developmental perspectives. *American Psychologist*, 29, 336-341.

Hayden, M.G. (1913). Terms of disparagement in American dialect speech. *Dialect Notes*, 4, 194-223.

Hayes, J. J. (1976). Gayspeak. *Quarterly Journal of Speech*, 62, 256-266.

Helffrich, S. (1962). Broadcast censorship: Past, present, future. *Televisic Quarterly*, 1(4).

Helfrich, H. (1979). Age markers in speech. In Scherer and Giles (Eds.), *Socic markers in speech*. Cambridge: Cambridge University Press.

Hellmann, J.M., Jr. (1973). I'm a monkey: The influence of the Black America blues argot on the Rolling Stones. *Journal of American Folklore*, 8(367-373.

Hemphill, M.R., & Pfeiffer, A.L. (1986). Sexual spillover in the workplace: Testin, the appropriateness of male-female interaction. *Women's Studies i Communication*, 9 (Fall), 52-66.

Hendrick, C., & Hendrick, S. (1983). *Liking, loving, & relating*. Belmont, CA Brooks/Cole.

Henningsen, H. (1957). Taboo-words among seamen and fishermen. *The Mariner's Mirror*, 43(4), 336-337.

Herek, G. M. (1989). Hate crimes against lesbians and gay men. *Americar Psychologist*, 44(6), 948-955.

Hermann, Imre. (1949). The giant mother, the phallic mother, obscenity. *Psychoanalytic Review*, 36, 302-307.

Hertzler, Joyce O. (1965). *A sociology of language*. New York: Random House.

Hess, E. H. (1965). Attitude and pupil size. *Scientific American*, 212, 46-54.

Heubusch, N. J., & Horan, J. J. (1977). Some effects of counselor profanity in counseling. *Journal of Counseling Psychology*, 24(5), 456-458.

Hochman, G. (1980). The disease that makes you curse. *Science Digest Special*, Sept/Oct, 88-116.

Holland, D., & Quinn, N. (Eds.). (1987). *Cultural models in language and thought*. New York: Cambridge University Press.

Holland, D., & Skinner, D. (1987). Prestige and intimacy. In D. Holland and N. Quinn (Eds.), *Cultural models in language and thought*. New York: Cambridge University Press.

Hollander, R. (1960). Compulsive cursing: An approach to factors in its genesis, development, and pathology. *Psychiatric Quarterly*, 34, 599-622.

Homer, J. (1979). *Jargon: How to talk to anyone about anything*. New York: Times Books.

Honigmann, John. (1944). A cultural theory of obscenity. *Journal of Criminal Psychopathology*, 5, 715-733.

Iowes, D. (1964). Application of the word-frequency concept to aphasia. In A. V. S. De Reuck and M. O'Connor (Eds.), *Disorders of language*. Boston: Little, Brown and Co.

Iunter, E.R. & Gaines, B.E. (1938). Verbal taboo in a college community. *American Speech*, 13, 97-107.

Iymes, D. (1964). *Language in culture and society*. New York: Harper and Row.

Iymes, D. (1960). Lexicostatics so far. *Current Anthropology*, 1(1), 3-44.

Iymes, D. (1971). The contribution of folklore to sociolinguistic research. *Journal of American Folklore*, 84(331-334), 42-50.

Infante, D.A., & Wigley, C.J., III. (1986). Verbal aggressiveness: an interpersonal model and measure. *Communication Monographs*, 53, 61-69.

Inge, T.M. (1990). *Comics as culture*. Jackson, MS: University Press of Mississippi.

Jackson, Bruce. (1966). White dozens and bad sociology. *Journal of American Folklore*, 79(312), 374-377.

James, J. (1972). Two domains of streetwalker argot. *Anthropological Linguistics*, 14(5), 172-181.

Jay, T.B. (1976). Impressions formed from taboo adjective descriptions. Unpublished Doctoral dissertation, Kent State University.

Jay, T.B. (1977). Doing research with dirty words. *Maledicta: The International Journal of Verbal Aggression*, 1(2), 234-256.

Jay, T. B. (1978a). A plea for help. *Interfaces: Linguistics and Psychoanalysis Newsletter*, 10, 14-15.

Jay, T. B. (1978b). Are you confused about dirty words? Presented at the Interdisciplinary Conference on Linguistics, Louisville.

Jay, T.B. (1978c). Are you confused about dirty words? North Adams, MA: North Adams State College. (ERIC Document Reproduction Service No. ED 158 610)

Jay, T. B. (1979). A bibliography of research on dirty word usage. *Catalogue of Selected Documents in Psychology*, 9, 77.

Jay. T. B. (1980a). A frequency count of college and elementary school students' colloquial English. *Catalogue of Selected Documents in Psychology*, 10, 1.

Jay, T. B. (1980b). Sex roles and dirty word usage: A review of the literature and reply to Haas. *Psychological Bulletin*, 88(3), 614-621.

Jay, T. B. (1981). Comprehending dirty word descriptions. *Language and Speech*, 24(1), 29-38.

Jay, T. B. (1985). The role of obscene speech in psychology. *Interfaces*, 12 (3, 75-91.

Jay, T. B. (1986, April). 2170 Obscene words: Who, what, where, when. Presented at Eastern Psychological Association, New York.

Jay, T. B. (1987). A maledicta bibliography. *Maledicta*, 9, 207-224.

Jay, T. B. (1988, March). Beer drinking in American film. Presented at Popular Culture Association meeting, New Orleans.

Jay, T. B. (1989, March). The emergence of an obscene lexicon. Presented at Eastern Psychological Association, Boston, MA.

Jay, T. B. (1990a, March). The evolution of cursing in American film. Presented at meeting of Popular Culture Association, Toronto.

Jay, T. B. (1990b, March). What are "fighting words"? Presented at Eastern Psychological Association, Philadelphia.

Jay, T. B., & Burke, T. (1980, April). Male and female differences in dirty word usage. Presented at Eastern Psychological Association, Hartford, CT.

Jay, T. B., & Danks, J. H. (1977). Ordering of taboo adjectives. *Bulletin of the Psychonomic Society*, 9, 405-408.

Jeffers, H.P., & Levitan, D. (1971). *See Parris & die: Brutality in the U.S. Marines*. New York: Hawthorn.

Jespersen, Otto. (1922). *Language: Its nature, development, and origin*. New York: Henry Holt and Co.

Jesser, C.J. (1978). Male responses to direct verbal sexual initiatives of females. *The Journal of Sex Research*, 14, 118-128.

Joesten, J. (1935). Calling names in any language. *American Mercury*, 36, 483-487.

Joffe, N. (1948). The vernacular of menstruation. *Word*, 4, 181-186.

The Jonathan David dictionary of popular slang. (1980). Middle Village, NY: Jonathan David.

Johnson, Burges. (1948). *The lost art of profanity*. New York: The Bobbs-Merrill Company.

Johnson, Falk. (1950). The history of some "dirty" words. *American Mercury*, 71, 538-545.

Johnson, F.L., & Fine, M.G. (1985). Sex differences in uses and perceptions of obscenity. *Women's Studies in Communication*, 8, 11-24

Johnson, G.B. (1927). Double meaning in the popular Negro blues. *Journal of Abnormal and Social Psychology*, 30, 12-20.

ohnson, R. D. (1973). Folklore and women: A social interactional analysis of the folklore of a Texas madam. *Journal of American Folklore*, 86, 211-224.

ones, L. V., & Wepman, J. M. (1966). *A spoken word count.* Chicago: Language Research Associates.

oreen. The bitch manifesto. (1973). In Koedt, A., Levine, E., & Rapone, A. (Eds.), *Radical feminism.* New York: Quadrangle, 50-59.

Kalcik, S. (1975). Like Ann's gynecologist or the time I was almost raped. *Journal of American Folklore*, 88(347-350), 3-11.

Kanner, L. (1944). A philological note on sex organ nomenclature. *Psychoanalytic Quarterly*, 14, 228-233.

Keker, J.W. & Want, W.L. (1970). Offensive speech and the FCC. *The Yale Law Journal*, 79(7), 1343-1368.

Kemper, S. (1984). When to speak like a lady. *Sex Roles*, 10, 435-444.

Key, M.R. (1972). Linguistic behavior of male and female. *Linguistics*, 88, 15-31.

Key, M.R. (1975). *Male/Female behavior.* Metuchen, NJ: Scarecrow Press.

Kiesler, S., Siegel, J., & McGuire, T. W. (1984). Social psychological aspects of computer-mediated communication. *American Psychologist*, 39(10), 1123-1134.

The Kinsey Institute for Research in Sex, Gender & Reproduction, Inc. 416 Morrison Hall, Indiana University, Bloomington, IN 47405.
Note - good source of bibliographies on a variety of topics.

Klerk, V. de. (1990). Slang: A male domain? *Sex Roles*, 22(9/10), 589-606.

Klofas, J., & Cutshall, C. (1985). Unobtrusive research methods in criminal justice: Using graffiti in the reconstruction of institutional cultures. *Journal of Research in Crime and Delinquency*, 22(4), 355-373.

Klofas, J., & Cutshall, C. (1985). The social archeology of a juvenile facility: Unobtrusive methods in the study of institutional cultures. *Qualitative Sociology*, 8(4), 368-387.
Note - full version of *JRC&D* immediately above.

Koedt, A., Levine, E., & Rapone, A. (1973). *Radical feminism.* New York: Quadrangle.

Kottke, J. L., & MacLeod, C. D. (1989). Use of profanity in the counseling interview. *Psychological Reports*, 65, 627-634.

Kramarae, Cheris. (1981). *Women and men speaking: Frameworks for analysis.* Rowley, MA: Newbury House.

Kramer, C. (1974). Women's speech: Separate but unequal? *The Quarterly Journal of Speech*, 60, 14-24.

Kreutzer, J. S., Schneider, H. G., & Myatt, C. R. (1984). Alcohol, aggression and assertiveness in men: Dosage and expectancy effects. *Journal of Studies on Alcohol*, 45(3), 275-278.

Kroeber, A.L. (1952). *The nature of culture*. Chicago: The University of Chicago Press.

Kroeber, A.L. (1960). Yurok speech uses. In Stanley Diamond (Ed.), *Culture in history: Essays in honor of Paul Radin*. New York: Columbia University Press.

Kucera, H., & Francis, W. N. (1967). *Computational analysis of present-day American English*. Providence: Brown University Press.

Kulik, J.A., Sarbin, T.R., & Stein, K.B. (1971). Language, socialization, and delinquency. *Developmental Psychology*, 4(3), 434-439.

Kunene, D.P. (1958). Notes on Hlonepha among southern Sotha. *African Studies (Johannesburg)*, 17(3), 159-183.

Kutner, N.G. & Brogan, D. (1974). An investigation of sex-related slang vocabulary and sex-role orientation among male and female university students. *Journal of Marriage and the Family*, 36(3), 474-483.

LaBarre, Weston. (1955). Obscenity: An anthropological appraisal. *Law and Contemporary Problems*, 20, 533-543.

LaBarre, Weston. (1939). The psychopathology of drinking songs. A study of the content of the "normal unconscious". *Psychiatry*, 2, 203-212.

Lachman, R., Shaffer, J. P., & Hennrikus, D. (1974). Language and cognition: Effects of stimulus codability, name-word frequency, and age of acquisition on lexical reaction time. *Journal of Verbal Learning and Verbal Behavior*, 13, 613-625.

Lakoff, Robin. (1973). Language and woman's place. *Language in Society*, 2, 45-80.

Larsen, V.L. (1963). Psychological study of colloquial menstrual expressions. *Northwest Medicine*, 62, 874-877.

Lawrence, Barbara. (1974). Dirty words can harm you. *Redbook*, May 143, 33.

Lawrence, D.H. (1957). *Lady Chatterley's lover*. New York: Grove Press.

Leach, E. (1966). Anthropological aspects of language: Animal categories and verbal abuse. In E.H. Lenneberg (Ed.), *New directions in the study of language*. Cambridge: MIT Press, 23-63.

Leach, E. (1958). Concerning Trobriand clans and the kinship category "tabu". In Jack Goody (Ed.), *The development cycle in domestic groups*. Cambridge: The University Press.

_eerhsen, C. (1988). Push-button pleasures, dial-tone dreams. *Rolling Stone*, 532, 71-73.

Leff, L. J., & Simmons, J. L. (1990). *The dame in the kimono.* New York: Grove Weidenfeld. Hollywood censorship 1920-1960.

Legman, G. (1968). *Rationale of the dirty joke.* New York: Grove.

Legman, G. (1975). *No laughing matter: Rationale of the dirty joke (second series).* New York: Bell.

Legman, G. (1977). A word for it! *Maledicta: The International Journal of Verbal Aggression*, 1(1), 9-18.

Legman, G. (1990). "Unprintable" folklore? The Vance Randolph collection. *Journal of American Folklore*, 103, 259-300.

Lerman, P. (1967). Argot, symbolic deviance, and subcultural delinquency. *American Sociological Review*, 32, 209-224.

Leslau, W. (1952). A footnote on interlingual word taboos. *American Anthropologist*, 54, 274.

Leslau, W. (1959). Taboo expressions in Ethiopia. *American Anthropologist*, 61, 105-107.

Lesser, R. (1978). *Linguistic investigations of aphasia.* London: Arnold.

Lewis, Mallie. (1974). Appelant vs. City of New Orleans. *The Criminal Law Reporter*, 14(20), 3097-3101.

Ley, D., & Cybriwsky, R. (1974). Urban graffiti as territorial markers. *Annals of the Association of American Geographers*, 64(4), 491-505.

Ley, R. G., & Bryden, M. P. (1979). Hemispheric differences in processing emotions and faces. *Brain and Language*, 7, 127-138.

Loewy, Arnold H. (1967). Free speech: The "missing link" in the law of obscenity. *Journal of Public Law*, 16, 82-106.

Lovaas, O.I. (1961). Interaction between verbal and nonverbal behavior. *Child Development*, 32, 329-336.

Love, A. M., & Deckers, L. H. (1989). Humor appreciation as a function of sexual, aggressive, and sexist content. *Sex Roles*, 20(11/12), 649-654.

Lowry, D. T., Love, G., & Kirby, M. (1981). Sex on the soap operas: Patterns of intimacy. *Journal of Communication*, Summer, 90-96.

Lucca, N., & Pacheco, A. M. (1986). Children's graffiti: Visual communication from a developmental perspective. *The Journal of Genetic Psychology*, 147(4), 465-479.

Mabry, Edward. (1975). A multivariate investigation of profane language. *Central States Speech Journal*, 26, 39-44.

Mabry, Edward. (1974). Dimensions of profanity. *Psychological Reports*, 35 387-391.

Macnamara, J. (1982). *Names for things*. Cambridge, MA: The MIT Press.

Macy, John. (1923). A cursory view of swearing. *The Bookman*, 57(6), 593-600.

Mahler, M. & Rangell, L.A. (1943). Psychosomatic study of maladie des tics (Gilles de la Tourette's disease). *Psychiatric Quarterly*, 17, 579-603.

Maledicta: The International Journal of Verbal Aggression, P.O. Box 14123, Santa Rosa, CA 95402-6123.

Malovich, N. J., & Stake, J. E. (1990). Sexual harassment on campus: Individual differences in attitudes and beliefs. *Psychology of Women Quarterly*, 14, 63-81.

Manning, S.K., & Melchiori, M.P. (1974). Words that upset urban college students: Measured with GSRs and rating scales. *The Journal of Social Psychology*, 94, 305-306.

Martindale, C. (1977). Syntactic and semantic correlates of verbal tics in Gilles de la Tourette's Syndrome: A quantitative case study. *Brain and Language*, 4, 231-247.

Masters, K. (1988). Rating game. *Premiere*, September, 64.

Masters, W.H., Johnson, V.E., & Kolodny, R.C. (1988). *Human sexuality*. Glenview, IL: Scott, Foresman and Co.

McCabe, A., & Lipscomb, T. J. (1988). Sex differences in children's verbal aggression. *Merrill-Palmer Quarterly*, 34, 389-401.

McGhee, P. E. (1979). *Humor: Its origin and development*. San Francisco: W.H. Freeman.

McGinnies, E. (1949). Emotionality and perceptual defense. *Psychological Review*, 56, 244-251.

McKinney, K. (1990). Sexual harassment of university faculty by colleagues and students. *Sex Roles*, 23(7/8), 421-438.

McMillan, J. B. (1980). Infixing and interposing in English. *American Speech*, 55(3), 163-183.

Mead, B.T. (1951). What do you tell parents concerned about their children using "dirty words"? *Medical Aspects of Human Sexuality*, 4(4), 98-107.

Mechling, J. (1984). High Kybo floater: Food and feces in the speech play at a Boy Scout camp. *The Journal of Psychoanalytic Anthropology*, 7(3), 256-268.

Mencken, H.L. (1944). American profanity. *American Speech*, 19(4), 241-249.

Mencken, H.L. (1962). *The American language: An inquiry into the development of English in the United States.* New York: Alfred A. Knopf.

Michael, R. P. (1957). Treatment of a case of compulsive swearing. *British Medical Journal*, 5034, 1506-1508.

Miller, M.E. & Solkoff, N. (1965). Effects of mode of response and sex of experimenter upon recognition thresholds of taboo words. *Perceptual and Motor Skills*, 20, 573-578.

Milner, J.S. & Moses, T. (1972). Sexual responsivity as a function of test administrator's gender. *Journal of Consulting and Clinical Psychology*, 39(3), 515.

Montagu, Ashley. (1942). On the physiology and psychology of swearing. *Psychiatry*, 5, 189-201.

Montagu, Ashley. (1967). *The anatomy of swearing.* New York: Macmillan Publishing Co.

Mooney, L. A., & Brabant, S. (1990). The portrayal of boys and girls in six nationally-syndicated comic strips. *Sociology and Social Research*, 74(2), 118-126.

Mosher, D.L., & Proenza, L.M. (1968). Intensity of attack, displacement and verbal aggression. *Psychonomic Science*, 12(8), 359-360.

Motley, M. T., Camden, C. T., & Baars, B. J. (1981). Toward verifying the assumptions of laboratory-induced slips of the tongue: The output-error and editing issues. *Human Communication Research*, 8(1), 3-15.

Motley, M. T., Camden, C. T., & Baars, B. J. (1982). Covert formulation and editing anomalies in speech production: Evidence from experimentally elicited slips of the tongue. *Journal of Verbal Learning and Verbal Behavior*, 21, 578-594.

Motley, M. T., & Camden, C. T. (1985). Nonlinguistic influences on lexical selection: Evidence from double entendres. *Communication Monographs*, 52(2), 124-135.

Mulac, A. (1976). Effects of obscene language upon three dimensions of listener attitude. *Communication Monographs*, 43, 300-307.

Mulcahy, F. D. (1976). Gitano sex role symbolism and behavior. *Anthropological Quarterly*, 49(2), 135-151.

Murphy, M.G. (1984). Euphemism in Russian. *Journal of Russian Studies*, 48, 3-8.

Murphy, R.P. (1978). Sociolinguistics in the movies: A call for research. *Anthropological Linguistics*, 20(5), 226-233.

Murray, H.A. (1938). *Explorations in personality: A clinical and experimental study of fifty men of college age.* New York: Oxford University Press.

Murray, S. O. (1979). The art of gay insulting. *Anthropological Linguistics*, 21, 211-223.

Murray, S. O. (1980). Lexical and institutional elaboration: The 'species homosexual' in Guatemala. *Anthropological Linguistics*, 22(4), 177-185.

Murray, T.E. (1985). The language of singles bars. *American Speech*, 60, 17-30.

Murray, T. E., & Murrell, T. R. (1989). *The language of sadomachism: A glossary and linguistic analysis.* New York: Greenwood Press.

Nadel, S.F. (1954). Morality and language among the Nupe. *Man*, 54, 55-57.

Nahemow, L., McCluskey-Fawcett, K. A., & McGhee, P. E. (Eds.). (1986). *Humor and aging.* New York: Academic.

Narancic, V.G. (1972). The psychology of swearing among sportsmen. *Journal of Sports Medicine and Physical Fitness*, 12, 207-210.

Neal, A.G. (1986). Animism and totemism in popular culture. *Journal of Popular Culture*, 19(2), 15-23.

Nelsen, E.A. & Rosenbaum, E. (1972). Language patterns within the youth subculture: Development of slang vocabularies. *Merrill-Palmer Quarterly of Behavior and Development*, 18, 273-285.

Nerbonne, G. P., & Hipskind, N. M. (1972). The use of profanity in conversational speech. *Journal of Communication Disorders*, 5, 47-50.

New dictionary of American slang. (1987). (by R. L. Chapman). New York: Harper & Row.

Nothman, F.H. (1962). The influence of response conditions on recognition thresholds for tabu words. *Journal of Abnormal and Social Psychology*, 65(3), 154-161.

Obscene remarks to a police officer: "disorderly conduct," "disturbance," "improper diversion," or poor taste? (1960). *Minnesota Law Review*, 45, 137-150.

O'Connell, B.E. (1977). Women's reaction to wolf-whistles and lewd remarks. *Medical Aspects of Human Sexuality*, 10, 58.

Oftedal, M. (1973). Notes on language and sex. *Norwegian Journal of Linguistics*, 27, 67-75.

Oliver, M. M., & Rubin, J. (1975). The use of expletives by some American women. *Anthropological Linguistics*, 17(5), 191-197.

O'Neal, E.C., Brunault, M.A., Carifio, M.S., Troutwine, R., & Epstein, J. (1980). Effect of insult upon personal space preferences. *Journal of Nonverbal Behavior*, 5(1), 56-62.

Osborn, C. A., & Pollack, R. H. (1977). The effects of two types of erotic literature on physiological and verbal measures of female sexual arousal. *Journal of Sex Research*, 13(4), 250-256.

Osgood, C.E., Suci, G., & Tannenbaum, P. (1957). *The measurement of meaning.* Urbana: University of Illinois Press.

Osthus, K. D. (1986). Fighting words and vagueness standing--State v Groves. *Creighton Law Review*, 19, 439-461.

Paletz, D.L., & Harris, W.F. (1975). Four-letter threats to authority. *The Journal of Politics*, 37(4), 955-979.

Panel on Folk Literature and the Obscene. (1962). *Journal of American Folklore*, 75, 189-264.

Paradise, L. V., Cohl, B., & Zweig, J. (1980). Effects of profane language and physical attractiveness on perceptions of counselor behavior. *Journal of Counseling Psychology*, 27, 620-624.

Patrick, G.T.W. (1901). The psychology of profanity. *Psychological Review*, 1901, 8(2), 113-127.

Pattison, R. (1987). *The triumph of vulgarity.* New York: Oxford University Press.

Pei, M. (1949). *The story of language.* New York: Lippincott.

Pei, M. (1973). *Double-speak in America.* New York: Hawthorn.

Piaget, J. *The language and thought of the child.* Translated by M. Gabain. New York: Meridian.

Pollak, F. (1970). Pornography: A trip around the halfworld. In Douglas A. Hughes (Ed.), *Perspectives on pornography.* New York: St. Martin's, 170-196.

Pollio, H., & Edgerly, J. W. (1976). Comedians and comic style. In A. Chapman and H. Foot (Eds.), *Humor and laughter: Theory, research and applications.* New York: Wiley.

Postman, L., Bronson, W. C., & Gropper, G. L. (1953). Is there a mechanism of perceptual defense? *Journal of Abnormal and Social Psychology*, 48, 215-224.

Preston, K., & Stanley, K. (1987). "What's the worst thing...?" Gender-directed insults. *Sex Roles*, 17(3-4), 209-218.

Randall, R. S. (1970). *Censorship of the movies.* Madison, WI: The University of Wisconsin Press.

Randolph, Vance. (1928). Verbal modesty in the Ozarks. *Dialect Notes*, 6, 57-64.

Ranson, S.W. & Clark, S.L. (1959). *The anatomy of the nervous system (10th Ed.).* Philadelphia: W.B. Saunders Company.

Read, A.W. (1934). An obscenity symbol. *American Speech*, 9(4), 264-278.

Reisner, M.F., Reeves, R., & Armington, J. (1955). Effect of variations in laboratory procedure and experimenter upon the ballistocardiogram, blood pressure, and heart rate in healthy young men. *Psychosomatic Medicine*, 17(3), 185-199.

The report of the commission on obscenity and pornography. (1970). New York: Bantam.

Ressner, J. (1990, August 9). On the road with rap's outlaw posse. *Rolling Stone*, 19-20,24, 73-74.

Note - The 2 Live Crew Obscenity trials in Florida

Rieber, R. W., Wiedemann, C., & D'Amato, J. (1979). Obscenity: Its frequency and context of usage as compared in males, nonfeminist females, and feminist females. *Journal of Psycholinguistic Research*, 8(3), 201-223.

Risch, B. (1987). Women's derogatory terms for men: That's right, "dirty" words. *Language in Society*, 16, 353-358.

Roscoe, B., & Evans, J. A. (1986). Desk top graffiti. *College Student Journal*, 20(2), 221-224.

Ross, H.D. (1962). Use of obscene words in psychotherapy. *Archives of General Psychiatry*, 6, 123-131.

Ross, H.E. (1969). Patterns of swearing. *Discovery: The Popular Journal of Knowledge*, November, 479-481.

Rothwell, J. D. (1971). Verbal obscenity: Time for some second thoughts. *Western Speech*, 35, 231-242.

Rothwell, J.D. (1982). *Telling it like it isn't.* New York: Prentice-Hall. Chapters on verbal taboo, sexism, & racism.

Rozin, P., & Fallon, A. E. (1987). A perspective on disgust. *Psychological Review*, 94(1), 23-41.

Rumenik, D., Capasso, D., & Hendrick, C. (1977). Experimenter sex-effects in behavioral research. *Psychological Bulletin*, 84, 852-877.

Sagarin, E. (1962). *The anatomy of dirty words.* New York: Lyle Stuart.

Saltzman, A. (1988). Hands off at the office. *U.S. News & World Report*, August 1, 56-58.

Sanders, J. S., & Robinson, W. L. (1979). Talking and not talking about sex: Male and female vocabularies. *Journal of Communication*, 29(2), 22-30.

Sanders, M.S. (1969). Viewpoints: What is the significance of crude language during sexual relations? *Medical Aspects of Human Sexuality*, 3(8), 8-14.

Sandwith, M., & Evans, J. D. (1977). "Taboo word" norms. *Perceptual and Motor Skills*, 44, 865-866.

Scherer, K.R., & Guiles, H. (Eds.). (1979). *Social markers in speech*. Cambridge: Cambridge University Press.

Schill, T., Emanuel, G., Pederson, V., Schneider, L., & Wachowiak, D. (1970). Sexual responsivity of defensive and nondefensive sensitizers and repressors. *Journal of Counseling and Clinical Psychology*, 35, 44-47.

Schwartz, G. & Merten, D. (1967). The language of adolescence: An anthropological approach to the youth culture. *The American Journal of Sociology*, 72(5), 453-468.

Scott, J. E., Eitle, D. J., & Skovron, S. E. (1990). Obscenity and the law: Is it possible for a jury to apply contemporary community standards in determining obscenity. *Law and Human Behavior*, 14(2), 139-150.

Sechrest, L., & Olson, K. (1971). Graffiti in four types of institutions of higher education. *The Journal of Sex Research*, 7(1), 62-71.

Segalowitz, S. J. (1983). *Two sides of the brain*. Englewood Cliffs, NJ: Prentice-Hall. Includes discussion of relation between brain and use of emotional words.

Seward, J. (1983). *Japanese in action*. New York: Weatherhill.

Sewell, E. H., Jr (1984). Appreciation of cartoons with profanity in captions. *Psychological Reports*, 54, 583-587.

Shannon, C. E., & Weaver, W. (1949). *The mathematical theory of communication*. Urbana, IL: University of Illinois Press.

Shantz, D. W. (1986). Conflict, aggression, and peer status: An observational study. *Child Development*, 57, 1322-1332.

Shapiro, A. K., Shapiro, E. S., Brunn, R. D., & Sweet, R. D. (1978). *Gilles de la Tourette syndrome*. New York, Raven Press.

Shapiro, B. J. (1969). The subjective estimation of relative word frequency. *Journal of Verbal Learning and Verbal Behavior*, 8, 248-251.

Shimanoff, S.B. (1985). Expressing emotions in words: Verbal patterns of interaction. *Journal of Communication*, 35(3), 16-31.

Shulman, J. H. (1990). Now you see them, now you don't: Anonymity versus visibility in case studies of teachers. *Educational Researcher*, 19(6), 11-15. Considers the use of students' foul language in school reports

Shuster, Janet. (1987). Grammatical forms marked for male and female in English. Unpublished paper, University of Chicago.

Siegman, A.W. (1956). Some factors associated with the visual threshold for taboo words. *Journal of Clinical Psychology*, 12(3), 282-286.

Simkins, L., & Rinck, C. (1982). Male and female sexual vocabulary in different interpersonal contexts. *The Journal of Sex Research*, 18 (2), 160-172.

Singer, D., Avedon, J., Hering, R., McCann, A., & Sacks, C. (1977). Sex differences in the vocabulary of college students. *The Journal of Sex Research*, 13(4), 267-273.

Skinner, B. F. (1957). *Verbal behavior.* Englewood Cliffs, NJ: Prentice-Hall.

Smal-Stocki, R. (1950). Taboos on animal names in Ukrainian. *Language*, 26, 489-493.

Smith, A. (1966). Speech and other functions after left (dominant) hemispherectomy. *Journal of Neurology, Neurosurgery and Psychiatry*, 29, 467-471.

Smith, Alfred. (1951). Swearing. *Journal of Sex Education*, 4(4), 256-260.

Smith, P.M. (1979). Sex markers in speech. In Scherer & Giles (Eds.), *Social markers in speech.* Cambridge: Cambridge University Press.

Smith, T. W. (1984). The polls: Gender and attitudes toward violence. *Public Opinion Quarterly*, 48, 384-396.

Soocher, S. (1990, August 9). 2 Live Crew: Taking the rap. *Rolling Stone*, 19, 22-23.

Sources of information and materials relating to human sexuality. Bibliography from Information Service, Institute for Sex Research, 416 Morrison Hall, Indiana University, Bloomington, IN 47401.

Spears, R. A. (1981). *Slang and euphemism.* Middle Village, NY: Jonathan David.

Spears, R. A. (1985). On the etymology of DIKE. *American Speech*, 60 (4), 318-327.

Spender, Dale. (1980). *Man made language.* London: Routledge & Kegan Paul.

Sporn, J. (1985). Content regulation of cable television: "Indecency" statutes and the First Amendment. *Rutgers Computer & Technology Law Journal*, 11, 141-170.

Staley, C. M. (1978). Male-female use of expletives: A heck of a difference in expectations. *Anthropological Linguistics*, 20(8), 367-380.

Stanley, J. P. (1970). *Homosexual slang.* American Speech, 45, 45-59.

Steadman, J.M., Jr. (1935). A study of verbal taboos. *American Speech*, 10, 93-103.

Steinberg, C. (1982). *Reel facts.* New York: Vintage.

Stelmack, R.M., & Mandelzys, N. (1975). Extraversion and pupillary response to affective and taboo words. *Psychophysiology*, 12, 536-540.

Stevens, James. (1925). Logger talk. *American Speech*, 1(3), 135-140.

Stocker, T. L., Dutcher, L. W., Hargrove, S. M., & Cook, E. A. (1972). Social analysis of graffiti. *Journal of American Folklore*, 85, 357-366.

Stoke, S.M., & West, E.D. (1931). Sex differences in conversational interests. *Journal of Social Psychology*, 2, 120-126.

Stone, L. (1954). On the principle obscene word of the English language (an inquiry, with hypothesis, regarding its origin and persistence). *International Journal of Psychoanalysis*, 35(1), 30-56.

Strainchamps, Ethel. (1971). Our sexist language. In Vivian Gornick and Barbara K. Moran, (Eds.), *Woman in sexist society*. New York: Basic Books, 240-250.

Stross, B. (1975). Metaphor in the speech play of Tzeltal children. *Anthropological Linguistics*, 17(6), 305-323.

Sutton-Smith, B., & Abrams, D.M. (1978). Psychosexual material in stories told by children: The fucker. *Archives of Sexual Behavior*, 7, 521-543.

Symonds, C. (1972). A vocabulary of sexual enticement and proposition. *The Journal of Sex Research*, 8, 136-139.

Taub, D. E., & Leger, R. G. (1984). Argot and the creation of social types in a young gay community. *Human Relations*, 37(3), 181-189.

Taylor, B.A. (1975). Towards a structural and lexical analysis of 'swearing' and the language of abuse in Australian English. *Linguistics*, 164, 17-43.

Tedford, T.L. (1985). *Freedom of speech in the United States*. New York: Random House.

Terpstra, D. E., & Baker, D. D. (1987). A hierarchy of sexual harassment. *The Journal of Psychology*, 121(6), 599-605.

Thomas, D.R., Shea, J.D., & Rigby, R.G. (1971). Conservatism and response to sexual humor. *British Journal of Social and Clinical Psychology*, 10, 185-186.

Thomas, M. (1951). Sexual symbolism in industry. *International Journal of Psychoanalysis*, 32, 128-133.

Thorndike, E., & Lorge, I. (1944). *The teacher's word book of 30,000 words*. New York: Columbia University, Teacher's College Press.

Thorne, B., & Henley, N. (Eds.). (1975). *Language and sex: Difference and dominance*. Rowley, MA: Newbury House Publishers.

Toch, H. (1969). *Violent men*. Chicago: Aldine.

Tourette Syndrome Association, P O Box 533, Bayside, NY, 11361.
Note - information available on this compulsive swearing syndrome.

Truax, A. (1989). Sexual harassment in higher education: What we've learned. *The NEA Higher Education Journal*, 5(1), 25-38.

Uhrbrock, R.S. (1935). The vocabulary of a five-year-old. *Educational Research Bulletin*, 14(4), 85-97.

Ullman, S. (1959). *The principles of semantics (2nd ed.)*. Oxford: Basil Blackwell and Mott, Ltd.

Van Lancker, D. (1972). Language lateralization and grammars. *UCLA Working Papers in Phonetics*, 23, 24-31.

Vetter, H. J. (1969). *Language behavior and communication: An introduction*. Itasca, Ill.: Peacock. Chapter 12 on Language and taboo.

Vetterling-Braggin, Mary. (1981). *Sexist language: A modern philosophical analysis*. Littlefield, Adams & Co.

Vissing, Y. M., & Straus, M. A. (1989). Verbal aggression by parents and psycho-social problems of children. Paper presented at the meeting of the Society For the Study of Social Problems.

Vokey, J.R., & Read, J.D. (1985). Subliminal messages: Between the devil and the media. *American Psychologist*, 40(11), 1231-1239.

Walsh, R.H., & Leonard, W.M. (1974). Usages of terms for sexual intercourse by men and women. *Archives of Sexual Behavior*, 3(4), 373-376.

Walters, R. G. (1974). *Primers for prudery: Sexual advice to Victorian America*. Englewood Cliffs, NJ: Prentice Hall.

Ward, E., Stokes, G., & Tucker, K. (1986). *Rock of ages: The Rolling Stone history of rock & roll*. New York: Summit.

Warnock, E. (1918). Terms of disparagement in the dialect speech of high school pupils in California and New Mexico. *Dialect Notes*, 5, 60-73.

Waterman, R. A. (1949). The role of obscenity in the folk tales of the "intellectual" stratum of our society. *Journal of American Folklore*, 52, 162-165.

Webster, Hutton. (1942). *Taboo: A sociological study*. California: Stanford University Press.

Webster's ninth new collegiate dictionary (1985). Springfield, MA: Merriam-Webster.

Weisstein, N. (1973). Psychology constructs the female. In Koedt, A., Levine, E., & Rapone, A. *Radical feminism*. New York: Quadrangle, 178-197.

Wells, J. W. (1989). Sexual language usage in different interpersonal contexts: A comparison of gender and sexual orientation. *Archives of Sexual Behavior*, 18(2), 127-143.

Wells, J. W. (1990). The sexual vocabularies of heterosexual and homosexual males and females for communicating erotically with a sexual partner. *Archives of Sexual Behavior*, 19(2), 139-147.

Wentworth, H., & Flexner, S. (1934). *Dictionary of American slang*. New York: Thomas Y. Crowell & Co.

Whiting, B., & Edwards, C. P. (1973). A cross-cultural analysis of sex differences in the behavior of children aged three through 11. *The Journal of Social Psychology*, 91, 171-188.

Wiley, D. A., & Locke, D. C. (1982). Profanity as a critical variable in counseling. *Counselor Education and Supervision*, 21(3), 245-252.

Williams, L.J., & Evans, J.R. (1980). Evidence for perceptual defense using a lexical decision task. *Perceptual and Motor Skills*, 50, 195-198.

Williams-Hunt, P.D.R. (1952). Comment on interlingual word taboo. *American Anthropologist*, 54, 274-275.

Wilson, W. (1975). Sex differences in response to obscenities and bawdy humor. *Psychological Reports*, 37, 1074.

Winner, E., & Gardner, H. (1977). The comprehension of metaphor in brain-damaged patients. *Brain*, 100, 717-729.

Winslow, D.J. (1969). Children's derogatory epithets. *Journal of American Folklore*, 82(325), 255-263.

Wober, J. M. (1980). Offense and defense in the home: Some reasons for viewers' reactions to bad language on television. Special report, Independent Broadcasting Authority, Audience Research Department, 70 Brompton Road, London, SW3 1EY

Wolfenstein, Martha. (1954). *Children's humor: A psychological analysis*. Glencoe, IL: The Free Press.

Woodrow, K. M. (1974). Gilles de la Tourette's disease - A review. *American Journal of Psychiatry*, 131(9), 1000-1003.

Worthington, A. (1964). Differential rates of dark adaptation to "taboo" and "neutral" stimuli. *Canadian Journal of Psychology*, 18, 257-265.

Wright, G.H. (1956). The names of the parts of the body: A linguistic approach to the study of the body-image. *Brain*, 79, 188-210.

Wurm, S.A., & Muhlhausler, P. (1982). Registers in New Guinea pidgin. *International Journal of the Sociology of Language*, 69-86.

Yang, N., & Linz, D. (1990). Movie ratings and the content of adult videos: The sex violence ratio. *Journal of Communication*, 40(2), 28-42.

Yee, S., Britton, L., & Thompson, W.C. (1988). The effects of rock music on adolescents' attitudes and behavior. Presented at the meeting of the Western Psychological Association.

Zipf, G. K. (1949). *Human behavior and the principle of least effort*. Cambridge: Addison-Wesley.

Zwicky, A.M., Salus, P.H., Binnick, R.I., & Vanek, A.L. (1971). *Studies out in left field: Defamatory essays presented to James D. McCawley*. Edmonton: Linguistic Research, Inc.